Portugal's Revolution: ten years on

T0381607

Portugal's Revolution: ten years on

HUGO GIL FERREIRA

AND

MICHAEL W. MARSHALL

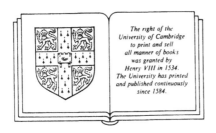

The right of the
University of Cambridge
to print and sell
all manner of books
was granted by
Henry VIII in 1534.
The University has printed
and published continuously
since 1584.

CAMBRIDGE UNIVERSITY PRESS

Cambridge
London   New York   New Rochelle
Melbourne   Sydney

CAMBRIDGE UNIVERSITY PRESS
Cambridge, New York, Melbourne, Madrid, Cape Town, Singapore,
São Paulo, Delhi, Dubai, Tokyo, Mexico City

Cambridge University Press
The Edinburgh Building, Cambridge CB2 8RU, UK

Published in the United States of America by Cambridge University Press, New York

www.cambridge.org
Information on this title: www.cambridge.org/9780521154857

First published 1986
First paperback edition 2010

A catalogue record for this publication is available from the British Library

Library of Congress Cataloguing in Publication Data

Ferreira, Hugo Gil.
Portugal's revolution.
Bibliography: p.
Includes index.
1. Portugal - History - Revolution, 1974 - Causes.
2. Portugal - History - Coup d'etat, 1975. 3. Portugal -
Politics and government - 1 9 7 4 - . 4. Revolutionists -
Portugal - Interviews. 5. Portugal - Social conditions -
20th century. I. Marshall, Michael W. II. Title.
DP68I. F47 1986 946.9'o44 85-29067

ISBN 978-0-521-32204-1 Hardback
ISBN 978-0-521-15485-7 Paperback

For Karin, Claudia, Paula and Pedro

For my brother, Peter, and for Colette, Eliska, Jennifer, Joan, Dylan, Emily and Sylvie

For Artur Baptista

For Portugal's post-coup idealism

Contents

Glossary

AD	Aliança Democrática, Democratic Alliance
ANP	Acção Nacional Popular, National Popular Action
AOC	Aliança Operária Camponesa, Farm-workers' Alliance
APU	Aliança Povo Unido, United People's Alliance
ARA	Acção Revolucionária Armada, Armed Revolutionary Action
ASDI	Associação Socialista Democrática Independente, Association of Independent Social Democrats
BR	Brigadas Revolucionárias, Revolutionary Brigade
CADC	Centro Académico da Democracia Cristã, Academic Centre of Christian Democrats
CAP	Confederação dos Agricultores Portugueses, Confederation of Portuguese Farmers
CCO	Centro de Coordenação de Operações, Centre of Coordination of Operations
CCP	Comissão Coordenadora do Programa, Co-ordinating Committee of the Programme (of the MFA)
CDE	Comissão Democrática Eleitoral, Democratic Election Committee
CDS	Centro Democrático Social, Social and Democratic Centre
CEUD	Comissão Eleitoral de Unidade Democrática, United Democratic Election Committee
CIP	Confederação das Indústrias Portuguesas, Confederation of Portuguese Industries
CGT	Confederação Geral do Trabalho, General Confederation of Work
CGTP	Confederação Geral dos Trabalhadores Portugueses, General Confederation of Portuguese Workers

CODICE	Comissão de Dinamização Central, Central Committee for Dynamisation
COPCON	Comando Operacional do Continente, Operation Command for the Continent
CR	Conselho da Revolução, Council of Revolution
CS	Conselho de Estado, Council of State
CUF	Companhia União Fabril, United Fabril Company
DGS	Direcção-Geral de Segurança, Department of General Security
FAP	Frente de Acção Popular, Front of Popular Action
FNLA	Frente Nacional para a Libertação de Angola, National Front for the Liberation of Angola
FPLN	Frente Patriótica de Libertação Nacional, Patriotic Front for National Liberation
FRELIMO	Frente de Libertação de Moçambique, Mozambique Liberation Front
FRS	Frente Republicana Socialista, Republican Socialist Front
FUR	Frente de Unidade Revolucionária, United Revolutionary Front
JSN	Junta de Salvação Nacional, Junta of National Salvation
LUAR	Liga Unitária de Acção Revolucionária, League of United Revolutionary Action
MDLP	Movimento Democrático para a Libertação de Portugal, Democratic Movement for the Liberation of Portugal
MDP/CDE	Movimento Democrático Português, Portuguese Democratic Movement
MES	Movimento da Esquerda Socialista, Movement of the Socialist Left
MFA	Movimento das Forças Armadas, Armed Forces Movement
MLSTP	Movimento para a Libertação de São Tomé e Príncipe, Liberation Movement for São Tomé and Príncipe
MPLA	Movimento Popular de Libertação de Angola, Popular Movement for the Liberation of Angola
MRPP	Movimento Reorganizativo do Partido do Proletariado, Movement for the Reorganisation of the Party of the Proletariat

MSP	Movimento Socialista Popular, Popular Socialist Movement
MUD	Movimento de Unidade Democrática, United Democrat Movement
MUNAF	Movimento de Unidade Nacional Anti-Fascista, Movement of Anti-Fascist Unity
ORA	Organização Revolucionária da Armada, Revolutionary Organisation of the Navy
PAIGC	Partido Africano para a Independência da Guiné e de Cabo Verde, African Party for the Independence of Guinea and Cape Verde
PAP	Plano de Acção Política, Plan for Political Action
PCP	Partido Comunista Português, Portuguese Communist Party
PDC	Partido da Democracia Cristão, Christian Democratic Party
PIDE	Polícia Internacional e de Defesa do Estado, International Police for the Defence of the State
PPD	Partido Popular Democrata, Popular Democratic Party
PPM	Partido Popular Monárquico, Popular Monarchist Party
PRP	Partido Revolucionário do Proletariado, Revolutionary Party of the Proletariat
PS	Partido Socialista, Socialist Party
PSD	Partido Social Democrata, Social Democratic Party
PVDE	Polícia de Vigilância e Defesa do Estado, Police of Vigilance and Defence of the State
SEDES	Sociedade de Estudos de Desenvolvimento Económico e Social, Society for the Study of Economic and Social Development
UDP	União Democrática Popular, Popular Democratic Union
UEDS	União da Esquerda Democrática Socialista, Union of the Social Democrat Left
UNITA	União Nacional para a Independência Total de Angola, National Union for the Total Independence of Angola
UON	União Operária Nacional, National Workers' Union

UPA	União dos Povos de Angola, Union of the Angolan People
ZIRA	Zona de Intervenção da Reforma Agrária, Zone of Intervention of the Agrarian Reform

Acknowledgments

We would like to thank the following for many valuable discussions and for their time in reading some of the original draft manuscripts: Dr P. Costa, Dr M. G. Emílio, Dr P. Fernandes, Dr R. Gillespie, Ms J. Hinves, Dr S. Hollingworth and Ms J. O. Peachey. Dr Richard Gillespie, of the Politics Department, Newcastle University was especially helpful with much constructive criticism throughout the preparation of the book. We are also indebted to the 'captains' for the interview material.

Special thanks must go to Colonel Artur Baptista and Ms J. O. Peachey: without their help it is doubtful whether the book would have been produced.

Finally, we would like to thank our colleagues, families and friends, who have encouraged us throughout: especially Karin, Colette and Jennifer, whose unfailing enthusiasm for the project was much appreciated.

Introduction

25 April 1984 was exactly ten years after the coup d'état which was brought about by young army captains, ending some fifty years of right-wing dictatorship. This book marks the first decade since the coup and the authors consider it unique because they had access to many of the officers who were directly involved in the overthrow of the Salazarian regime. In over ninety hours of tape-recorded interviews, the officers revealed their reasons for taking part in the revolution and their reactions to the subsequent events. In editing and analysing the tapes the authors tried to be as impartial as possible and they considered it was essential to conduct interviews with both left and right-wing officers who were involved in the shaping of Portugal's political evolution over the decade.

Since a large section of the book is original interview material, it is the authors' intention that it should act as a primary source for any subsequent study on the coup d'état and revolution, and it is hoped that, as well as being educational, the book is an exciting insight into the making of contemporary Portuguese history.

The book was written by two authors with widely differing backgrounds. One of them, Hugo Gil Ferreira, was born in a small town of seven hundred people in the Portuguese colony of Angola. He lived there until he was thirteen and then moved with his family to Lisbon to grow up under the Salazar/Caetano regime. Like many of the Portuguese middle class, he and his family passively opposed the regime (although in the 1950s, he became more active as a student leader, when undergraduates attempted to re-open one of the students' unions). In 1961 he was conscripted and saw active service as a doctor in Angola during the Colonial War, where he met some of the officers who were later to be important in the 1974 coup d'état. As it happened, he was in Britain from 1973 to 1976, carrying out research at Cambridge University. The other author, Michael Marshall, was

born in the south of England. Later, abandoning a career as a
navigating officer in the merchant navy, he entered university in
his mid-twenties and, after obtaining a doctorate, continued his
research at Cambridge, where he met and became friends with
Hugo Ferreira.

Some of their more personal reasons for writing this book are
as follows:

Hugo Gil Ferreira: one of my motivations was a deeply-felt sense
of gratitude to the officers of the Armed Forces Movement (MFA)
who brought down a regime which I considered had impover-
ished my life – an impoverishment which seemed to spread into
every aspect of the Portuguese culture. As time passed and the
economic problems of the country grew worse, the MFA officers
were often blamed for the ills that beset the country. However,
the MFA only had power for approximately eighteen months
during the 1974–84 period, and so one of my aims was an
attempt to clarify the role of the military in Portuguese politics
during that decade.

I was in England in 1974 and, when I heard there had been a
coup and the old regime had fallen, I was elated. Subsequent
fears, with the news of the appointment of Spínola as the new
President, were quickly dispelled when I heard that all political
prisoners were to be freed and politicians like Álvaro Cunhal and
Mário Soares had returned to the country. I had worried about
Spínola's appointment, since, while serving simultaneously in
Angola with him, I had been dissatisfied with the way he had
conducted the war.

In the weeks that followed the coup I again became alarmed at
the reports in the British media of the rise of a new military
dictatorship. When I went to Portugal in June 1974 and then on
three separate visits during the next two years, my fears were
allayed. At that time I considered that the majority of the MFA
were sincere in their wishes to restore democracy to the country.
It did not seem as if they wanted either a communist state or the
spread of anarchism; a view that was not generally shared by
much of the media of the western democratic nations. Thus,
another reason for writing this book was to examine the sincerity
of the MFA's intention.

My experience of the professional army during the Colonial

War led me to believe that above all else the soldiers wanted to end the war. They wanted to end it as quickly as possible and to minimise the loss of life on both sides, an aim which I believe they carried out successfully. It was while I was in Angola that I acquired a respect for a number of the professional army officers, especially at the rank of captain, and began to think that the army was the only force capable of bringing down the Salazar/Caetano regime.

Michael Marshall: I had visited Portugal under the Salazar regime and eight years after the coup d'état returned to live in Lisbon. The differences were startling. During Salazar's time Portugal had seemed ordered, pristinely clean and the people somewhat subdued. On my return in 1982, I was immediately struck by the degree and intensity of the political activity; throughout the country fly-posters, street banners, hoardings and painted slogans declared that this or that party was the only one capable of uniting and serving the people. In Lisbon there were many walls and buildings beautifully coloured with political graffiti. Painted on almost every lamp-post were red and white carnations, symbols of the revolution. The graffiti and paintings were often underwritten with such catch-phrases as: 25 ABRIL SEMPRE (25 April always); I DE MAIO PARA CUMPRIR ABRIL (1 May to fulfil April), and O POVO UNIDO JAMAIS SERÁ VENCIDO (The united people will never be defeated).

Shortly after my arrival in 1982 I visited a magnificent memorial that stands on the banks of the river Tagus. The memorial commemorates the voyages of the fifteenth-century discoverers; maritime explorers who navigated their small caravelas across the Atlantic to Brazil, Africa and around and beyond the Cape of Good Hope. Opposite the memorial is the sixteenth-century Jeronimos cathedral, one of Lisbon's most famous sights and another imposingly beautiful monument to the Portuguese explorers. But I was soon to be confronted with the incongruities of this city, for, within a short distance from the cloisters and formal cathedral gardens, I came across a crowded, rubbish-strewn shanty-town. Near the single water tap that appeared to act as a supply for at least twenty families (black immigrants from the former Portuguese African colonies), the red flag of the Portuguese Communist Party (PCP) was almost defiantly flying, with its discreetly-placed yellow hammer and sickle in the top left-hand corner. There were a lot of political slogans, most of them hastily scrawled on the walls and pavements. Amongst much else was: VOTA OTELO (Vote Otelo); AD RUA (Democratic Alliance, get out) and PCP NO GOVERNO (PCP in government).

During my stay, Portugal became a fascination. Debate was very much alive, political graffiti were everywhere and strikes were sometimes spontaneous and often political. The country was still undergoing far-reaching changes following the 1974 coup d'état and incongruities did not only exist within the cities. Sophisticated Lisbon contrasted dramatically with the almost third-world conditions of the outlying rural districts. Thus, one of my reasons for writing this book was to analyse in some depth both the contemporary Portuguese way of life and its economic and socio-political evolution throughout the post-coup decade.

After nearly two years of residency, it seemed to me that both Portugal and the rest of the world had not been just to the coup and the revolution. Discussions with many of those who had been involved in the events of 25 April 1974 as army officers, political activists and well-wishing onlookers often took a negative turn and showed that they had almost all been overwhelmed by the revolution. By 1984 some had begun to think that the quality of life had been better under Salazar; that there had been more economic and political stability, less inflation, better transport and cleaner towns and cities. It was as if the coup of 1974 had created a run-away train. 'Democracy is fine', one man said to me, 'but the freedom is very frightening.' Thus, another reason for writing the book was to examine the 1974 coup and the following revolution and, as objectively as possible, to assess the positive achievements that had taken place in Portugal in the subsequent decade.

1   *Setting the scene*

At dawn in Lisbon on 25 April 1974 the leading tank of the spearhead of the armoured columns that slowly moved towards the city centre met an old lady setting up her flower stall. She smiled and gently tossed a red carnation at the tank commander and so symbolised a revolution. The carnation was to become the emblem of the MFA.

Introduction

Interviews with those men who played influential parts in the Portuguese revolution, and coup d'état of 25 April 1974, form an important part of this book. They describe their roles in, and their feelings towards, the course of events that was to change modern Portuguese history. There is a need to place these interviews in context, for it is an interesting paradox that an authoritarian regime was overthrown by its own armed forces.

Part 1, then, describes Portugal before 25 April 1974. It sets out to show the effects of fifty years of Salazarism on the people of Portugal. It describes what it was like to live in the country or in the cities before 25 April; how the regime ran the economy and how Salazar was able to isolate Portugal from the rest of the world. The history of fifty years of military and civil dissent in the regime is summarised and the reasons outlined for the growth of unrest in the armed forces. This growth eventually led to the Armed Forces Movement (MFA) and the overthrow of the regime.

Salazar and the New State

In 1974 an authoritarian regime had existed for just under fifty years. It had been established in 1926 when a right-wing military coup overthrew a democratically elected government. This coup,

5

which overthrew the First Republic (1910–26), was really a succession of coups which first began in Braga in the north of the country on 28 May 1926. Here General Gomes da Costa declared his intent to overthrow the First Republic. In Lisbon the threatened government resigned and, almost immediately, handed over power to a naval commander, Mendes Cabeçadas. Then General Gomes da Costa marched on Lisbon and took control of the country. A power struggle ensued between a number of different factions which eventually resulted in the arrest of Gomes da Costa, his deportation to the Azores and the emergence of General Oscar Carmona as the new leader and President of Portugal. The success of these coups was not due to the power and efficiency of the military machine, but rather to the apathy of most Republicans who seemed unconcerned by the military's intervention into politics. The coups were, like most Portuguese revolutions, bloodless.

The new right-wing military government removed professional politicians from power, privatised the public sector and set about 'morally rearming' Portugal. However, they ran the country into an economic crisis and for help they turned to a group at Coimbra university who had suggested a path towards economic recovery. In 1928 one of the leaders of the Coimbra group, a law professor, was appointed minister of finance. In office he had some success in curing the economic ills of the country, and quickly realised that the military government was divided and insecure. He set out to gain power from within and in 1932 this professor became prime minister; his name was António de Oliveira Salazar. In 1933 Salazar created the 'New State' (Estado Novo). The constitution of the New State was approved by a majority in a national referendum. Although, on the surface, this new constitution gave democratic freedom to the people, there were built-in provisions which Salazar was able to use to systematically erode the normal democratic rights of the Portuguese. From 1933 onwards all political parties were abolished and workers' trade unions were substituted by state-run organisations.

Censorship was very much in evidence: all meetings, political or cultural, had first to be cleared by the state censors, as did all newspapers, plays, musicals, television programmes and radio broadcasts. No one could be appointed to a state position without first being investigated by the secret police. In 1956 a law was passed which allowed the state to arrest and imprison people for an indefinite period in the 'interests of national security'. Prison camps were set up in Portuguese colonies for political and military dissidents.

Salazar was to remain prime minister for almost forty years by a simple electoral device. In theory, in the New State, the prime minister was chosen and appointed by the President of the Republic. But, before each presidential election, the prime minister with his collaborators would select the candidate of whom they most approved, and since elections were rigged, he was always elected. Not surprisingly, the new President of the Republic would reappoint Salazar as prime minister.

During the first fifteen to twenty years of the New State other authoritarian regimes – nazism in Germany and fascism in Italy – rose and fell in Western Europe. Just before the Second World War, Portugal supported Franco in the Spanish Civil War and in 1939 the Salazar and Franco regimes signed a mutual defence treaty, the Iberian Pact, which was to last until the Portuguese coup d'état in 1974. Salazar, often labelled a fascist by outside powers, was, right up until the 1960s, able to deal skilfully with governments with different political leanings from his own. Thus, during the Second World War, he managed to keep Portugal neutral, although his personal inclinations strongly favoured the Axis powers. He withdrew visible support for them when he saw that they were losing the war, although that did not stop him from proclaiming an official half day of mourning, following Hitler's suicide. In the latter stages of the war, in order to appease the Allies, he gave Britain a military base in the Azores. In 1949, because of the western world's fear of the spread of communism, and Salazar's consistent anti-communist stand, Portugal joined with other western nations to become a founder member of NATO. In 1955, as a result of the negotiations between non-communist and communist blocs, Salazar's Portugal was admitted to the United Nations.

The first sign that the strength of the New State was weakening did not appear until 1958. A disenchanted but prestigious general, a previous supporter of the regime, General Humberto Delgado, led the *oposição* (under Salazar, all the parties opposing the regime were known as the *oposição*) to oppose the official candidate in the presidential elections. As usual, the regime's official candidate, Admiral Américo Thomaz, was re-elected. However, public support for Delgado was so massive that Salazar had to take notice. In order to prevent this public display of disaffection from occurring a second time, the regime changed the rules of the presidential elections. From 1959 onwards the President was to be elected by a special body whose composition was to be determined, although indirectly, by the government, that is, by Salazar.

The Colonial War and military dissent

The weakening of the Salazarist regime was largely due to the Colonial War and the rise of dissent in the regime's armed forces. To understand the reasons for the military coup of 25 April 1974, an analysis of the causes of the war and the rise of this dissent is necessary.

After the First World War, Portugal had managed to keep most of its colonies. The most wealthy colonies, Angola and Mozambique, were in Africa. These colonies were enormous and they provided an important source of foreign currency to support Salazar's regime. Labour was black, abundant and cheap and with this labour the colonies were able to provide Portugal with important commodities, such as oil, cotton, diamonds, coffee, sizal and iron ore. Portugal could then export and sell these commodities at enormous profits. A small, extremely wealthy section of Portuguese society controlled this exploitation of the colonies. This section was composed of five families – Champalimaud, Mello, Quina, Queiroz Pereira and Espiríto Santo, who owned a large slice of the Portuguese economy. They worked hand in hand with Salazar and were protected by the regime's laws which prevented the formation of any new competitive industries. These laws were especially strict in the colonies. The overall effect of this was that Portugal did not industrialise to anything like the same extent as the rest of Western Europe. In 1974, 86 per cent of all Portuguese firms employed less than ten workers. The large firms, not owned by the five families, belonged to the multinational conglomerates that came to Portugal to benefit from the low-wage policies of the regime.

After the Second World War, at a time when other nations' colonial empires were being dismantled, Portugal came under pressure to give independence to its colonies. But the regime desperately needed them, and, rather than let them go, passed a law in 1951 whereby the colonies became Portuguese 'overseas territories'. Portuguese whites who were born in the colonies were upgraded from 'second-line' Portuguese with limited rights to fully-fledged Portuguese citizens. The expressions 'Portuguese colonies' or 'Portuguese colonial empire' were banned from official documents and from the media. Despite this, blacks living in these overseas territories were still discriminated against. Marcello Caetano, who was to replace Salazar as the regime's head in 1968, said that the blacks were to be organised and enclosed in an economy directed by the whites.

In 1961 the Portuguese possessions in Goa were annexed by India. The Portuguese military in India was vastly outnumbered by the Indian army and had to surrender. The army, humiliated by this defeat, resented Salazar for refusing to negotiate with Nehru and obtain some form of face-saving settlement. Salazar was not upset by the loss of these poor, Indian colonies, but he had every intention of holding on to the rich African territories (especially Angola and Mozambique). In order to hold on to these African colonies he thought it essential that his regime should not be blamed for handing over any parcel of Portuguese overseas territory to any foreign country. He thus attributed the loss of the Indian possessions to the military, and court-martialled many senior Portuguese army officers. His handling of the army in India was to produce bitter resentment that his regime was to pay for years later.

In the year when Portugal lost its possessions in India, trouble started for the Salazar regime in the African colony of Angola. Portugal had had a presence in Africa for over five hundred years. It began in the fifteenth century when Portuguese explorers, encouraged by Prince Henry the Navigator, rounded the most western African cape. By the beginning of the next century they controlled the Cape Verde Islands, thousands of miles of the west coast and they had built a chain of forts and small towns on the east coast. During the next four centuries the Portuguese were to export millions of Africans to the slave markets of the world and move inland to colonise vast tracts of land.

In line with the policy of other powerful colonising nations like France and Britain, their African policy was to try and assimilate the black Africans into the Portuguese culture. It was a policy that always favoured the white settlers. In Angola, before the Colonial War, to become an *assimilado* a black African had to have an income and prove that he/she could read and write Portuguese. Such requirements were never applied to the white settlers who were often illiterate.

There was a history of opposition to Salazar's regime in Angola by black intellectuals, but the secret police, ever watchful, were ruthless and effective in controlling any anti-colonial dissent. However, in December 1956 the MPLA (Movimento Popular de Libertação de Angola, Popular Movement for the Liberation of Angola) was formed by black and white intellectuals, left-wing progressives and communists. Its leader was Agostinho Neto who was later to become the first President of the Republic of Angola.

In 1961 the MPLA stormed the prison of São Paulo in the capital Luanda and at the same time became politically active in the north. In the same year the UPA (União dos Povos de Angola, Union of the Angolan People), under the leadership of Holden Roberto, began to attack the rich plantations of the white settlers. Holden Roberto left Angola and formed a government in exile, which raised arms and money abroad, some from the USA. The government organised and sustained a new guerilla movement, the FNLA (Frente Nacional para a Libertação Angola, National Front for the Liberation of Angola), after the UPA was dissolved following international divisions.

Later (in 1968) Jonas Savimbi, ex-Minister of Foreign Affairs in Roberto's government, in exile, formed another group, UNITA (União Nacional para a Independência Total de Angola, National Union for the Total Independence of Angola). They argued for democracy based upon majority rule. The party attracted lower-middle-class white settlers and had support from tribes in southern Angola.

In 1961 the generals of the Portuguese military high command, under the leadership of Botelho Moniz, sensed trouble in Angola and the other colonies and tried to force Salazar into retirement. They were unsuccessful, for he managed to rally the support of most of his ministers and most of the important military units in the Lisbon area. Dissident generals were dismissed and Salazar, with the help of newly appointed, now compliant generals, was able to set in motion the Colonial War.

By 1963 and 1964 guerilla attacks had been launched in the other Portuguese colonies in Africa, Guinea-Bissau and Mozambique. The guerilla movement in Guinea-Bissau had been formed in September 1956 in the capital Bissau. Its ideology became essentially Marxist and initially it was largely made up of urban workers and assimilados. Their leader was the charismatic Amílcar Cabral who was from the Cape Verde Islands and the movement, PAIGC (Partido Africano para a Independência da Guiné e de Cabo Verde, African Party for the Independence of Guine and Cape Verde) demanded independence for the islands as well as for Guinea-Bissau.

PAIGC was well organised. In January 1963 it became active in the south of Guinea-Bissau and by July of the same year it was well entrenched in the northern forests. By 1973 the liberation movement claimed that it controlled nearly two-thirds of the country, but that year saw the death of its leader, Amílcar Cabral. He was killed in Conakry, the capital of the neighbouring country Guinea, by Portuguese agents who were probably acting under General Spínola's orders.

Mozambique's guerilla movement FRELIMO (Frente de Libertação de Moçambique, Mozambique Liberation Front) was formed outside the country. In July 1962 in Tanzania three independent groups were persuaded by Eduardo Mondlane to form FRELIMO with the aim of establishing a popular social democracy in Mozambique. In September 1964 FRELIMO attacked the Portuguese on four fronts. By 1969 Mondlane had been killed by Portuguese agents but FRELIMO now controlled a quarter of Mozambique. It had established contact with the MPLA and PAIGC, mainly through the efforts of Amílcar Cabral in Guinea-Bissau.

From 1964 onwards for a period of ten years Portugal was to wage war against these liberation movements in the three colonies. From an army of some ten thousand men, defending its vast colonial empire in peacetime, grew an army of almost two hundred and twenty thousand men in 1972. This was about 2 per cent of the population, and then the total number of officers in the armed forces was estimated to be seven thousand, of which four thousand were in the army.

In 1968 Salazar overbalanced and fell off a chair, and as a result had to be operated on for a cerebral haemorrhage. During the recovery from the operation, he had a stroke which left him almost incapacitated. Salazar's man, President Thomaz, appointed another law professor, Marcello Caetano, as prime minister. Although Caetano said that a more liberal Social State would replace the old New State, his real intentions became clear with his attitudes towards the colonies. He never said that he would dismantle the Portuguese colonial empire.

In 1969 parliamentary elections were held in which for the first time the oposição openly criticised the Colonial War. Although the polling stations had observers from all the parties, the electoral roll had been fixed by the regime in such a way as to ensure the return of the old order. Among the elected MPs, who were all of course from Caetano's Social State party (Acção Nacional Popular, National Popular Action), a few formed a wing with the declared aim of liberalising the regime from within. Most of these MPs resigned as a result of clashes between Caetano and the extreme right, but by 1984 almost all had held important positions within the Portuguese governments since the 1974 coup.

Marcello Caetano never had the same powers as Salazar. Throughout his premiership he constantly fought with President Thomaz and his right-wing supporters. He never really took control of the forces that, under Salazar, had so successfully repressed the rise of Portuguese democracy. Salazar's control was through the military and paramilitary units. The military consisted of the usual three branches – air force, army and navy. The paramilitary were the Republican Guard, the regular police force, the secret police and a voluntary Legionnaire Corps. This corps which had been formed originally to defend the regime, helped General Franco during the Spanish Civil War – some eight thousand legionnaires died in Spain fighting Franco's cause. Officers of the military could be drafted to any of the paramilitary units, and many held important command posts within the paramilitary. Caetano's loss of control of the forces of repression was due to an increasing political awareness that occurred with time in the armed forces. This awareness really started when General Delgado was beaten in the Presidential elections, even though it was clear he had a large popular following. Delgado was a charismatic leader who had had a large following within the military. His murder by agents of the secret police fuelled disenchantment with the regime, a disenchantment which had begun when the military were blamed for the loss of the Indian possessions and continued when the professional officers were called time and time again to fight a Colonial War which many thought they could no longer win. By the early 1970s professional officers, above and including the rank of captain, had spent ten out of thirteen years fighting in the colonies.

Military discontent had shown itself when a number of attempts were made to either bring down or focus outside attention on the regime. For example, the year after the Delgado election, junior officers formed the Independent Military Movement and tried unsuccessfully to overthrow Salazar's government. Captain Henrique Galvão, a previous supporter of Salazar, with some fellow officers, hijacked a transatlantic liner in 1961. This was almost a single-handed, flamboyant attempt to highlight the iniquities of the Portuguese political system. The following year Captain Varela Gomes and some supporters took control of a Beja regiment in an attempt to overthrow the regime. Although all these plots failed, they were symbolic of a real dissatisfaction that existed within the armed forces.

By the late 1960s the Colonial War was going badly for Portugal, particularly in Guinea-Bissau, where the well-equipped guerilla movement (PAIGC), under Amílcar Cabral's leadership, continued to gather momentum with a large popular following and was even successful enough to infiltrate the Portuguese army. In an attempt to regain control of the situation, the regime appointed one of its most respected generals, António Spínola, as governor general and commander-in-chief of the colony. Caetano gave him special wide-ranging powers and Spínola used them to select some of the most able young officers to help him regain the colony. It was not long before he realised that the war could not be won by military means and that the only way to safeguard Portugal's interests was to win back the support of the populace. To this end he carried out a number of reasonably successful reforms and, through President Senghor of Senegal, he even managed to open negotiations with the guerillas. Conditions became ripe for a settlement, but Caetano absolutely refused to negotiate with the rebels. Spínola and his fellow officers were furious for they thought that, as had happened in India, the army was to be made a scapegoat for failing to destroy the enemy. This

resentment ran so high that many of the young officers in
Spínola's staff were to become prominent figures in the revolution of 1974.

Spínola's view of the Portuguese colonial problem was based
on studies carried out by his military staff. On his return to
Portugal, he published a book, *Portugal and the Future*, and prior
to its publication in February 1974, authorisation had been given
by the then chief of staff, General Costa Gomes. António
Spínola's book caused great interest in Portugal, for this was the
first time that an alternative to total victory in the Colonial War
had been considered. The book argued for a gradual evolution
from colonies to a Portuguese-speaking federation, in which the
old colonies would be given some autonomy. In March 1974, as a
result of the publication of the book and other clashes with the
regime, General Costa Gomes and Spínola were sacked. They
were finally removed from power because, unlike most other
generals, they refused to give their full loyalty and support to
Caetano's regime. This further opened up a split that already
existed between the older more senior ranks, and the younger
officers, for most of the junior officers supported Spínola. Such
was their disenchantment with the older generals that the young
officers would often refer to them as the rheumatic brigade!

Before the Colonial War, most army officers had been apolitical. This is not surprising, since they lived in a closed environment, in which political debate was forbidden. At the age of
eighteen or nineteen, they entered the Military Academy, where
they lived in isolation and were trained to avoid political discussion. At twenty-one, the young officers left the Academy, and
on arrival at their new barracks they censured any political
discussion that took place amongst the soldiers under their new
command. But in the Colonial War these officers came out of the
rigid military structure that existed back home in Portugal. In the
colonies they had to develop close relationships with the soldiers
under their command and they mixed with non-professional
conscripted officers, many of whom had come from the universities. They also came into contact with the white settlers, black
Africans and, for the first time, they were exposed to the ideas of
Karl Marx and international socialism through the propaganda
of their enemies. The result was an increased political awareness,
and the army officers most affected were those officers below the

rank of colonel, for it was they who were most involved in the fighting.

This politicisation was to split the higher from the lower officer ranks, a split which might have been further reinforced by the class differences that tended to exist between the ranks. The higher ranks were mostly from either the upper classes or senior civil servants from Lisbon and Oporto families or from the landed gentry, while the lower officer ranks were, typically, sons of poorly-paid civil servants or farm or shop owners. There was thus a possibility of a real class division existing inside the army officer corps. This division was probably less marked or even non-existent in the air force and the navy, because these two branches of the armed forces required more technically qualified officers and this tended to break down class barriers.

As the cohesion within the armed forces, and thus their strength, began to decline, the power of one of the branches of the paramilitary forces – the secret police – began to increase. After the right-wing coup of 1926 an embryonic secret police force had been set up. In 1933 Salazar formed the PVDE (Polícia de Vigilância e Defesa do Estado, Police of Vigilance and Defence of the State), which theoretically was to act as a frontier guard and watch-dog of any foreign infiltration into Portugal. In practice PVDE gathered political information on the Portuguese. The PVDE grew and, although its name was changed in 1945 to PIDE (Polícia Internacional de Defesa do Estado, International Police for the Defence of the State), it still gathered information on Portuguese dissidents. In 1969 Caetano changed the name again to DGS (Direcção-Geral de Segurança, Department of General Security) and for a while at least he curtailed some of its powers. However, this was only temporary, for it soon resumed its old role and became increasingly active in its intelligence operations. This increase in activity was in part due to the Colonial War. Units of the PIDE/DGS collaborated intimately with the armed forces prior to and during any military action.

Although the size of the secret police was never really known, it is possible that there were at least three thousand full-time agents, with probably ten times that number of informers. Not only did they use the normal electronic surveillance techniques, such as phone-tapping and bugging, but they also carried out torture and assassinations, as a means of obtaining and repressing information. From information obtained after the coup d'état in 1974, it is certain that PIDE/DGS agents murdered General Humberto Delgado after he had incurred the wrath of Salazar, when he opposed the regime's candidate in the presidential election.

A special relationship existed between the PIDE/DGS and the armed forces, and the secret police were never as active against the military as they were against the civilian population. This was because of the close cooperation that had to exist between the two forces, especially when on active service in the Colonial War, and, in addition, some officers in the military units were transferred to take command posts in these paramilitary units. The secret police might gather information about dissident officers, but military protocol did not allow them to intimidate or torture these officers. Thus young officers were able to organise themselves and voice opinions against the regime without undue fear of reprisals from the PIDE/DGS. This was important, as we shall see later, in allowing these young officers to set the events in motion that were to bring about the coup d'état of 25 April 1974.

Up to this point the causes of the Colonial War and the rise of dissent within the armed forces have been analysed. It now becomes appropriate to consider the socio-economic situation which existed in Portugal prior to the revolution.

The Church and the state

Portugal is and was a Roman Catholic country, and, as in so many other countries, Church and state have, and had, a special relationship. Like the military, the Church supported the Salazar/Caetano regimes and, in return, high-ranking church officials were accepted within its power structure. Salazar was a life-long close friend of Cardinal Cerejeira, the Patriarch of Lisbon, who was a powerful figure in the Portuguese Catholic Church. As students in the 1920s, they had both been very active politically. Both, in fact, had been leaders of the Centro Académico de Democracia Cristã, Academic Centre of Christian Democracy (a pressure group with strong monarchic leanings). Salazar was a Roman Catholic, but he managed to keep his New State and the Catholic Church somewhat apart, creating a rather peculiar relationship. Although officially the Portuguese were free to practise any religion, in fact only Catholicism was taught at school, although class attendance was not compulsory. Salazar allowed a Catholic university to be created in Lisbon, but the regime never recognised its degrees. The Church ran and owned a number of schools, yet the state never subsidised them. The regime accepted that Catholic marriages could legally be dissolved only by papal decree, though it accepted that marriages certified in registry offices could be dissolved by a court order.

The state allowed the Church a great deal of access to the media. It controlled a radio station, owned several newspapers and was a major share-holder of Portuguese television. In return, the Church was often seen to be a supporter of the state. For example, its support for the Colonial War was implied when the clergy blessed the soldiers before they embarked for the colonies.

It is fair to say that the Church did not always blindly accept the regime's policies. In the 1960s mainly as a result of the Colonial War some intellectual Roman Catholics in Lisbon openly criticised the policies of Salazar's New State. In 1958 in the north of the country the bishop of Oporto, D. António Gomes, voiced his disapproval of Salazar's policies. He wrote an open letter, criticising Salazar for his attempts to identify the New State with the Church. The bishop argued that the Catholic hierarchy should not compromise itself as it would result in a weakening of the power of the Church. Salazar's reply was to exile the bishop abroad for ten years. When Marcello Caetano took over from Salazar as prime minister, much of the 'liberal wing' of his parliament consisted of Roman Catholics.

The economy under Salazar

Under Salazar, up to the late 1950s, Portugal was essentially an agricultural country, and most people lived either by farming or, on the Atlantic coast, by fishing. The farming, which was mostly subsistence, was antiquated and the fishing was labour intensive and based upon century-old techniques. The products that were exported (for example, sardines, wine, cork and olive oil) were sold abroad at prices well below their true world-market value to large foreign companies. Salazar's regime kept the cost of living low by paying low wages to industrial workers and especially to farm workers. He tightly controlled the money supply and so prevented capital investment and industrial expansion. This meant there was always a supply of cheap labour. His economic policy successfully balanced the budget so that from 1928 onwards public expenditure was balanced by the state's income from taxes. Between 1929 and 1970 the GNP rose at an average annual rate of 7 per cent from two billion escudos to twenty-nine billion escudos. However the balance of payments (trade balance) was only positive between 1940 and 1945. From 1945 there was an increasing deficit.

The main result of this primitive monetarist policy was that to survive, firms had to be either very small or very large. This led to the evolution of massive corporations or monopolistic empires. One of them, CUF (Companhia União Fabril), owned almost two hundred companies, which included banks, insurance companies, shipping lines, large chemical factories and shipyards. CUF accounted for almost 10 per cent of the total wealth generated by the country and large corporations, such as CUF, were solely in the hands of the five families mentioned earlier. On the other hand, 86 per cent of all the other industrial firms were very small in that they employed less than ten workers. The large corporations provided many of the ministers of Salazar's governments, and as a result legislation was produced to keep and protect these large monopolistic empires. Not only did these groups provide ministers, but often ex-government ministers would enter into key positions within these corporations.

Under Salazar the economic life of the country was organised around the corporations of both employers and employees. Although these corporations were in theory independent, they were effectively run by the state, since appointments to key jobs were always politically vetted by the regime. There was even a Ministry of Corporations to co-ordinate and oversee their activities. The employers' corporations were the *grémios* and the regime decided that grémios were the only legal representative of the employers and would only deal with them. Different grémios dealt with different sectors of the economy, and business and managerial decisions made by the grémios for a certain sector of industry would bind all firms in that sector, whether or not the firm was a member of a grémio. Such was the power of the grémios that they could even force employers to join their respective grémios.

The workers were organised in *sindicatos* (unions), which were also controlled by the regime, and Salazar's government vetted all the major appointments. These sindicatos had no real bargaining power, as they were unable to use their most powerful weapon – the withdrawal of labour. Under Salazar it was illegal for workers to go on strike. Through its control of the grémios and the sindicatos, the regime was able to control wages, prices, the job market and thus the cost of production.

The regime resisted any form of major industrialisation until the late 1950s. Then, owing to some foreign investment, its need to process raw materials from the colonies, and in an attempt to increase agricultural productivity, some industrialisation occurred. This resulted in a movement of people from rural to urban areas. One major effect of this migration was the politicisation of agricultural workers, as they mixed with their more sophisticated, industrial counterparts. Urban migration further depleted the land labour force and worsened the agricultural situation.

Despite urban migration, the legacy of Salazar's lack of industrialisation can be seen clearly by examining the distribution of the work force. In 1974 Portugal had a population of eight million. Of these, two hundred thousand men were fighting the Colonial War. Then, about 31 per cent of the total work force were involved in agriculture, while 36 per cent were involved in industry. These figures may be directly compared to the United Kingdom, for example, where the corresponding figures were 2.7 per cent and 45.7 per cent. Compared to most other countries in Western Europe, a large proportion of the work force in Portugal was still on the land.

Portugal is divided in the middle by the river Tagus, which runs westwards across the country to enter the sea at Lisbon. In the early 1970s, most of the people living in the north of the country were smallholders, and they made up about 60 per cent of the total population. They were poor, they barely scraped a living from their farms, they were politically conservative and much influenced by the Church. South of the Tagus the farms were large and often owned by absentee landlords (*agrários*). Some of these farms were so large that 3 per cent of the total number of farms in Portugal occupied two-thirds of the cultivated land. In the Alentejo region, south of the Tagus, many farm workers worked part-time which meant that there was always a substantial body of unemployed labour. Since the 1930s these Alentejo workers had been politically active and the underground Portuguese Communist Party (PCP) had many supporters.

Between 1960 and 1972 large numbers of agricultural workers left the country in order to avoid being conscripted for the Colonial War, and to seek better social and economic conditions elsewhere. They went to the Northern European countries, to Canada, to the United States and to Venezuela. It is estimated that during the period some one and a quarter million Portuguese left the country, mostly illegally. These emigrants represented a large proportion of the work force, which meant that many regions were depleted of healthy, active men. With all these young men leaving in the early 1970s, only 10 per cent of the agricultural work force was under thirty-five years old.

The rural area's work force was thus composed of mainly the old or the very young, and these people were largely illiterate. In the early 1970s, of the total population in Portugal (older than fifteen years), 30 per cent were illiterate, but 60 per cent of this figure was made up of rural workers. This partially explains why, after 1974, the revolution largely failed to politicise and influence the inner rural areas. These areas were so cut off by poor communication, cultural habits and a way of life that had remained unchanged for generations that, even though television sets were to be seen in these areas, many country people said that they were completely unable to understand what was being transmitted. However, in the Alentejo region, thanks mainly to the PCP, the agricultural workers were highly politicised, and after April 1974, as we shall see later in part 2 and in the interviews, these workers brought about radical changes in the agricultural industry in this region.

Housing, health and education

The rapid growth in the early 1970s of the industrial belts mainly around Lisbon and Oporto created serious housing problems which persist even now. The housing shortage was so acute that in 1960 about forty thousand people lived in under ten thousand slum dwellings in the Lisbon area. Thus there was extreme overcrowding; they lacked both sewers and running water and ventilation was acutely inadequate. Throughout the 1960s and 1970s, housing became one of the worst problems that town dwellers had to face, and the situation was exacerbated by the lowest rate of house building in Europe. In 1974, about one-third of Portuguese families were without a house. For those with houses things were not much better. In 1900 only fourteen in a hundred dwellings were connected to a water supply. By 1970 the situation had not greatly improved: only thirty-three in every hundred dwellings were connected to the water supply.

The overcrowding and poor sanitation which were the result of the urban migration inevitably led to the spread of contagious diseases and general poorer health. At this time the health system in Portugal was abysmal and there was no real national health scheme. Most areas lacked qualified medical staff, as in the early 1970s about 80 per cent of all the doctors and nurses were to be found working in the three main cities – Lisbon, Oporto and Coimbra. Infant mortality (about 45 for 10,000 live births) was approximately four times that of, for example, Holland and the number of people suffering from infectious diseases, such as tuberculosis or intestinal infections, was almost twenty times greater in Portugal than in Holland.

Although the regime forced some Portuguese to pay for health care through the *Caixas de Previdência*, they received very little in return for their money. It says a lot about the regime that it allowed part of this collected money to be lent at low interest rates to the profitable companies that controlled large sectors of the Portuguese economy. However, until the late 1970s, most of the Portuguese paid nothing to the Caixas scheme and received nothing in return. Thus, for example, whenever farm workers, fishermen or construction workers who were not in the scheme were ill they had to pay for any medical treatment they received. Most workers were so poor that they could not afford any treatment.

Health care was not the only area in which Portugal lagged behind the rest of Europe. Education was inaccessible to large sectors of the population. In the early 1970s, more than one-third of the Portuguese older than fifteen were illiterate, and almost 60 per cent of the Portuguese urban and rural councils did not have secondary schools. Of the schools that did exist 40 per cent of these were in improvised buildings. Education was usually for the social elite. In the middle 1960s, of those who went to secondary school, only 4.2 per cent were the children of farm or industrial workers. Between 1960 and 1970 Portugal spent less on education than any other country in Europe.

Everyday life under the Salazar regime

Portugal under the Salazar regime was a subdued country ruled by old military men and faceless bureaucrats who were all under Salazar's thumb. The emphasis was on obedience to the New State. The state looked strong, solid and invincible and much of its architecture had the same feel. Huge, tomb-like buildings were often surrounded by tall, stone columns bearing eagles and laurel leaves sculptured in granite. The universities and technical schools looked like gigantic army barracks. Not surprisingly, the achievements of the regime were mainly in the area of civil engineering. It was particularly effective in bridge, dam and road building, improving communications and producing hydro-electric power. Thus in 1926 there were only 26,000 kilometres of road, but by 1974 the regime had built some 8,000 more kilometres. During this period (1930–74) there was a ten-fold increase in the number of kilometres of telephone lines laid (8,000–80,000) and energy production increased rapidly from 89 million kilo-watt hours in 1930 to 77 billion kilo-watt hours in 1974.

Although lagging well behind the rest of Europe, some 10,000 primary schools were built between 1926 and 1974 and several universities and technical colleges were created. The new university of Lisbon, Lisbon technical university, and the universities of Braga, Aveiro and Évora were all built under the Salazar/Caetano regime.

In order to run the New State, administrative buildings were constructed along with army installations. Sports stadiums as well as some council houses and hospitals were built. The ports were improved and some limited industrialisation took place, mainly to process material from the colonies. To this end the regime built oil refineries and steel works, and there was a chemical industry which was involved in the production of cement, fertilizer, plastics, sulphuric acid and nitrogen. In addition, there were rubber factories, paper mills and a pharmaceutical industry.

To live in Portugal during this period was to live in a country isolated from the rest of the world. The media was so heavily censored that the Portuguese never had a true picture of the state of the country. Political debate was non-existent and most Portuguese were unable to relate their personal, social and economic problems to the policies of the government. The state encouraged non-political activity, such as football, in largely successful attempts to distract the attention of the populus from the regime's socio-economic problems.

Corruption and nepotism were everywhere. For instance, in the universities many professors were the sons or other relations of the previous professors. As a rule, jobs and promotions were obtained through whom you knew, rather than on merit. Police and civil servant wages were low, and it was well known that for many a large proportion of their income would come either from bribes or from other jobs. These jobs were frequently related to their official capacity. Thus local officials in town councils were often involved in land speculation.

In this environment to protest about the nature of things was extremely difficult. Because of censorship, individuals were unable to mobilise public opinion. Within institutions, since everyone was surrounded by corruption, no one knew to whom they could turn. It is possible that, since large numbers of the population were involved in this morass of corruption and nepotism, support for the regime lasted as long as it did. However, not everyone accepted the status quo. There had been a history of civilian protest against the regime going back as far as 1927.

Civilian dissent in the Salazar/Caetano regime

Often civilian protest went hand in hand with military protest. In 1927 the Oporto revolt occurred. Junior officers and civilians mainly from the left-wing trade union CGT (Confederação Geral do Trabalho, General Confederation of Work) rebelled in both Oporto and Lisbon. The rebellion was unsuccessful and the leaders had to flee the country, escaping to France and forming the Paris League for the Overthrow of the Dictatorship. But in exile they were as unsuccessful as they had been at home. One outcome of the Oporto revolt was that the CGT and the Portuguese Communist Party (PCP) were outlawed by the regime. In 1928 civilians and officers from two regiments in Lisbon with the support of officers from Setubal and Lisbon attacked military units but failed to gain popular support. In 1931 some officers who had been arrested and deported to Madeira, the Azores and Guinea-Bissau for their part in the Oporto revolt organised an uprising. This was supported by workers and students in Portugal and officers and soldiers in two Lisbon regiments. Again the uprisings were quickly suppressed and the regime was given an excuse to increase its political repression.

In 1934 the labour laws creating a corporative state (corporations, grémios and sindicatos) were passed. As a reaction to these laws, workers attempted a general strike. Although not completely successful, it gathered wide support throughout the country and anti-regime violence flared. In Marinha Grande, in the north, armed workers captured the town. Railways, the Coimbra power station and police stations throughout the country were bombed. But again the uprising was crushed and it was followed by arrests and deportations. In reply, workers formed an underground trade union movement under the influence of the Portuguese Communist Party (Intersindical).

In 1936 the Spanish Civil War broke out and Salazar supported Franco by sending troops and naval vessels. Franco was to support Hitler, and Franco's infamous Blue Division, which invaded Russia along with the German army, was to have Portuguese soldiers. Among these Portuguese soldiers was General Spínola who was later to become President of the Republic after the 25 April 1974 coup. In 1936, however, part of Salazar's navy mutinied. The communists in the navy (ORA, the Revolutionary Organisation of the Navy) with the support of militant workers captured shore bases and two vessels anchored in the river. Their aim was to steam away and join the Spanish Republican navy, but before they could move, the vessels were shelled from shore-based batteries and the mutiny collapsed. The dissidents were sent to prison camps on the Cape Verde Islands. In the following year, anarchists failed to kill Salazar with their preferred weapon – the bomb.

As the Second World War progressed, because of Salazar's personal inclinations, Portugal, although outwardly neutral, strengthened military, economic and social ties with the Axis, and civilian opposition to the regime weakened. There were strikes in 1942, 1943 and 1944, but each time the workers were increasingly repressed. Factories were closed, workers imprisoned and tortured.

In 1941 the Portuguese Communist Party was reorganised under the leadership of Álvaro Cunhal, who was to lead the party for the next forty years. From then onwards it grew into the most effective opposition in the country. It had a strong base among the Alentejo farm workers and the industrial workers, and the party was totally dedicated to the overthrow of the regime. Most of its leaders underwent torture and many were imprisoned for large numbers of years – Álvaro Cunhal for thirteen years. In 1943 MUNAF (Movimento de Unidade Nacional Anti Fascista, Movement of Anti-Fascist Unity) was created under the leadership of General Norton de Matos. With civilian and military units, the movement planned a further coup, but the regime's secret police was excellent and the plans were discovered before the coup even took place.

The end of the Second World War saw the defeat of fascism, but because Salazar had supported the Axis countries during the early part of the war, he was forced, by external pressures, to carry out some 'democratisation'. For the first time in twenty years, the oposição was allowed to challenge the regime. Parliament was dissolved and parliamentary elections were called. The MUD (Movimento de Unidade Democrática, United Democratic Movement) was formed, but electoral rigging, tampering with electoral rolls and restricted access to the media prevented any MUD candidate from being elected. After these so-called elections, supporters of MUD were actively persecuted and imprisoned. Despite this, MUD went underground, and was even able to form a youth wing. The oposição was gradually becoming aware that it had some support and some strength. The regime also realised this and in reply Salazar strengthened, reorganised and recruited more secret police.

In spite of Salazar's attempts to crush the civilian opposition, in 1946 and 1947 there were strikes in the textile and ship-building industries. In 1947 Salazar removed twenty-two of the best professors in the universities. They were replaced by 'trustworthy' academics, loyal to the regime.

In March 1948 Salazar passed a law outlawing MUD.

Throughout the next two decades the oposição was to become split into two main groups: on the one hand there was the Communist Party and its sympathisers and on the other a heterogeneous group, amongst which were to be found the old republicans and future founder members of the Socialist Party (PS). During these twenty years the PCP was well organised but at election periods the two camps would emerge and form the oposição. However, it was the PCP that always drove the opposition to the regime and only at election times would the two groups emerge and unite. Eventually many PCP members were to leave the party and form and join other groups. Mário Soares, later to be a founder member of the PS and Portugal's first prime minister under the new constitution, was originally a member of the PCP. At the onset of the Colonial War in 1961 many republicans supported Salazar's colonial policies and this was to fragment the oposição for a short period.

In 1949 Norton de Matos was the oposição's candidate in the presidential elections. He withdrew as a result of the difficulties raised by the regime throughout the election, and General Oscar Carmona was re-elected as President, as he had been since 1928. In 1956 a law was passed by the regime which allowed people to be kept in prison for an indefinite period of time without trial.

As a result of the death of President Carmona, presidential elections were again held in 1951, but the oposição withdrew because of harassment and as a protest against the undemocratic regime. About 10 per cent of the Portuguese people voted in this election. Seven years later presidential elections had to be held again. This time the oposição's candidate was General Humberto Delgado. He was immensely popular, but despite his huge following from the liberal military and such diverse groups as the monarchists and the Portuguese Communist Party, the regime's candidate was elected – Admiral Américo Thomaz. Threatened by the support given by the oposição to Delgado, which said that its first political act would be to throw out Salazar, Salazar abolished direct presidential elections. Humberto Delgado was shot by PIDE/DGS secret service agents in Spain, much to Franco's displeasure, and with the outbreak of the Colonial War in 1961, the civilian opposition weakened and started to splinter.

Student unrest started in 1962 in the Lisbon universities. To avoid political persecution and the Colonial War, many of these students fled the country. Some of them, together with other political emigrants and members of the Portuguese Communist Party, who were already living abroad, formed the FPLN (Frente Patriótica de Libertação Nacional, Patriotic Front for National Liberation). This front had the support of the Algerian president and throughout the 1960s the FPLN broadcast daily anti-government propaganda from Algeria.

Parliamentary elections were held in 1965, and the oposição criticised the regime's colonial policies. However, frustrated by the inability to bring about any effective change within the regime, the opposition became increasingly violent. Three urban guerilla groups were formed: LUAR (Liga Unitária de Acção Revolucionária, League of United Revolutionary Action) was created in 1967 by the Communist Party, which also organised the ARA (Acção Revolucionária Armada, Armed Revolutionary Action) in 1970. The BR (Brigadas Revolucionárias, Revolutionary Brigade) was formed in 1971 by the FPLN. In the same year the NATO Communications Centre was blown up by the BR and the ARA attacked a PIDE Bureau, destroying an aeroplane hangar in the raid.

With the removal of Salazar from power, coupled with increasing military unrest (there were to be some 25,000 desertions before the Colonial War was over), civilian opposition became stronger and more active. In 1969, during elections, the two anti-regime electoral fronts emerged. They organised themselves into the CDE (Comissão Democrática Eleitoral, Democratic Election Committee), which had strong links with the Communist Party, and the CEUD (Comissão Eleitoral de Unidade Democrática, United Democratic Election Committee). A few months after the coup d'etat on 25 April 1974, the CDE became a political party, the MDP/CDE (Movimento Democrático Português, Portuguese Democratic Movement). The CEUD had many politicians who were to later form the Socialist Party.

The result of the 1969 elections was that the official regime candidates were, as usual, elected. But from then on new pressure groups and parties continued to form. Possibly as an outcome of the student unrest that was occurring in Europe and America, many Portuguese young people became interested in the ideologies of the ultra left, and in 1970 a Maoist group was born, the MRPP (Movimento Reorganizativo do Partido do Proletariado,

Movement for the Reorganisation of the Party of the Proletariat).
It had a large following among students and young industrial
workers. Also in that year a pressure group, SEDES (Sociedade de
Estudos de Desenvolvimento Económico e Social, Society for the
Study of Economic and Social Development), made up of economists, lawyers and technocrats, was formed as many of the
intellectual middle classes had become dissatisfied with the
regime. Many of its members were left-wing Catholics and some
had formed the liberal wing of the Caetano regime. Three years
later, in 1973, the PRP (Partido Revolucionário do Proletariado,
Revolutionary Party of the Proletariat) was formed from the BR.
Exiled Portuguese met in West Germany and created the Socialist
Party in 1972, a party that was to play a major role in the next
chapter of Portuguese history.

The years 1973 and 1974 saw effective workers' strikes
throughout the country, as the civilian opposition grew from
strength to strength. In 1973 Caetano, feeling threatened by the
liberal wing of his party and unable to stand their continued
criticism of his policies, forced the main leaders to resign from the
National Assembly. Caetano's grip on the political situation was
clearly weakening when in April 1973 the oposição met openly
and defiantly in the town of Aveiro. By then it was clear that
Caetano was not going to allow any constitutional liberalisation
of the regime. Many Portuguese realised that change might only
be brought about by a radical transfer of power. The stage was set
for revolution and this was to be brought about through the
Armed Forces Movement and the coup d'état of 25 April 1974.

The lead-up to 25 April

The event that really brought together large numbers of middle-
rank and junior officers was a government-organised congress in
Oporto in June 1973. This Congress of Combatants was an
attempt by the government to try to increase support for its
Colonial War in Africa. The regime intended the congress to pass
motions that called for an increase in the war effort. However,
officers in Guinea-Bissau, who had been under Spínola's
command (among them Ramalho Eanes and Otelo Saraiva de
Carvalho), disagreed with these motions. They contacted like-
minded officers in Portugal and formed themselves into a group.
The military hierarchy refused this group permission to register

its disapproval of the motions at the congress. In reply, the group collected over four hundred signatures in support of a document which stated that, since most of the officers on active service were not allowed to speak at the congress, any motions passed would be invalid.

This highlighted the schism that existed between the lower and higher officer ranks, for the generals, who had all been appointed by the regime, were staunch supporters of the Colonial War. The schism led some junior officers to think of forming an association through which they could voice their professional complaints. A meeting was convened in September 1973, at Évora in south-eastern Portugal, in response to a law passed by the regime in July. The association was called the Movement of Captains and the new law was to be a disastrous one for the regime. It enabled non-professional (conscripted) officers to enter the ranks of the professional officers by attending the Military Academy for just over a year. This was seen by the professional military as a serious erosion of their status, for all professional officers had had to attend a four-year course at the Academy. Moreover, these conscripted officers, after attending a one-year course, would have accelerated promotion, since their years of military service served before attending the Academy were to be counted in establishing their officer seniority. Thus professional officers felt discriminated against by the government, and considered the law to be particularly unfair: it was they who had been fighting the Colonial War for the regime for some twelve years.

Although the Movement of Captains was ostensibly not about political grievances, it was used by a group of officers to further their political aims. These officers believed that the only way to end the Colonial War was to bring down the Caetano regime. A Movement of Captains was set up in each of the colonies of Guinea-Bissau, Angola and Mozambique, and all three movements kept in close communication with the one in Portugal.

In October 1973 parliamentary elections were held, and as usual they were rigged. Major Melo Antunes, a prominent figure in the Movement of Captains, became a member of the oposição, under the CDE banner. In December of the same year Colonel Fabião publicly denounced a right-wing coup that was in the process of being organised by General Kaulza de Arriaga, the once military commander of Mozambique. One of the aims of this coup was to remove Generals Costa Gomes and Spínola from office. These generals supported the Movement of Captains from their senior positions of general chief of staff and vice-general chief of staff respectively.

On 5 March 1974 the young officers met at Cascais, a seaside resort near Lisbon, and they agreed to collaborate with Generals Spínola and Costa Gomes. (They needed Spínola as a figurehead for the movement, and also the support of regiments loyal to him.) But later in the month, the two generals were dismissed for their refusal to support the regime. This moved some officers in the Movement of Captains, which was now called the Movement of the Armed Forces, into open rebellion. An infantry regiment from the town of Caldas da Rainha marched on Lisbon, thinking that support would come from other military units, but it did not, and almost two hundred young officers were arrested. Among them was Captain Vasco Lourenço, one of the founders of the MFA, who was deported to the Azores. As a result of Vasco Lourenço's deportation, Major Otelo Saraiva de Carvalho took over the operational side of the MFA. He planned and led the military operation that eventually brought down some fifty years of authoritarian regime. He decided that the coup should take place on 25 April. No troops loyal to the MFA would surround army barracks, as it was hoped that the uncommitted armed forces would follow. By 11 pm on 24 April 1974 the MFA leaders had a small army complete with tanks and armoured vehicles at the alert and ready to move. Not long after midnight a song by Jose Afonso was broadcast by a Lisbon radio station:

> Grândola, brunette town
> Land of brothers,
> Town, it's the people who give you the power.
> A friend in every corner,
> Equality on every face.
> In the shadow of the ageless oak tree,
> I swear to choose your power as my companion.

The song, which seemed to carry with it some of the ideals of the young MFA captains, was the signal for the columns to move. By 3 o'clock the centre of Lisbon was occupied. The 25 April coup had arrived. The rest of the armed forces and the Portuguese people were to follow the tanks on to the streets.

2 *The coup d'état and revolution*

Introduction

This part is divided into three: a chronology, the interviews, and an analysis section. It deals only with the coup d'état, the revolution and the immediate post-revolutionary period. It is generally considered that the Portuguese revolution ended on 25 November 1975, but for completeness the immediate post-revolutionary period is dealt with and the chronology extended to the end of 1976. (In part 3 a brief survey of Portugal's history is included up to April 1984.) The chronology is extensive and covers the period from 25 April 1974 to December 1976 so that the interviews are seen in context and can be better understood. It is not proposed that the chronology be studied in depth, rather that it is used to give greater insight into the interviews.

The interviewees use dates to refer to historical events. This is something that the Portuguese often do when they refer to a sequence of historical events. For example, when Portugal became a Republic on 5 October 1910 (as a result of a military and civilian revolution which deposed the king) this whole sequence of events is referred to as 5 October. In Lisbon today one can find many streets named after dates which represent historical events. Even the famous bridge that crosses the river Tagus has been renamed Ponte 25 de Abril in memory of the 1974 coup d'état. Previously it had been known as Ponte Salazar. In the revolutionary period that followed the coup d'état there were three key events which are known, even officially, as 28 September 1974, 11 March 1975 and 25 November 1975. The dates refer to a whole series of events rather than just to the events of that day.

Just after the chronology, a number of block diagrams are included which show a breakdown of the power structure that prevailed after the three key events. There are also tables which

31

show the composition of the various committees and councils which make up this power structure. A quick glance at these tables shows that the interviews cover most of the officers who played decisive roles in the revolution.

In the presentation of the interviews the officers have been loosely grouped together. This grouping is an arbitrary one and based upon an analysis of their roles throughout the revolution and the way in which they interpreted the course of the revolution. All those interviewed were men of action and were true to their political beliefs. The grouping is loose because each of the groups that was chosen could be applied to each officer. Nevertheless they were classified because it was considered that these were the dominant characteristics of their personalities.

To help understand the armed forces' hierarchy, appendix 7 gives a detailed outline of the structure of the armed forces: the ranks are somewhat different from those in the British armed forces.

Chronology, 1974–6

Since the chronology is extensive, focus is first given to the three key events by describing them in brief.

After the 25 April 1974 coup d'état, António de Spínola became the new interim President. He appointed many of his supporters to positions of power in the Council of State (CS table 1, block diagram 1). The MFA had set up a seven-person Junta of National Salvation (JSN) to run the country with the Council of State acting as a sort of second chamber. The Council of State was made up of the members of the JSN and fourteen others, all the seven members of the Comissão Coordenadora do Programa, Co-ordinating Committee of the Programme of the MFA (CCP) and seven meritorious Portuguese citizens (see table 1 for composition). Legislative and executive decisions were to be made by a provisional government which was later to be dissolved after the new Constitution had been written and a democracy established. The prime minister of the first provisional government was Palma Carlos, a law professor from Lisbon university. Within the government there was a spread of political opinion from communists, socialists, moderates and independents. The leader of the Socialist Party, Mário Soares, was the minister of foreign affairs; and the leader of the Communist Party, Alvaro Cunhal, was a minister without portfolio.

28 SEPTEMBER 1974

The first provisional government was almost unable to act, split irrevocably with different ideologies. The result was a power struggle between President Spínola and the MFA and its Programme Co-ordinating Committee. One of the major disagreements was decolonisation. Spínola wanted a loose federation of the colonies of Portugal (so-called neo-colonial solution), while the MFA sided with the independence movements that were fighting in the colonies and wanted to give them full independence. On 27 September 1974 Spínola attempted to sweep himself into power on the wave of a massive uprising of the 'silent majority'. Outmanoeuvred, his attempt failed, and he cancelled the demonstration. On 30 September he resigned his presidency and was replaced by General Costa Gomes.

Throughout the whole of 1974 until 11 November 1975, when the last and most important colony became independent, one of the most important aims of the MFA was rapid decolonisation.

11 MARCH 1975

Spínola's resignation was a victory for the MFA and the military became increasingly, although often unwillingly, involved in politics. In an attempt to regain power, Spínola and his supporters attempted a counter-coup in the hope that many of the uncommitted military would follow. His base was to be the Tancos air force base north of Lisbon. Anticipated support would be from the commandos under Almeida Bruno, the Tancos paratroopers, and the air force under Mendes Dias. In the event, on 10 March 1975, the counter-coup was probably prematurely triggered and the hoped for military support never arrived. Spínola fled the country for Spain, France and then Brazil.

25 NOVEMBER 1975

The departure of Spínola speeded up the leftward momentum of the revolution. The mass movement gathered force, and a new prime minister, Vasco Gonçalves, legislated Portugal leftwards. However, democratic elections for the Constitutional Assembly applied a brake to the swing. Then, following a period of intense political activity (the 'hot summer'), the power of the mass movement and its military supporters was eventually curbed. With the colonies now all independent, the Colonial War ended, and the armed forces were ready to re-establish order; they abandoned their association with the left. The middle-ground civilian political parties were beginning to flex their new-found muscles, and on 25 November 1975 tanks were on the Lisbon streets again, this time under the operational command of Ramalho Eanes. The operational commander of the 25 April 1974 coup, Otelo Saraiva de Carvalho, ended up under house arrest. Eanes was to become Portugal's first President under the new Constitution, and 25 November saw the beginning of the end of the MFA as a political force. The civilian parties, especially the Socialist Party, were to become increasingly more powerful. The leader of the PS, Mário Soares, was to become Portugal's first prime minister under the new Constitution.

1974

25 April   The coup d'état.
                      Laws were passed dismissing President Américo Thomaz, Caetano's parliament, the old government, the Council of State and the district and colonial governors. The secret police (PIDE/DGS), the Portuguese Legion, the youth movement (Mocidade Portuguesa), and Caetano's official party, Acção Nacional Popular, were all disbanded.

26 April   The day after the coup and the country was run by the Junta of National Salvation (JSN) which commanded all the armed forces and appointed the first and second provisional governments. The JSN also elected the first and second presidents and passed all the laws until the Council of the Revolution was formed.
                      Spínola went on television and announced the

MFA Programme (appendix 1) which had been written by the Political Committee of the MFA in conjunction with Spínola and Costa Gomes. The Political Committee was renamed The Co-ordinating Committee of the Programme of the MFA on 25 April 1974 (see block diagram 1). Most members of the MFA preferred to keep a low profile at this time.

An amnesty law for political crimes against the old regime was passed.

27 April   After some hesitation on the part of the JSN all political prisoners were freed from the prisons of Caxias and Peniche: it was public pressure that forced the JSN to act. A law was passed whereby delegates of the JSN were to be appointed to all government ministries.

29 April   MFA officers of the navy met to discuss the removal of all pro-regime naval officers and later some officers were removed from office.

The stock exchange was closed.

A law defining the *saneamentos* (cleansing) of the armed forces was passed.

First occupations of private houses occurred in Lisbon.

1 May   The May Day demonstrations took place – the largest public demonstrations ever held in Portugal.

5 May   The far left tried, unsuccessfully, to block new army recruits being sent to the Colonial War and from this moment onwards the ultra left became increasingly active in the revolutionary process.

6 May   The social democrat PPD (Partido Popular Democráta, Popular Democratic Party) was founded as there were no parties representing

the middle ground or the right wing in Portuguese politics.

13 May   The Intersindical in the district of Braga was formed as a confederation made up of representatives from all the trade unions. The Intersindical was to become known as the 'CGTP Intersindical' as it was seen, by the workers, to be a continuation of the CGT (which was originally formed in 1919 as part of the worldwide anarcho-syndicalist movement) and was a confederation of the Portuguese trade unions (sindicatos). In Salazar's New State this union movement was destroyed and replaced by state-controlled sindicatos. In Caetano's Social State a number of independent unions emerged and they were important in co-ordinating the workers after the 25 April coup, since they were already reasonably well organised and had had some political experience. The PCP and the Intersindical co-operated closely with one another throughout the course of the revolution.

A law defining the new set of conditions under which Salazar's old Constitution should be followed was passed.

14 May   Censorship was officially abolished.

15 May   Spínola was officially proclaimed President.

This day marked the first confrontation between Spínola and the MFA when Spínola ordered the arrest of Colonel Varela Gomes as he said Gomes was interfering with captured PIDE/DGS files. The MFA forced Spínola to release Gomes and so revealed that Spínola was not in control of the MFA.

16 May   The first provisional government was sworn in under Prime Minister Palma Carlos. The government included the PS, PCP, MDP/CDE, PPD and SEDES.

26 May   Minimum salary was established at 3,300 escudos per month. The last days of May saw the first strikes for better wages and conditions in the underground, the bus services, the postal services and the bakeries.

31 May   The Council of State, which was created from the JSN, the CCP and seven Portuguese citizens, was sworn in (table 1). The creation of this Council had been proposed in the MFA political programme (appendix 1) and its composition was chosen by Spínola. He attempted to give himself a majority vote on the Council, but in the Palma Carlos crisis (see below), the Council voted against Spínola. This led to the resignation of Palma Carlos.

8 June   First MFA meeting at Manutenção Militar. The MFA considered that it was being diluted by infiltrators and that it was losing control of the decolonisation process, so it decided to tighten membership control and to create MFA delegates in the military units. A special body linking the CCP with the general chief of staff was also created.

13 June   Second MFA meeting at Manutenção Militar where the minister of economic affairs described the state of the economy and argued that there should be a wage freeze. Here Spínola attempted to dissolve the MFA and become more powerful. The attempt failed and this was the first public confrontation between Spínola and the leaders of the MFA. Vasco Gonçalves pledged support to Spínola provided that Spínola implemented the MFA political programme. Sá Carneiro, the leader of PPD, proposed that a 'state of siege' be declared and that full powers should be given to Spínola.

17 June	Collapse of the first provisional government which led to the resignation of Palma Carlos. The government claimed it needed special powers as it was unable to govern.
19 June	After meeting President Nixon in the Azores, Spínola affirmed that 'there is a total identity of spirit between Nixon and Portugal'.
24 June	A document from the general chief of staff of the armed forces, Costa Gomes, was circulated amongst the armed forces which proposed the integration of all the armed forces into the MFA but this document was never really enforced.
8 July	COPCON (Commando Operacional do Continente, Operational Command for the Continent) was created by law. In theory COPCON was an extremely powerful body, capable of calling out any military unit in the country in order to protect the integrity of the Portuguese state. It was later to play an important role in the process of the revolution. The formation of COPCON was a tactical move by the CCP aimed at reducing Spínola's influence in the armed forces. The CCP was concerned with the manner in which he had dealt with Caetano and Thomaz and they worried at his attempts to increase his support in the military by speaking at units stationed throughout the country.
9 July	The Palma Carlos crisis. Prime Minister Palma Carlos's attempted resignation resulted in the collapse of the first provisional government.
11 July	Palma Carlos resigned.
13 July	Otelo Saraiva de Carvalho was given command of COPCON and also made commander of the Lisbon military region.

18 July   Spínola failed on a number of occasions to choose a new prime minister, which showed that he needed the participation of the MFA in government.

Formation of the second provisional government with Vasco Gonçalves as prime minister. The government included the PPD, PCP, PS and SEDES.

The MFA began to emerge as the leading political force in the country and even created its own propaganda division – the Fifth Division (see block diagram 2).

24 July   Rosa Coutinho was appointed president of the governing junta of Angola; later he became high commissioner of Angola. He and his aides were later able to negotiate with the three liberation movements and bring about the so-called Alvor agreement.

27 July   Spínola acknowledged that full independence would be given to the colonies which was a retreat from his original plan of a federal solution to the colonial problem. It showed that he was losing influence and power, especially as the negotiations with the liberation movements in the colonies were being conducted solely by the MFA, with the aim of giving them full independence.

9 August   Re-establishment of diplomatic relations with Russia.

10 August   The right to strike was officially recognised by the Council of State. Before this date, there had been strikes and so recognition can be seen as an example of legislating after events had taken place (another example of this is the Agrarian Reform law, see appendix 6, and below).

17 August	The old regime's state corporations (sindicatos, grémios etc., see part 1) were abolished.
26 August	An agreement was signed between Portugal and the PAIGC movement of Guinea-Bissau.
7 September	An agreement was signed between Portugal and the FRELIMO movement of Mozambique. Rádio Mozambique was taken over by white settlers as part of the intensification of the political unrest amongst the settlers opposed to the MFA's decolonisation programme. This unrest was part of a reaction against the MFA which eventually led to the 28 September counter-coup.
9 September	Admiral Victor Crespo was appointed high commissioner to Mozambique.
10 September	Guinea-Bissau became independent of Portugal. Speech by Spínola in which he opposed anarchism and called on the 'silent majority' for support. The day before, a committee to organise demonstrations by the 'silent majority' had been formed. The central banks of Portugal (Bank of Portugal), Angola (Bank of Angola) and Mozambique (National Overseas Bank) were nationalised.
26 September	Prime Minister Vasco Gonçalves was publicly insulted at a bull-fight in Lisbon, which he had been pressurised to attend by President Spínola. At the bull-ring the public applauded Spínola.
27 September	The government authorised a demonstration by the 'silent majority'.
28 September	Public demonstrations by the 'silent majority' were frustrated by road blocks set up by left-wing elements around Lisbon. Also COPCON

intervened to prevent these demonstrations from taking place. This date marked the collapse of Spínola's influence in the armed forces. A number of public figures (among them General Kaulza de Arriaga) were arrested by COPCON for their alleged involvement in right-wing counter-coups.

29 September   Spínola tried, through the Brazilian embassy, to involve the USA and NATO in his attempted bid for power but, for unknown reasons, he abandoned this line of action. He resigned as President and the JSN nominated General Costa Gomes as the new President and Vasco Gonçalves to be prime minister in the third provisional government.

30 September   Costa Gomes became the new President of the Republic of Portugal. Spínola announced his resignation in a televised speech.

The third provisional government took office under Prime Minister Vasco Conçalves; the government included the PCP, PS and the PPD.

The Committee of Twenty (Superior Council of the Movement) was formed by the MFA (see block diagram 3 and table 1) and it was decided that its members had to belong to the MFA. They were taken from the CCP, the JSN and the first provisional government. This Committee led to the Council of the Revolution following the failure of the 11 March counter-coup (see below).

The formation of the Committee of Twenty marked the time when there was a reorganisation of the MFA into a more structured body. The Committee was the co-ordinating body of the MFA and it included all those who held important civilian and military positions. The reorganisation resulted in the formation of an

MFA assembly and councils for all the different branches of the armed forces.

9 October   The industrial laws of the previous regime (see part 1), which had protected the powerful monopolistic groups, were abolished.

12 October   Government delegates were appointed to the banks in an attempt to control the economy (the flight of currency abroad, for example).

25 November   Government delegates were appointed to private firms.

26 November   An agreement that recognised the independence of São Tomé and Príncipe was signed.

31 November   The Council of State passed a law which recognised the existence of political parties.

6 December   The MFA assembly discussed the Melo Antunes plan for the economic recovery of Portugal. This plan was written by a group of economists under the chairmanship of Melo Antunes. It was considered to be a moderate plan, based upon a mixed economy and did not include large-scale nationalisations.

The plan, which saw a role for some of the old monopolistic groups, was criticised by the left wing of the MFA, but it was supported by Vasco Gonçalves and approved by his provisional government. (It was published in the press on 21 February 1975.) Although Vasco Gonçalves supported the plan, he did argue, however, that any economic transformations should have the workers' support. The plan was also supported by the employers' confederation, the CIP (Confederação das Indústrias Portuguesas, Confederation of Portuguese Industries).

In December UDP (União Democrática

Popular, Popular Democratic Union), a Marxist group, was created. Its founder members came from a number of Marxist groups which originally came from an offshoot of the PCP – the FAP (Frente de Acção Popular, Front of Popular Action).

17 December   The agreement between Portugal and the liberation movement of São Tomé and Príncipe, MLSTP (Movimento Libertação de São Tomé e Príncipe, Liberation Movement for São Tomé and Príncipe) was signed.

31 December   The revised structure of the MFA was announced and explained in a press conference (Committee of Twenty, MFA assembly, councils for different branches of armed forces).

1975

11 January   President Costa Gomes publicly announced that elections would be held in April for the Constitutional Assembly which would write Portugal's new Constitution.

13 January   The Committee of Twenty advocated the principle of the Unicidade Sindical, which stated that each trade was to be represented by only one trade union.

14 January   Public demonstrations in favour of Unicidade Sindical. However, the PS, the PPD and the CDS (Centro Democrático Social, Social and Democratic Centre formed in July 1974), believed that the Unicidade Sindical was an attempt by the MFA to give control of the trade union movement to the PCP; the communists had a strong influence in most of the trade unions.

The PCP became legal, the first civilian party to become so.

15 January   The Alvor agreement: an agreement between the three liberation movements in Angola and the Portuguese government on the steps to be taken to achieve independence. In the end this agreement did not work because of the civil war that broke out between the three liberation movements. The war was largely brought about by the intervention of foreign powers: the Cubans supported the MPLA, the USA supported FNLA, and South Africa supported UNITA.

16 January   Public demonstration by PS supporters opposed to the principle of Unicidade Sindical.

17 January   Frank Carlucci arrived in Lisbon as US ambassador. It was later argued that by supporting the PS, he was to play a decisive role in the political struggle that eventually led to the coup on 25 November.

20 January   The principle of Unicidade Sindical was made law.

26 January   CDS Congress in Oporto was stopped by left-wing demonstrators.

1 February   Sanches Osório was elected secretary general of the PDC (Partido da Democracia Cristão, Christian Democrat Party). This party was formed at the beginning of 1975 and is distinct from the CDS. Both parties claimed to be within the Christian democratic movement, although only the CDS was recognised by the international Christian democrat movement. The PDC was later to be accused of being involved in the 11 March coup by supporting Spínola.

15 February   An agreement with the Vatican was signed which allowed marriages that were performed

in church to be dissolved in a civilian court. The agreement was the result of political pressure on the government.

11 March   Spínola and his supporters attempted a military coup. Their aeroplanes bombed the light artillery regiment RALI but the coup failed and Spínola escaped to Spain in a military helicopter. On the night of 11 March, the MFA assembly met and for the first time it included sergeants and privates. (The Group of Nine, see below, were to call this assembly the 'wild assembly'.)

13 March   Civilian members of the Council of State resigned.

14 March   The Committee of Twenty (or the Superior Council of the Movement) was renamed the Council of the Revolution, and enlarged to twenty-eight members (see table 2 and block diagram 4).

     Nationalisation of all the banks. These nationalisations were opposed by Melo Antunes, as they did not agree with his economic plan and they created a split between Melo Antunes (and his supporters) and the supporters of Vasco Gonçalves (Gonçalvists).

15 March   Nationalisation of all the insurance companies was ordered by the Council of the Revolution.

17 March   The PDC, the Maoist party, MRPP, and the AOC (Aliança Operária Camponesa, Farm-workers' Alliance) were banned.

20 March   The Council of the Revolution was sworn in, in the presence of the President of the Republic.

24 March   Spínola and his supporters from the 11 March counter-coup were officially expelled from the army.

26 March	The fourth provisional government was sworn in with Vasco Gonçalves as prime minister (block diagram 4). It included the PS, the PCP, the PPD, the MDP/CDE and members of the MFA.
31 March	Unemployment benefit was brought in.
3 April	The composition of the MFA assembly was defined by law.
10 April	The Council of the Revolution approved the economic measures of the new government.
11 April	The first pact between the MFA and the political parties was signed. This pact (see appendix 2) stated that the forthcoming electoral results could not be used to decide power sharing among the parties and the MFA. This, in effect, was saying that the MFA political programme would be implemented regardless of any electoral results.
14 April	A law was passed regulating house occupations.
15 April	Electricity, oil and transport were nationalised. Legalisation was created for the expropriation of land in the Alentejo region (see appendix 6). Land occupations had already taken place.
25 April	Elections for the Constitutional Assembly were held. The Assembly was to write Portugal's new post-revolutionary Constitution. Results were as follows:

UDP   0.8%(1)
PPD   26.4%(81)
MDP/CDE 4.1%(5)
CDS   7.7%(16)
PCP   12.5%(30)
PS   37.9%(115)

(The number of delegates is shown in parentheses. Percentages are percentages of the total number of votes cast. UDP was the Popular Democratic Union, União Democrática Popular. It was an ultra-left-wing group with Maoist leanings.)

These results marked the start of the bid for power by the PS, as they realised that they had the largest following amongst the electorate. Until these elections the size of the following of each of the political parties was unknown.

30 April   A law was passed recognising CGTP Intersindical. A law was also passed recognising employers' associations.

1 May   Onset of a political crisis. There was a clash between the PS and the communist-dominated confederation of the Portuguese trade unions, CGTP Intersindical. (The CGTP Inter. is like the TUC in the United Kingdom, but it is a more powerful body.)

Originally CGTP Intersindical proposed to have a workers' demonstration on May Day in Lisbon and not invite any of the political parties; although party representatives would be there, they would not speak. However, the PS disagreed and organised a separate demonstration, the theme being its opposition to the MFA–parties pact (see 11 April 1975). The PS march eventually converged on 1 May stadium, where the workers' demonstration, organised by Intersindical, was listening to May Day speeches. Mário Soares (the leader of the PS) was intent on speaking, but he was prevented from gaining access to the platform.

12 May   In Angola, the MPLA and FNLA started a civil war.

21 May   Ultra-left-wing workers of the *República* news-
              paper ejected the management, as they argued
              that the paper was an organ of the PS. The
              journalists sided with the management, claiming
              that not only was the paper independent, but it
              was one of the few newspapers in Lisbon that
              was independent of the PCP. The PS accused the
              PCP of being behind the workers' protest.
                 The MFA minister of information supported
              the management, as did the prime minister,
              Vasco Gonçalves. Gonçalves proposed that the
              newspaper be given back to the management,
              and also that a member of the MFA be installed
              to ensure that the newspaper did not become
              counter-revolutionary. COPCON tried to nego-
              tiate with the ultra-left-wing workers, but
              without success and eventually negotiations
              broke down. COPCON closed the newspaper
              when asked to by the management. After this
              'the *República* newspaper affair' was to be used
              by the PS as a warning of the dangers of a
              communist take-over of the country.

22 May   There were public demonstrations by PS sup-
              porters against the closure of the *República*
              newspaper and PS ministers of the Gonçalves
              government decided to boycott cabinet meetings
              until the *República* was reopened.

27 May   New divorce laws were passed.

2 June   The Constitutional Assembly met for the first
              time and set about writing a new Portuguese
              Constitution.

16 June   Council of the Revolution decided to hand the
              República newspaper back to the workers.
                 Minimum salary raised to 4,000 escudos a
              month.

The previous regime's grémios were transformed into employers' associations.

18 June   There were public demonstrations against the Church's attempt to shut down the Church-owned Rádio Renascença by cutting off its electricity supply. Rádio Renascença had previously been occupied by the left and had been broadcasting left-wing propaganda.

19 June   The Council of the Revolution published a plan for political action (PAP, Plano de Acção Política). This was an attempt to reach a compromise between three factions in the MFA: the Gonçalvists, the followers of Otelo and the political moderates. These moderates were to become the Group of Nine.

23 June   Otelo was nominated as full commander of COPCON and to be responsible only to the President of the Republic, General Costa Gomes.

25 June   Independence of Mozambique.

1 July   The government decided to return Rádio Renascença to the Church.

3 July   The Council of the Revolution opposed the nationalisation of Rádio Renascença.

5 July   Independence of Cape Verde Islands.

8 July   The General Assembly of the MFA published a document known as the 'Alliance of the People and the MFA'. It proposed parallel civilian and military structures based upon 'direct democracy'. The MFA–People's Alliance caused a great deal of controversy, both within the armed forces and the political parties and was never

implemented; it was really the Gonçalvists reacting against the PAP.

10 July

The PS and the PPD criticised the MFA–People's Alliance document, and PS ministers left the government, arguing that the government was dominated by the PCP; moreover, they were dissatisfied by the way in which it had handled the *República* newspaper affair.

11 July

The Council of the Revolution expelled the dissenting PS ministers from the government.

12 July

Independence of São Tomé and Príncipe.

15 July

The MPLA were the victors in the civil war in Angola.

16 July

The Council of the Revolution appointed Costa Gomes, Vasco Gonçalves and Otelo to write a new MFA political programme, to be finally approved by the Council.

17 July

The PPD withdrew from government in support of PS.

19 July

The PS were prevented from holding demonstrations in Lisbon against the Vasco Gonçalves government.

20 July

Several headquarters of the PCP and the MDP/CDE were bombed by the right-wing Maria da Fonte movement. The Maria da Fonte movement was named after a mid-nineteenth-century revolutionary movement that was composed of aristocrats, high-ranking officers, clergymen and workers: its aims were the downfall of a totalitarian government. The twentieth-century movement arose in the north and was supported by the Church and a number of anti-communist groups. It has been alleged that it had links with the MDLP (see Sanches Osório interview, p. 85) and the Group of Nine.

23 July The infantry branch (the largest branch) of the MFA met at Mafra. It was voted that the MFA assembly be altered to allow proportional representation for all the branches of the MFA, that the Fifth Division be dissolved (see below, 25 August), that the MFA assembly should be only a consultative body, and that there was no objection if Prime Minister Gonçalves were to be replaced by another person.

24 July The army assembly met, and was presided over by Fabião. Vasco Lourenço failed to get the army assembly to accept the previous day's decisions.

25 July The Gonçalvists managed to call a full MFA assembly. Vasco Gonçalves presented a political programme that bore little relation to his commitment to the Council of the Revolution (see above). Vasco Lourenço forced him to withdraw his programme. Finally the MFA assembly nominated Costa Gomes, Otelo and Vasco Gonçalves to form a Directorate to lead the country and the Council was to act as a consultative body. The Directorate never met.

29 July The Agrarian Reform law was passed.

30 July The Directorate was officially created.

7 August Publication of the Document of the Nine (see appendix 4) by the Group of Nine. The Group of Nine was a heterogeneous group which had strong links with the PS. It also included important military officers, such as the commanders of the north (Pires Veloso, see 12 September), centre (Franco Charais) and south (Pezarat

Correia) military regions outside Lisbon. These officers were important in allowing the 25 November coup to take place.

8 August The fifth provisional government was sworn in, with Vasco Gonçalves as prime minister. The major parties were the PCP and MDP/CDE.

11 August The members of the Group of Nine were suspended from the Council of the Revolution. It was argued that the Document of the Nine was published without first being discussed in the Council of the Revolution and the more left-wing members of the Council considered that this was an act of treason and they were strong enough to expel the Group of Nine from the Council.

12 August CUF, one of the largest of the monopolistic economic groups under Salazar, was nationalised.

The COPCON Document was published, in an attempt by the left to answer the case made by the Nine. Essentially the COPCON Document (appendix 5) was a plan of action based upon a popularist's point of view, while the Document of the Nine (appendix 4) was a social democratic analysis of the political situation. The COPCON Document was influenced by the civilian ultra left, in particular the PRP (see part 1).

20 August There were public demonstrations in Lisbon in support of the COPCON Document.

22 August The Alvor agreement was suspended, because of the political instability in Angola.

25 August The Fifth Division, the propaganda wing of the MFA, was closed down by COPCON and the

President of the Republic as it was said to be under the control of the PCP and no longer obeying the orders of the army hierarchy. The Fifth Division was a department of the general staff under General Costa Gomes and had organised the 'cultural dynamisation programme', published the MFA bulletins and other propaganda material and had had regular radio and television broadcasts.

The PCP realised that Gonçalves's downfall was imminent and, in a change of tactics, made an alliance with the ultra left and formed the FUR (Frente de Unidade Revolucionária, United Revolutionary Front). However, the support for FUR was limited to Lisbon and the Alentejo region and, a few days later, the PCP withdrew from the organisation. The MDP/CDE stayed in.

28 August   The Council of the Revolution appointed Pinheiro de Azevedo as prime minister and Vasco Gonçalves as the general chief of staff of the armed forces. Pinheiro de Azevedo was seen as a left-winger and received the full support of the left.

31 August   South Africa invaded southern Angola and in 1984, almost ten years later, it still had a presence in Angola.

1 September   The Constitutional Assembly proposed to give votes to all those over eighteen.

5 September   The army assembly met at Tancos and withdrew support for Vasco Gonçalves as general chief of staff. As a result Gonçalves resigned and fell from power and this was the first victory for the political moderates and the Group of Nine.

7 September   Attempted coup by white settlers in Mozam-
                 bique in order to block the Lusaka agreement
                 between the liberation movement and Portugal.
                 This agreement gave full independence to
                 Mozambique. The coup failed.

10 September   Government created the IARN (Institute for the
                 Aid of National Refugees). This institute had a
                 budget of some 300 million US dollars to help
                 the hundreds of thousands of Portuguese
                 refugees returning from the colonies (the *retor-
                 nados*).

11 September   The Council of the Revolution was reduced
                 from twenty-nine to nineteen members as the
                 Gonçalvists were expelled.

12 September   Pires Veloso was appointed commander of the
                 northern military region.

17 September   A general strike was held in the Alentejo region
                 in support of the Agrarian Reform (Reforma
                 Agrária).

19 September   The sixth provisional government was sworn in
                 under Prime Minister Pinheiro de Azevedo. It
                 included the PS, the PPD and the PCP.

27 September   The Spanish embassy was attacked and set on
                 fire and COPCON was accused of not inter-
                 vening to prevent the attack.

29 September   Prime Minister Pinheiro de Azevedo ordered the
                 military occupation of the television and radio
                 broadcasting stations.

15 October   The sixth provisional government shut down
                 Rádio Renascença.

16 October   Timor was invaded by Indonesia.

21 October   Following public demonstrations the govern-
                    ment reopened Rádio Renascença which
                    started broadcasting with a left-wing bias.

26 October   The three liberation movements in Angola
                    refused to form a government of national unity.

30 October   Several regimental assemblies throughout the
                    country protested against the right-wing poli-
                    cies of the government and the Council of the
                    Revolution.

3 November   A law creating trial by jury was passed.

7 November   Rádio Renascença was destroyed by para-
                    troopers from the Tancos base acting under
                    orders from the Council of the Revolution.
                    Public outrage followed and this led the para-
                    troopers to question the authority of the chief
                    of staff of the air force. The paratroopers
                    claimed that this was the second time they had
                    been deceived. The first time was when, on 11
                    March, they were involved in the siege of the
                    Lisbon light artillery regiment RAL1. Unrest in
                    the paratroop regiment led to 123 officers
                    leaving the regiment on 10 November and
                    the events of 25 November. The officers had
                    been ordered by the chief of staff of the air
                    force to assemble at the American base at Cor-
                    tegaça and here they formed a company. In the
                    lead-up to the 25 November coup, fighter
                    planes, helicopters and ammunition were
                    assembled at the base without the knowledge
                    of COPCON.

9 November   There was a joint PS and PPD demonstration in
                    support of the sixth provisional government.

10 November   One hundred and twenty-three paratroop officers abandoned the Tancos base for the Cortegaça base.

Construction workers went on strike about wages and conditions.

11 November   Angola became independent under the MPLA with Cuban support.

12 November   Construction workers sieged parliament and the government and again COPCON was accused of not intervening, this time to defend the government.

13 November   The sixth provisional government conceded to the demands of the construction workers.

14 November   The Tancos paratroopers denounced the right-wing connections of the officers who had left the base. The left-wing press accused the officers of having connections with the CIA, through the Brazilian embassy.

16 November   The PCP, the CGTP Intersindical and other organisations demonstrated against the government.

19 November   The sixth provisional government went on strike as a protest against the unrest in the country!

20 November   General Franco died.

FUR organised a demonstration against the sixth provisional government.

21 November   Otelo agreed to give up his command of the Lisbon military region to Vasco Lourenço, but Lourenço claimed that he would be unable to control the military units in the Lisbon area.

Later officers in COPCON reacted against
Vasco Lourenço's appointment.

22 November   There were public demonstrations in Lisbon
which demanded the reinstatement of Otelo.

24 November   The Council of the Revolution stated that Otelo
was to be replaced by Vasco Lourenço as com-
mander of the Lisbon military region. Otelo
pledged his support to Vasco Lourenço.
   The right-wing Confederation of Portuguese
Farmers, Confederação dos Agricultores Portu-
gueses (CAP) organised a blockade of the roads
to the north of the country in the town of Rio
Maior, near Lisbon. It was claimed by some that
this was the first move to put Lisbon under siege.

25 November   Successful coup led by the Group of Nine.
President Costa Gomes declared a state of emergency. The coup was precipitated by the paratroopers from the Tancos base, who invaded the
air force bases of Montijo, Monte Real, Ota,
and Tancos at 5.45 am. The military operation
(carried out by the *operacionais*, operationals)
was commanded by Lieutenant-Colonel Eanes,
although President Costa Gomes was formally
in command. They ordered the commandos to
lay siege to those air force bases that were
occupied by the paratroopers. The commandos
attacked the military police in Lisbon who
quickly surrendered.

26 November   COPCON closed down.
   Melo Antunes defended the presence of communists in the government.

27 November   Paratroopers surrendered to the commandos
and left the air force bases.
   COPCON officers were arrested.

28 November   Otelo resigned from COPCON, Fabião resigned as chief of staff of the army and both men automatically left the Council of the Revolution.

30 November   Rosa Coutinho, Otelo, Fabião, Almada Contreiras and Filgueiras Soares all left the Council of the Revolution. Eanes became a member of the Council of the Revolution after his appointment to chief of staff of the army.

2 December   The state of emergency was lifted.

3 December   A number of left-wing journalists were dismissed from their posts in the nationalised newspapers.

5 December   Melo Antunes stated that, 'the participation of the communists was indispensable to the construction of a democratic and socialist Portugal'.

7 December   Eanes was appointed chief of staff of the army.

9 December   Nationalised newspapers had new editorial appointments.

28 December   Rádio Renascença was returned to the Church.

1976

5 January   A law was passed that limited the Agrarian Reform to the south of Portugal.

8 January   Eanes started to tour military units in the north of the country. This day marked the emergence of Eanes as a national political figure.

12 January   The stock market reopened.

19 January   Otelo released his account of the events of 25 November.

29 January	Left-wing party headquarters (MDP/CDE and PCP) were bombed in Braga and Covilhã.
2 February	There was a national strike against these bomb attacks.
3 February	The sixth provisional government returned the first of a number of large companies to the private sector.
5 February	The Federal Republic of Germany gave a large loan to Portugal.
9 February	The Council of the Revolution reaffirmed its confidence in the sixth provisional government.
16 February	President Costa Gomes recognised that there was now a new understanding between the MFA and the political parties.
22 February	Portugal finally recognised Angola's independence. This late recognition by Portugal was to harm future relations between the two countries.
26 February	A new pact was signed between the MFA and the political parties (Pacto MFA–Partidos, see second MFA–Parties Pact, appendix 3). The pact defined the role of the Council of the Revolution in the new Constitution. The Council, instead of being the final legislative body, now had only the power to send legislation back to Parliament for further consideration. However, it was still the supreme authority in relations with the armed forces. It was responsible for laws in the armed forces, for organisation and for discipline.
3 March	Otelo was released from prison.

5 March	Eanes officially announced his candidacy for the presidential elections.
8 March	Fifteen political parties began to contest the 250 seats at the new Legislative Assembly (the Portuguese Parliament).
29 March	The Constitutional Assembly continued to write the new Portuguese Constitution. One of the articles of the new Constitution states that governments cannot be overthrown.
2 April	The proclamation of the Constitution of the Portuguese Republic. This would come into effect in June this year when a new President would be elected.
6 April	The European Economic Community, EEC, gave Portugal a loan of 200 million US dollars.
7 April	The MFA assembly confirmed its dedication to a socialist Portugal.
22 April	In a bomb attack against the Cuban embassy, two died.
25 April	Elections for the Legislative Assembly were held. The turn-out was 83 per cent compared with 95 per cent on the same date the year before. Results were as follows:

PCP/MDP	14.6%
PPD	24.0%
PS	35.0%
UDP	1.7%
MRPP	0.7%
PPM	0.5%
CDS	15.9%

(PPM – Partido Popular Monárquico, Popular Monarchist Party).

10 May   Admiral Pinheiro de Azevedo announced his candidacy for the forthcoming presidential elections.

18 May   Octávio Pato, the PCP parliamentary leader, presidential elections.

24 May   Otelo announced his candidacy for the forthcoming presidential elections.

27 May   President Costa Gomes decided that he would not rerun for President.

3 June   The Legislative Assembly was officially opened.

23 June   Pinheiro de Azevedo had a heart attack and was effectively out of the presidential campaign.

27 June   Presidential elections were held with the result that Eanes became Portugal's first democratically elected President for some fifty years. Results were as follows:

Eanes	61.5%
Otelo	16.5%
Pinheiro	14.4%
Pato	7.6%
Turn-out	75%

14 July   Eanes was sworn in as Portugal's new President.

16 July   Eanes invited Soares to be prime minister and form the first democratic government of the new Constitution.

23 July   The first constitutional government was sworn in. Mário Soares was prime minister in a minority government.

11 August   Spínola returned to Portugal and was not arrested.

16 September   Portugal was admitted to the Council of Europe.

23 September   Appointment of eighteen new administrative governors. In Portugal there are eighteen administrative districts that were, and are, responsible to central government. Each district has a governor, whose main role is the maintenance of law and order.

30 September   Legislation was passed which abolished the Unicidade Sindical. Now each trade could be represented by more than one trade union.

2 October   The PPD became the PSD (Partido Social Democrata, the Social Democratic Party). The PSD made several attempts to affiliate to the international social democratic movement, but without success. The PS was successful. Later the PSD affiliated to the international liberal movement.

24 October   Otelo was imprisoned for twenty days. This was because he attended political meetings while still a member of the armed forces.

2 November   Lopes Cardoso was dismissed as minister of agriculture in Soares's government. He had been a keen supporter of the Agrarian Reform programme of the MFA.

4 December   The government stated that there would be 'freedom' in the Alentejo region, which meant that it would dismantle some of the Agrarian Reform. This was to be carried out by the new minister of agriculture, António Barreto (Barreto's Law).

12 December   First elections for the local authorities.

13 December   Results, country-wide, were as follows:
               CDS   15.9%
               PSD   24.7%
               FEPU   17.9%
               (Mainly PCP and MDP/CDE)
               PS   33.5%

29 December   Prime Minister Soares stated that the Portuguese
               economy should be based upon a free-market
               economy.

TABLES AND BLOCK DIAGRAMS

Table 1. *Composition of the Council of State and of the Committee of Twenty*

(a) *The Council of State* 31 May 1974		
Citizens	*JSN*	*MFA*
Freitas do Amaral	Pinheiro de Azevedo	Victor Alves*
Henrique de Barros	Rosa Coutinho	Melo Antunes
Almeida Bruno	Costa Gomes	Almada Contreiras
Isabel Magalhães Colcaco	J. Silverio Marques	Victor Crespo
Rafael Durão	Galvão de Melo	Vasco Gonçalves*
Ruy Luis Gomes	Diogo Neto	Costa Martins*
Azeredo Perdigão	Spínola	Pereira Pinto

* were replaced in the second provisional government by Vasco Lourenço,
Franco Charais, Pinto Soares, Canto e Castro

(b) *The Committee of Twenty* (from 28 September 1974)			
	Air force	*Army*	*Navy*
Co-ordinating	Canto e Castro	Franco Charais	A. Contreiras
Committee of the MFA	P. Pinto	Vasco Lourenço	Judas
Programme (CCP)		P. Soares	
Junta of	Mendes Dias	Carlos Fabião	P. Azevedo
National	Pinho Freire	Costa Gomes	R. Coutinho
Salvation (JSN)		F. L. Pires	(or S. Ribeiro)
Ministers (or	Costa Martins	Victor Alves	V. Crespo
equivalent)		Melo Antunes	
		Vasco Gonçalves	
		Otelo S. Carvalho	

Table 2.   *Composition of the Councils of the Revolution*

(a) *First Council of the Revolution* (after 11 March 1975)		
Air force	*Army*	*Navy*
Canto e Castro[17]	Victor Alves[4]	Pinheiro de Azevedo†
Graça Cunha[1]	Melo Antunes[4]*	Almada Contreiras
Mendes Dias[2]	Otelo Saraiva Carvalho*	Ramiro Correia[1]†
Pinho Freire[2]	Sousa e Castro	Rosa Coutinho*
Costa Martins[4]	Franco Charais*	Victor Crespo[4]*
Costa Neves	Pezarat Correia*	Martins Guerreiro
Pereira Pinto[1]	Corvacho[2]	Miguel Judas[1]
Morais e Silva	Carlos Fabião*	
	Costa Gomes*	
	Vasco Gonçalves*	
	Marques Junior*	
	Vasco Lourenço*	
	Macedo[1]	
	Fisher L. Pires[3]*	
	Pinto Soares[5]	
	Ferreira Sousa[1]	

(b) *Second Council of the Revolution* (after Tancos Assembly 5 September 1975)		
Air force	*Army*	*Navy*
Canto e Castro	Victor Alves	Pinheiro de Azevedo[7]
Graça Cunha[6]	Melo Antunes	Almada Contreiras
Pinho Freire	Otelo Saraiva Carvalho	Ramiro Correla
Costa Martins[6]	Sousa e Castro	Rosa Coutinho
Costa Neves	Franco Charais	Victor Crespo[6]
Pereira Pinto[6]	Corvacho[6]	Martins Guerreiro
Morais e Silva	Carlos Fabião	Felgueiras Soares[8]
	Costa Gomes	
	Vasco Gonçalves[6]	
	Marques Junior	
	Vasco Lourenço	
	Macedo[6]	
	Ferreira Sousa[6]	
	Pires Veloso[4]*	

(c) *Third Council of the Revolution* (after 28 November 1975)

Air force	Army	Navy
Canto e Castro	Melo Antunes	Pinheiro de Azevedo
Pinho Freire[13]	Otelo Saraiva	Almada Contreiras[16]
Costa Neves	Carvalho[12]	Ramiro Correia[12]
Morais da Silva	Sousa e Castro	Almeida e Costa[11]
Ribeiro Cardoso[15]	Franco Charais	Rosa Coutinho
	Pezarat Correia	Victor Crespo[14]
	Ramalho Eanes[11]	Souto Cruz[11]
	Carlos Fabião[12]	Martins Guerreiro
	Costa Gomes[10]	Miguel Judas[12]
	Marques Junior	Felgueiras Soares[12]
	Vasco Lourenço	
	Loureiro dos Santos[11]	
	Pires Veloso[13]	
	Rocha Vieira[13]	

Key

(1) Left after Tancos assembly meeting.
(2) Dias gave his place to Pinho Freire after 11 March 1975.
(3) Resigned from the CR in April 1975.
(4) Entered the CR after March 1975.
(5) Resigned in July 1975.
(6) Expelled from the CR by their corresponding assemblies (air force, navy and army) in September 1975.
(7) Became prime minister after Gonçalves.
(8) Replaced Pinheiro de Azevedo as chief of staff of the army.
(9) Replaced Corvacho as commander of the northern military region and as member of the CR.
(10) Left the CR in July 1976.
(11) Entered the CR because of their positions within the armed forces (i.e. chiefs of staff, etc.).
(12) Left after 25 November 1975.
(13) Departed from the CR because of a rule passed by the CR that disallowed simultaneous membership of the CR and certain military posts (for example, the commanders of the military regions).
(14) Re-entered the CR.
(15) Elected by the air force.
(16) Arrested following 25 November coup.
(17) Appointed as a substitute for Costa Martins.
   (After Almeida, 1979, vol. 1, p. 354)
* interviewed
† deceased

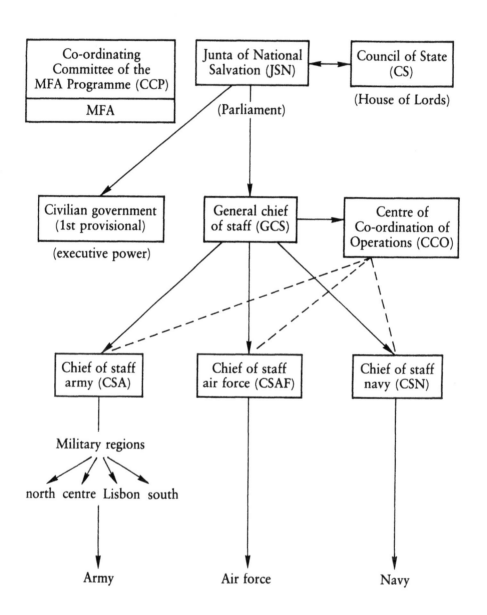

arrow direction indicates flow of power

BLOCK DIAGRAM I. POWER STRUCTURE AFTER 25 APRIL
1974

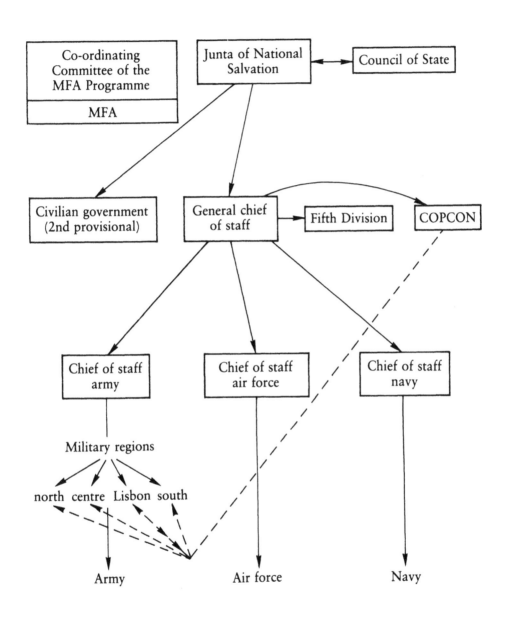

arrow direction indicates flow of power

BLOCK DIAGRAM 2. POWER STRUCTURE AFTER 18 JULY
1974

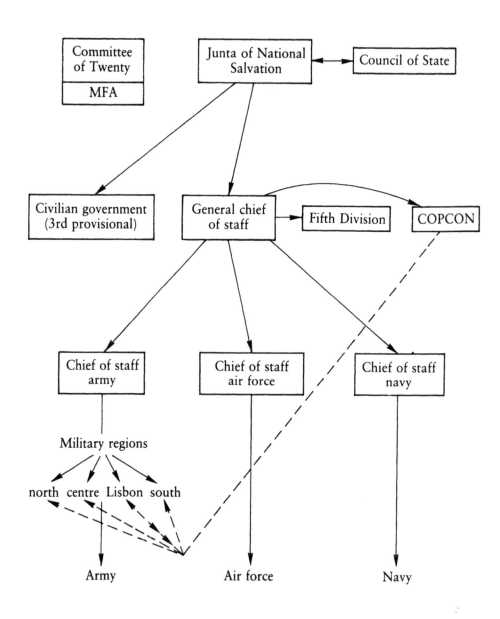

arrow direction indicates flow of power

BLOCK DIAGRAM 3. POWER STRUCTURE AFTER 28 SEPTEM-
BER 1974

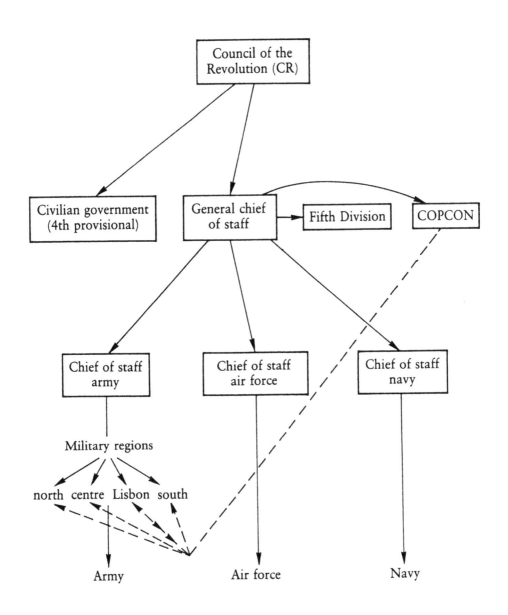

arrow direction indicates flow of power

BLOCK DIAGRAM 4. POWER STRUCTURE AFTER 11 MARCH
1975

The interviews

All the interviews were based upon the following questionnaire:

Question 1. Family details, place and date of birth, education.

Question 2. Military career to date.

Question 3. What was your attitude to the political regime before 25 April 1974?

Question 4. What was your involvement in the Movement of Captains, and your reason for joining the Movement?

Question 5. Was 25 April 1974 a revolution? If so, why?

Question 6. Did 25 April fail? If so, why?

Question 7. What was 28 September 1974?

Question 8. What was 11 March 1975?

Question 9. What was 25 November 1975?

Question 10. What were the relationships between the Group of Nine and COPCON just before 25 November? What was the role of COPCON in the revolutionary process?

Question 11. Was there a danger of a left-wing take-over on 25 November? Was the left wing identifiable with the PCP?

Question 12. Were foreign powers involved in Portugal before and after 25 April 1974? If so, what evidence is there?

Question 13. What was the role of the Church before and after the revolution? Did it hinder or aid the revolutionary process?

Question 14. What were the relationships between the military radicals and the civilian left?

Question 15. What were your views on the decolonisation process?

Question 16. Do you see any historical parallels between the Portuguese revolution and other revolutions?

Question 17. What are the major social and political changes that have occurred since 25 April 1974?

Question 18. Is the Portuguese revolution over? If so, when and why?

Question 19. Do soldiers make good revolutionaries?

Question 20. How do you see Portugal in the next ten years? What is the role of the army in the next ten years?

Question 21. What is the role of the Association of 25 April?

With this questionnaire it was possible to obtain the political outlook of the officers, to characterise their roles in the revolution and to obtain their current views on Portugal. The interviews that are presented in the book do not exactly follow the questionnaire. For reasons of space, not all their replies are included, but most of the above questions are answered, either directly or indirectly. Questions that were left out are summarised in the analysis sections, which follow the interviews. Sometimes additional questions were asked in order to examine more closely specific issues and the roles of particular officers in important events.

In order to have a better understanding of the interviews, a more detailed question-by-question analysis of the questionnaire follows. Each interview has a short biographical section for each officer. This was constructed from questions 1 and 2 and was included, firstly because it provides information on the cultural and political background of the officer, and is of interest in relation to his current political outlook. Secondly, these questions throw more light on the argument (see part 1) that a class division tended to exist between the higher- and the middle- and lower-ranking officers. Furthermore the information about their military careers contained in the biographies, and more loosely in other parts of the interviews, evaluates their abilities to cope with the rapidly changing events of the revolution and also reflects the stability of their political outlooks.

Questions 2 and 4 are intimately related, since together they show whether the involvement of the officer in the Movement of Captains was a direct political statement, or more simply a professional protest. They also provide important indications of the development of their political awareness. Questions 5 and 6, which deal with the coup d'état on 25 April 1974, assess the degree of political sophistication of the officer. The key events that followed the coup are dealt with in questions 7, 8 and 9 and provide comprehensive information about both the course of the revolution and the role the officers played in it. (These three questions were particularly effective, as in the interviews the officers gave a wealth of background information in their analysis of the significance of these three coups.)

Although question 10 at first sight seems a very specific question, the officer's perception of the relationship between the Group of Nine and COPCON was important, as COPCON was seen at that time to be one of the major driving forces of the revolution. The Group of Nine represented a body of opinion that considered the revolution to be out of control and losing the support of the people. This question is used to reveal to which group the officer belonged.

The PCP played a crucial role in the revolution because it was a well-organised party, with dedicated and politically experienced members. The anti-communism that had flourished in the Salazar/Caetano regime overspilled into the post-revolutionary period which meant that the Communist Party was always watched. Reactions against the PCP were often extreme and the common ground for diverse political groups. Question 11 essentially deals with the officers' perception of the PCP and the 25 November coup is a good focus point.

The involvement of foreign powers and the Church are dealt with in questions 12 and 13 which are self-explanatory. Question 14 is another important question which assesses the degree of politicisation of the officer, since, without doubt, there was a continuous interplay between the armed forces and the civilian political groups representing all shades of political opinion.

In part 1 it was concluded that the Colonial War was probably the most important issue in bringing about the fall of the Salazar/Caetano regime. Regardless of their political sympathies, most officers were opposed to the war, since they were forced to do successive tours of duty in a situation which seemed hopeless and in a war which could not be won. Question 15 tests the validity of these conclusions reached in part 1. Also it aims at analysing the relationship between their political sympathies and their attitudes towards the war.

The last six questions attempt to characterise the current political position of the officer. The last question concerning the Association of 25 April is of interest because the recently-formed Association of 25 April has been criticised as an attempt by the armed forces to continue their participation in Portuguese politics. The Association was formed after the Council of the Revolution was dissolved in 1982. It was formed as a cultural organisation and initially open only to members of the armed forces, but recently it has become open to civilians. It was named the Association of 25 April as its aims were to keep alive the ideals outlined in the Programme of the MFA (Appendix 1).

CLASSIFICATION OF THE INTERVIEWS

The questionnaire allowed classification of those interviewed into six groups: the idealists, the independents, the link-men, the organisers, the populists and the strategists. In order to carry this out, the replies were grouped according to the type of information they elicited from the interviewees. For social, political and educational background answers to questions 1 to 4 were used. Replies to questions 7, 8 and 9 allowed an examination of their attitudes to the key events of the revolution. They were used to plot their political path through the course of the revolution and analyse the roles they played. Replies to questions 5, 6, 10, 11, 14, 17 and 19 implicitly revealed the present political outlook of the officers. Their attitudes to the wider implications of the revolution were dealt with using questions 12, 13, 16 and 18. Their replies to the question on decolonisation (15) were important in politically classifying the officers, since decolonisation has often been given as one of the main reasons for a split that occurred within the MFA. Also, it revealed whether political attitudes changed once decolonisation had taken place. The way in which the officer views the contemporary role of the armed forces in Portugal was touched upon in replies to question 19.

An apology is due to those officers who consider that they have been wrongly grouped. The classification was somewhat arbitrary and partly carried out to give structure to the interview section.

THE IDEALISTS

These officers were often driven by a political vision of Portuguese society. Brigadier Correia had a vision of 'direct democracy' in Portugal. He envisaged that people would have control over their lives through a direct involvement at a local level. There would be a decentralisation of power and local councils would be the decision-making body for housing, health, education and cultural activities. Central government would still be responsible for security and foreign affairs. General Gonçalves's vision was for a caring and egalitarian society organised on Marxist principles. Sanches Osório, as a committed Catholic and democrat, believed in applying the principles of Christianity to politics.

    Pezarat Correia (PC)

    Sanches Osório (SO)

    Vasco Gonçalves (VG)

Brigadier Pezarat Correia. Born in Oporto in 1932. Grandfather and father were professional army officers. Father was anti-regime and participated in the Oporto revolt in 1927 (see part 1), was arrested and deported to Angola. Correia entered military college when ten years old and finished his education at the Military Academy. First saw active service in Goa in India in 1954. Fought in the Colonial War in Mozambique, Angola and Guinea-Bissau. Became commander of the eastern auxiliary forces in Angola where he first met the Movement of Captains. Although already a major became involved with the Movement. After 25 April 1974 was cabinet leader of the MFA in Angola. Pushed for the removal of General Silverio Marques in Angola and helped create conditions to enable the MFA to negotiate the independence of Angola with the three liberation movements. Returned to Portugal in January 1975 and joined the cabinet of the chief of staff of the army. After the attempted coup on 11 March was elected to the Council of the Revolution. Was commander of the southern military region as a temporary brigadier; one of his major tasks was to support the implementation of the Agrarian Reform. Member of the Group of Nine. After leaving the southern military region, remained in the Council of the Revolution as a colonel until its dissolution in 1982. In 1982 was promoted to brigadier. Is currently a brigadier in the army.

Interview

Q. How do you see 11 March 1975 and why was Spínola defeated?

A. The 11 March was an attempted coup by a fraction of the MFA: Spínola's supporters. Spínola had organised a group to stop and reverse the political situation, but he failed because he only had a small following and no support from the popular movement. After the failure of the coup, the paratroopers said publicly that they had been wrong. On 11 March, the day of the coup, I was at the general staff headquarters and I kept myself there all day.

Q. Was 25 April 1974 a revolution?

A. The 25 April was, I think, a military coup, but with certain peculiarities. It was innovatory as the MFA produced a political programme that was progressive and this programme enabled the MFA to mobilise popular support. The popular movement transformed the military coup into a revolution.

Q. What were the aims of the revolution?

A. The three objectives were: to democratise, to decolonise and to develop. If the military coup had only been a military take-over, the revolution would never have taken place. This is because democracy would have ended up as a militarily con-trolled regime, decolonisation would have ended up in the neo-colonial situation and development would only have involved the big corporations which had controlled the economy in the previous regime. The popular movement caused democrat-isation to be a movement of the people, a movement that was almost anarchic. The movement caused decolonisation to lead to the total independence of the colonies and development to lead to nationalisation. The popular movement was the basis of the Agrarian Reform, various public enterprises, etc.

Q. Is the revolution still going on?

A. I can't answer directly. The revolution did not develop correctly, as there was never a strong revolutionary force. The power struggles, even within the MFA, weakened it and this led to 25 November. But the Constitution that was approved in 1976 institutionalised the revolution. If the clauses in this Constitution had been carried out, ultimately, even under the law, there would have been a continuation of the revolution by constitutional

means. Unfortunately, once the Constitution came into effect, all
the governments were preoccupied with reversing the revolutionary process, and today there is no longer a revolution. I think 25
November 1975 was when the revolution lost steam.

Q. On 25 November did you think that there was any risk that
the communists would take over?

A. I think conditions had been created so that the communists
might have attempted to take power, but I think the major danger
was that the minority groups on the extreme left would have
created an anarchic situation. My main preoccupation was that
there could have been an extreme right-wing military coup. There
were demonstrations in the north of the country, supporting the
right and the Group of Nine intended to block any movement
from the extreme right. We explained this in the Document of the
Group of Nine.

Following 25 November the Group of Nine lost power through
the progressive dismissal of members of the Nine from positions
of responsibility within the military hierarchy. Also attempts
were made to make the Council of the Revolution less able to
intervene in the affairs of state. These actions against the Group
of Nine became increasingly successful. Gradually the chief
positions in the army were returned to the old hierarchy, who
had had nothing to do with 25 April 1974. These officers were
non-politicised officers, but under the umbrella of being non-
political they were often conservatives.

Q. What did you do in the lead-up to 25 November?

A. I had been appointed to the Council of the Revolution in
March 1975. In May 1975 the Council decided that there was a
need to strengthen the influence of the MFA and also that the
commanders of the military regions should be members of the
Council of the Revolution. This meant promoting officers from
the MFA into the upper echelons of the hierarchy of the armed
forces. The chief of staff of the army [Fabião] and the commander of COPCON [Otelo] were already members of the Council of
the Revolution. I was a lieutenant-colonel and was temporarily
promoted to brigadier and put in charge of the southern military
region, while Charais, another member of the Council of the
Revolution, was also temporarily promoted to brigadier and
appointed commander of the centre military region.

I was responsible to Fabião, although operationally I was

under Otelo, but I don't think that Otelo controlled COPCON. There was a fundamental problem in COPCON. In the Lisbon region the military units were populist and strongly influenced by the way Otelo behaved. On the other hand Otelo himself was under pressure from those units which were always challenging the military hierarchy. Outside Lisbon the military hierarchy was more permanently established. In relation to the military region under my command, I tried to advise Otelo as to the best way to deal with our local problems.

Q. Was there any disagreement between the Group of Nine and COPCON?

A. It was big. The Group of Nine was driven by the fact that in each military unit, each company wanted to transform itself into a power nucleus with the result that orders from COPCON were always challenged. Soldiers were even being persuaded not to carry out orders. The Group of Nine wanted the revolution to continue. It could not have gone on in that way so we had to make a stand.

Q. What was your involvement in the coup of 25 November?

A. I signed the Document of the Nine and was a member of the Group of Nine who organised themselves to face any coup that might arise. Such a coup took place on 25 November. We thought then that there was a need for a strong leadership of the revolution so that revolutionary transformations could be carried out. Although the 'Document' was a political statement, we knew that sooner or later military action against us would follow. A group of officers [the operationals], supporters of the Group of Nine, were involved in planning a military response to pre-empt any such attempt. As commanders of the southern and central military regions, Charais and myself collaborated with these officers. I had several meetings with Colonel Eanes before the November coup took place.

The 25 November took place in the early hours of the morning after the Council of the Revolution had been assembled. These meetings normally went on very late and usually I would sleep in my house in the Lisbon area, before returning to my command post at Evora the next day. On the morning of 25th I was unaware that the coup had taken place. I went to the head-quarters of the Council of the Revolution to deal with some outstanding business before returning to Evora and was told that the coup was 'on the streets'. By then, the operational group which had been set up and which included Colonel Eanes was assembled. So I went straight to the room in which it was assembled. From here I telephoned my headquarters in Evora which was going to give support to the counter-coup and got in my car and left. From my headquarters I kept in contact with the units of armoured cars that were sent under my command to Lisbon to be at the President's disposal. I also kept in contact with units that patrolled the southern region in order to keep the situation under control.

I believe that General Fabião should not have been replaced by General Eanes as chief of staff of the army following the 25 November coup. Once the anarchy in the Lisbon units had been controlled things would have been different. Fabião needed a military hierarchy he could trust. On 26 or 27 November I was in Evora, the military situation was under control and Melo Antunes telephoned me. He told me, 'We have met and decided that General Eanes is going to be chief of staff of the army. What is your opinion?' I answered, 'If you have already decided, I agree.' I think Eanes was chosen as he had controlled the military operations of 25 November and because he was trusted on account of his previous military career.

Q. Why did the people who signed the Document of Nine later lose power?

A. The men who signed had a socialist project for Portugal, whereby it would have been possible to have carried out profound economic and social changes and at the same time have a representative democracy. That project does not seem to interest the present political powers. Charais and myself kept our military regions ready to support any democratic project. But once the new Constitution had been approved in April 1976, the new assembly elected and General Eanes had become President, it was decided, on account of pressures from the military hierarchy, to remove us both as commanders of the military regions and replace us with the officers outside the Council of the Revolution.

Q. Are you implying that the present political power is not interested in a socialist and democratic regime?

A. They are not. I would say that the dominating class in Portugal today is the same as that before 25 April coup. The soldiers gave them the chance to hand over power legitimately, through elections, but the truth is that the people who were in opposition to the previous regime before 25 April 1974, such as the leaders of the PS, are now playing their games.

Q. Since you were closely involved in the Agrarian Reform, would you like to describe it?

A. In the south most of the farm workers lived without work throughout the whole of the year, yet the land was undercultivated because it was owned by a very few absentee landlords. The people in the Alentejo have always been militant revolutionaries and when 25 April came they saw an opportunity to change the established system. Initially they were hopeful that the new government would intervene on their behalf as they were convinced that their conditions were such that legislation could be carried out through the MFA Programme to help them. However, legislation was not forthcoming and at the same time the revolutionary process was being accelerated. The landowners created more difficulties, for example, some ran away, others did not organise harvesting, others renegued on workers' salaries, while others withdrew capital from their farms. All these factors coupled with high unemployment led the workers to make the first land occupations.

When I was appointed commander of the southern military region one of my tasks was to control these land occupations, and I was promised that legislation on the Agrarian Reform would follow. In July 1975 a law was passed regulating the expropriation of land [see appendix 6]. This law established that farms south of the Tagus, excluding the Algarve, with an area larger than 300 hectares of non-irrigated land or larger than 50 hectares of irrigated land could be expropriated by the state. This law did not propose dramatic changes and also, as the power structure was ill-defined, the workers were not confident that it would be applied. The workers were under pressure to occupy the land before the law was passed and so occupations were carried out in an anarchic way. There were even occupations of small farms which were not in agreement with the new law and small farmers who should have supported the Agrarian Reform began to oppose it.

Q. How many workers were involved in these land occupations?

A. In the Alentejo there were some 40,000 workers who were involved in the Agrarian Reform. It was a big problem for me for I felt that if we applied the law in an orderly manner we could accomplish an effective Agrarian Reform, but if we let the workers carry out those anarchic occupations we would endanger the whole process. The aim of the law was to give land to groups of workers who would then organise co-operatives.

It is obvious that simple land expropriation is not an Agrarian Reform. There is a need to change crops, organise financial help, provide technical know-how and organise the co-operatives in such a way that they become profitable. There was a danger that any initial false moves would result in reduced profitability and so condemn the whole process from the start. After 25 November I thought that the conditions had been created to bring about the reform. I had signed the Document of the Nine in the hope that such conditions might be created. I also felt that prior to 25 November I was unable to be an effective commander of my military region. Immediately after the coup we got results. We were able to correct irregular occupations and I thought that the first important steps towards a true Agrarian Reform had been taken.

Q. Did you use troops to apply the law of the Agrarian Reform?
A. No, there was no need as by then we had the power. We set up a Commission of Analysis in the Ministry of Agriculture. In this Commission there were representatives of the MFA and the decisions of the Commission were respected.

You should now understand why I said that civilian governments were backward-looking. The Agrarian Reform law was in agreement with the Constitution, that is, the Constitution had taken the Agrarian Reform into account [the Constitution laid down rules to implement the Agrarian Reform]. But the first socialist government passed a new Agrarian Reform law in 1977 [Barreto's law] which perverted the virtue of the original law. It enormously increased the size of the farms that could be privately owned and allowed the families of previous farm owners to now own land which had already been expropriated.

The socialist government cut financial support for the co-operatives so that they started to have problems and because of this some of the co-operatives returned land to the previous owners. After all that the region in which the Agrarian Reform had taken place was accused of not being productive. It is as if after cutting off a child's leg you say, 'Look he can't walk.' This second law was the so-called Barreto's law. The socialist minister who wanted to carry out the original Agrarian Reform law, Lopes Cardoso, was forced to resign and in 1976 I was removed as commander of the southern military region.

When Barreto's law was carried out, there was opposition from the workers and the forces of law and order had to intervene. From then on the process was controlled by the minister of agriculture and these people were linked with the Confederation of Portuguese Farmers (CAP) which is an association of big landowners. Today in the Alentejo there are large numbers of land reserves which have been handed back to the original landowners. The workers had invested in these reserves and now once again they are abandoned. Today there are probably more than 20,000 farm workers unemployed.

The Agrarian Reform was the most important social victory of the revolution. The original Reform law, not Barreto's law, followed the initiatives of the farm workers and corresponded more to the model originally advocated by the PS and less to the model proposed by the PCP. The PCP had proposed the expropriation of land and the creation of big state farms, while the PS advocated the creation of workers' co-operatives. In the end the workers brought about a solution similar to the PS proposal but did it with the PCP's support. The PS attacked what the workers did and aligned itself with the right. Because the Alentejo zone was under communist influence, the PS thought that by attacking Agrarian Reform they would erode the PCP's power in that area.

Q. Could you describe your political position?

A. I would like to see radical political changes in Portuguese society, but I don't think that the military make good revolutionaries. The officers belong to the bourgeois class and although they may have taken a stand as the MFA did, they are not the true revolutionary class. They end up facing internal contradictions and I think my own position shows up these contradictions. Because of my military training I am concerned about order and discipline, but because of my social conscience I would like to see certain changes made with order and discipline. Is this possible?

I would like to see every citizen have equal opportunities at birth and each select their responsibilities according to their potential. I believe that fundamental rights such as health, education, housing, social security and work should be assured for all. The scale of rewards for each individual should be according to their ability. I am against a political elite and power should be examined openly and there should be constitutional means of changing power, according to the needs of the country. I think that this is only possible through an extensive programme of decentralisation. Central offices could control major areas such as security and foreign affairs. But the solution of citizens' immediate problems, culture, housing, work etc. could all be resolved at an autonomous local level. Only in this way can citizens participate in the solution of their problems.

Major Sanches Osório. Born in 1940 in Lisbon. Father was a civil servant. Secondary education at the Military College. Entered the Military Academy in 1958 and trained as an engineering officer. In 1967 was posted to Angola as a captain. Was promoted to major whilst in Angola. On his return to Lisbon attended the General Staff School after a short period in the Tancos engineering unit. Was in the command post, with Otelo, in the engineering barracks at Pontinha on 25 April 1974. For a short while was spokesman for the Junta of National Salvation. Was military aid to Prime Minister Palma Carlos for a few days. Was director general of information in the second provisional government. Became minister of information. On 28 September 1974 asked for unlimited leave of absence from the army to become general secretary of the PDC. Following the 11 March 1975 coup left Portugal for Paris and became spokesman for the MDLP (Movimento Democrático para a Libertação de Portugal, Democratic Movement for the Liberation of Portugal), under Spínola's leadership. On his return to Portugal on 3 March 1976 was arrested and imprisoned for seven days. Was released and worked as a civil engineer. Was elected as a Member of Parliament for the CDS in 1980. Resigned from the CDS before term of office was finished and stayed in Parliament as an independent. Is currently director of a civil engineering firm.

Interview

Q. What was your attitude to the Salazar and Caetano regimes?
A. My family was always opposed to Salazar. I was influenced by General Norton de Matos during his presidential campaign. I was shocked by my grandfather's arrest at the age of seventy-two for being a Norton de Matos supporter. Since the age of ten I had been involved in the Saint Vincent Paul Catholic Movement. This had led me to visit many of the Lisbon shanty towns which made me aware of the prevailing social injustices.

In Angola in the Colonial War I saw a reversal of many of the innovating reforms that had been brought about by General Norton de Matos whilst he was high commissioner. I also saw that attempts to settle Portuguese citizens in Angola were being blocked by the fear that Angola would develop and demand independence. All this demonstrated the paralysis that had set into Portuguese politics.

Q. Why did you join the Movement of Captains?
A. I signed the document against the Oporto Congress of Combatants. I thought that the armed forces, who had been either implicit or explicit supporters of the previous regime, should be responsible for bringing about a political change, although I think that soldiers should only be involved politically under exceptional circumstances.

From the start I thought that the Movement of Captains should be political. I brought in Victor Alves and Charais and managed to involve the Church. This was to avoid any future conflict between Church and state that is a common feature of Portuguese history.

I helped set up the Cascais meeting of the Movement and was in the command post on the day of the coup, along with Otelo [army], Fischer Lopes Pires [army], Garcia dos Santos [communications] and Victor Crespo [navy].

Later on I became connected with the right. As a spokesman for the Junta of National Salvation, I was in close contact with Spínola, although my real political contacts with him did not start until 11 March. I also had close contacts with Prime Minister Palma Carlos. Thus I was a natural link between President Spínola and the prime minister. When the land occupations started in the Alentejo region, friends, who were landowners, appealed to me and I gave them my support. These are some of the reasons why people see me as a right-winger, although it was I, who, after the revolution, together with a PCP Central Committee member, Jaime Serra, chose the building for the headquarters of the Communist Party!

Q. Do you see 25 April as a revolution?

A. It was a revolution that was never finished and never went as deep as it should have done. This was due in part to the fact that revolutions in general cannot be controlled and the things that were changed were only on the surface. Those things that were changed were changed in the wrong direction.

The only real thing to come out of the revolution was freedom. We obtained a democracy and we are left with the freedom to express our thoughts. We did not manage to obtain the economic, educational and social changes that would have allowed us to fully benefit from 25 April. We did decolonise, but we did only what the foreign powers allowed us to do. The dramatic effects of decolonisation such as the exodus of the white settlers were the result of the shortcomings of Salazar's policies. The regime did not implement policies that allowed Portuguese people to settle effectively into the colonies.

The rest is something we have to put up with and be patient about, for the real revolution is only something that can come in the next generation. The economic and social changes were carried out too hastily during the course of the revolution. The only possible economic system viable in Europe is one based upon a mixed economy. Nationalisations should be carried out as part of an integrated economic plan by a democratic government and not by revolutionary means. The armed forces throughout the course of the revolution were politically ignorant and were manipulated by politicians.

The establishment of freedom and democracy was due to Marshal Costa Gomes, who managed to steer a difficult but intelligent course between the rival factions. He showed himself to be a sophisticated politician, who may be considered a traitor by many because he said 'yes' and 'no' to all. Without him, it would not have been possible to elect the Constitutional Assembly and to write and approve a new Constitution.

Q. How do you think General Spínola lost power?

A. We need to start at the MFA assembly meeting on 13 June

1974 [Manutenção Militar]. At this meeting Spínola asked for a vote of confidence. In reply, Vasco Lourenço got up and started his speech by pledging the support of the MFA to General Spínola, provided that Spínola carried out the MFA Programme. At the start of the speech there was a round of applause when Vasco Lourenço commended Spínola and at this point Spínola left the assembly hall, but Vasco Lourenço then went on to say that Spínola had to implement the MFA Programme, and this was approved by the assembly. Afterwards I went to Spínola and told him he had lost, but he replied that he had won. His defeat was to become clear on 28 September.

Spínola is a social democrat, but is always pulled back by his class origins. I suffer the same thing myself. I did not play an active role on 28 September but the day before, whilst still minister of information in his government, I accused Prime Minister Gonçalves of following the policies of the PCP. I resigned from Gonçalves's government, but in retrospect I think I should have stayed on.

In the following months everyone was conspiring against what was considered to be the excessive gains of the PCP but the dissenting groups were not co-ordinated. For reasons about which I am still unclear the attempted 11 March coup was prematurely triggered. Although I was not involved in the military operations of 11 March, I left the country with Spínola, as I had said that I would follow him if he had to leave. After the coup many people left Portugal, and many of us formed the MDLP under the leadership of Spínola in Paris.

I was the public relations officer of the MDLP. Within the organisation there were true democrats, as well as a lot of ultra-right-wingers who were included in the Movement for tactical reasons. All of us wanted to fight against an anarchic revolution. The proof of this was that after 25 November Spínola dissolved the MDLP. This coup stopped the anarchism from spreading. The coup came about because the PCP was pushing the far left into action [the paratroopers occupying the bases] and the Group of Nine used these occupations as a pretext to act.

On 28 September, as minister of information, I delivered a message over the radio which ordered the lifting of the road-blocks set up by left-wing elements [see part 2]. This message was signed by Prime Minister Vasco Gonçalves and myself. There

were only two copies of this message, one of them with me. After
11 March my office was searched and this document removed.
Q. What was the role of the Church before and after 25 April
1974?
A. Before 25 April the Church in the early days supported the
dictatorship, but later on it did criticise the regime. Salazar was a
Catholic and managed to keep Church and state separate, a
policy that should be pursued by present-day politicians. In the
latter stages of the regime the Church participated in student and
worker unrest through its young priests.

    After 25 April 1974 the Church at first played the role of an
observer. Later the bishop of Oporto voiced dissent against the
MFA. In the meantime the political parties had become aware of
the influence of the Church throughout the country and so they
wanted its support. This is dangerous as the Church is too old and
always gains the upper hand. For the Church, time does not
matter. The Church was not anti-revolution, but it was anti-PCP.
Today the Church speaks to the right through the bishop of
Bragança, to the centre through the patriarch of Lisbon and to
the left through the bishop of Setubal.
Q. What is the role of the newly-formed Association of 25 April?
A. I am a member. The Association is controversial for it is said
to be an association of crypto-communists. I don't think it is,
though it must have some communist military members. Its aims
are positive, provided it does not just remember the past. The
group of seminars to commemorate ten years after the revolution
now being organised may be useful because they allow an open
discussion of the future evolution of Portugal. The Association
can become a forum for debate about Portuguese society.
Q. How do you describe yourself politically?
A. I am a Christian democrat in the purest sense and not in the
sense of being a supporter of the Christian Democrats. Although
a member of the CDS, I voted for Eanes to become President, even
though he was not a CDS candidate. My hope is for a society
based upon consensus and one which allows me to make decisions on specific issues. I am also a monarchist in the British sense
of a constitutional monarchy that has no real power. The
Portuguese parliament has always worked badly, and at second
best the system should move towards a presidential system. I
consider that the last revision of the Constitution which
reinforced the parliamentary element was a mistake.

General Vasco Gonçalves. Born in Lisbon 1921. Father was an orphan from a poor background, who captained the Portuguese national football team, before becoming an accountant. Secondary education at a state school in Lisbon. Read engineering at a Lisbon university in order to fulfill the entry requirements for the Military Academy. Attended the Military Academy for four years, two of which were spent studying engineering at the Instituto Superior Técnico. Was an engineering officer in the army and in 1955 was posted as a captain to India, when the Indian incursions into Portuguese territories were taking place. Returned to Lisbon and from 1957 until 1965 was a professor at the Military Academy. As a major in an engineering regiment served in the Colonial War in Mozambique from 1965 until 1967. Then returned to Portugal, was promoted to lieutenant-colonel and assigned to the headquarters of the engineering branch of the army. In 1970 was on active service in Angola as a colonel and in charge of all military engineering services. In 1972 returned to Lisbon and the engineering headquarters. In 1973 was approached by members of the Movement of Captains. On 25 April was a member of the Co-ordinating Committee of the Programme of the MFA. In July 1974 became prime minister at General Spínola's request and with the support of the MFA. In September 1975, as a result of negotiations between the left-wing of the Council of the Revolution and the President of the Republic, he agreed to step down as prime minister and become the general chief of staff of the armed forces. However, as a result of the Tancos assembly (see chronology), he was not appointed general chief of staff. Is currently a general in the army reserves.

Interview

Q. In 1973 you were a colonel, so why were you approached by the Movement of Captains?

A. I had been against the regime since the Spanish Civil War, although I had not been active politically. On the whole engineering officers are less politically isolated from the outside world than other branches of the army, because they have to attend a university course. After 25 April engineering and administrative officers played a role in the revolutionary process that was out of proportion to the number of officers involved.

In Angola I organised weekly meetings in my headquarters to discuss the political situation which shows that even then I was not committed to the regime. As my contacts with the Movement of Captains increased, they became more aware of my political views, but I think that one of the reasons I ended up as one of the leaders of the MFA on 25 April 1974 was because I was a high-ranking officer.

The Movement of Captains included officers within a broad spectrum of political opinions. The Movement began as a professional movement, but as a result of the political background and, in particular, of the dissatisfaction with the Colonial War, it became a political movement with a programme – the MFA Programme.

Q. Why were you chosen as prime minister in July 1974?

A. I was chosen because in the first few months of the revolution, along with Melo Antunes, I had been very active in the Co-ordinating Committee of the MFA. Also I was a colonel.

During this period there had been a continuous fight between the MFA, and thus the Co-ordinating Committee, and Spínola and his followers. The political ideology of the Spínolists favoured the large economic monopolies and was a neo-colonial solution to the Colonial War. The MFA supported the popular movement and wanted to give independence to the colonies.

The Palma Carlos crisis [see chronology] was the first confrontation between the MFA and the Spínolists, and was an attempt by Spínola to take power. The crisis occurred because Palma Carlos proposed a referendum which had the intention of making Spínola powerful by confirming him as President of the Republic. General elections were also to be delayed until the end of 1976.

When Spínola realised that the Council of State (in which the MFA played a decisive role at that time) would not approve the two proposals, he withdrew them. Palma Carlos resigned and Spínola realised he had lost. During this period Spínola attempted to appoint another prime minister but in the end he was forced to choose me because I had the support of the MFA and some members of the Junta of National Salvation. I am not sure that by choosing me he was not out to burn both me and the Co-ordinating Committee of the MFA.

Q. Was 25 April a revolution?

A. On 25 April we made a military coup. This coup was followed by a very strong popular movement which in turn strengthened the progressive political elements within the MFA. The mass movement's political and social background was given to it by its political organisations and the trade union movement. The union movement followed the political line of the CDE [see part 1]. Within the MFA we really did not predict the strength and the power of the popular movement that followed the coup.

The MFA Programme followed in general the lines of the anti-fascist democratic movement expressed, for example, in the resolution passed at the Aveiro Congress of 1973 [see part 1]. The aims of the programme were simple: the end of the Colonial War, the formation of a Constitutional Assembly to write a new Constitution and the setting up of a democracy. It also mentioned measures that favoured the under-privileged and were against the economic monopolies [see appendix 1].

Q. Were there any detailed plans to nationalise the banks and insurance companies before 11 March coup?

A. Melo Antunes and myself had been supporters of the CDE and prior to 25 April, the CDE had advocated nationalisation and in addition Agrarian Reform. From the 25th onwards, many members of the MFA became aware that political solutions could not be carried out unless there were changes in the economy. The social democratic programme, written by Melo Antunes, and published on 21 February 1975, was accepted by a large part of the MFA. But it was opposed by others who demanded nationalisations. Personally, I thought the plan narrow at that time, but I did support it.

Before 11 March several attempts were made to control the banks by governmental appointments within the banks. But even so money being printed by the Bank of Portugal was still vanishing. Before 11 March the economic and finance ministers had said that bank nationalisations were technically possible. The 11 March gave us the decisive conditions to carry out nationalisations with the support of the workers in the banks. I should point out that in the months that followed the 11 March coup many nationalisations were emergency measures. They occurred because owners had left the workers without management, pay or work. A good example of this was in the cement industry.

When we nationalised no detailed plans had existed before 11 March. Melo Antunes criticised these nationalisations but in my opinion he had not realised that the political situation had caused his plan to be already outdated. [Gonçalves was eventually replaced as prime minister partly as a result of opposition against him from Melo Antunes, the Group of Nine and members of the Council of the Revolution.]

Q. What was your disagreement with the Group of Nine?

A. They were fundamentally an expression of different political beliefs. After 25 April there were three main political streams: 1) the liberals, who wanted to see the fall of the previous regime, but no fundamental economic changes; 2) the social democrats and the right-wing socialists, who incidentally have been in power since 1976, and who wanted an alliance between the petite bourgeoisie and the middle classes and the monopolistic groups. They wanted to curb the power of the monopolistic groups, who controlled the economy under Salazar; 3) the left-wing socialists and Catholics, the CDE, and the PCP, who all wanted to see these monopolistic groups destroyed in order to achieve true economic democracy. The Group of Nine belonged to the second stream. During the revolutionary process the left wing of the MFA found out that the third stream was the one in agreement with the philosophy of the MFA Programme to which the left wing of the MFA was committed.

My government was able to carry out a large number of revolutionary measures. In the end we lost, because Portugal is poorly industrialised with a small working class and a large bourgeoisie. Although the Document of the Nine looks like a left-wing document, at best it is naive since, at present, and in our country, the petite and fractions of the middle bourgeoisie alone will never make a progressive left-wing revolution.

I considered the publication of the Document of the Nine an act of treason against the revolution. I demanded the Group of Nine's expulsion from the Council of the Revolution. In retrospect I think this was the result of my principles and attitudes acquired from my military training. I nevertheless attempted to negotiate with the Group of Nine through my colleagues, but they [the Group of Nine] refused.

It is not surprising that the next government after mine (the sixth provisional government) which included members of the Group of Nine, such as Melo Antunes, Victor Alves, Victor Crespo, and Costa Bras, produced mainly right-wing legislation. The sixth government froze salaries, reversed some of the Agrarian Reform and appointed right-wingers to manage the nationalised banks.

Q. What were the disagreements between COPCON and your government?

A. Otelo commanded COPCON and Otelo is a complex figure. He was under the influence of the social democrats, Melo Antunes, for example, and the far left, the PRP. The COPCON had in general an anti-communist radicalism. While this radicalism also permeated the working class, here it had to contend with the experience of the workers. Its influence was therefore gradually eroded.

In the COPCON and in the armed forces in general radicalism often led to anarchism. One should remember that many officers were trained under the previous regime whose authority was based upon repression of the individual and not leadership. The policies of my government were frequently policies advocated by the PCP. This was not because I was a member of the PCP, but because we agreed with them. Nevertheless we were seen as communists. We tried to form an alliance with the more radical sectors, but we had no success.

Q. Do you think Otelo controlled COPCON?

A. It is difficult to say, because COPCON was a complex structure. We should not forget that the actions of COPCON extended beyond Lisbon. In the area where the Agrarian Reform took place the officers of the COPCON acted most positively in their support of the reform.

Q. Why did your government legalise the land occupations in the Alentejo region [Agrarian Reform], but not the house occupations that occurred in urban areas?

A. In the region where the Agrarian Reforms were made conditions were politically right for them to occur. I opposed the house occupations because I did not think it was the same situation in the urban areas. The house occupations were encouraged by some radical officers and should not be compared with the land occupations carried out by workers who had a long history of political struggle.

The house occupations created a panic among large sections, for example, the emigrants. [Many emigrants owned houses in Portugal which they had bought with capital earned abroad.] When I asked Otelo to reverse the house occupations he told me to do it myself with the help of the Republican Guard!

Q. What was the 25 November coup?

A. It was a counter-revolutionary coup. In my opinion, since I was not in power, the paratroopers' invasion of the air force bases was the result of provocation by the Group of Nine and their right-wing associations. It was a provocation because the sixth provisional government which included members of the Group of Nine, lacking power, ordered the paras to bomb Rádio Renascença. The lower-ranking paras carried out these orders, but protested after the event. As a result of this protest their officers left, and the chief of staff of the air force stopped the wages of the lower ranks. Only if the paras had been very politically aware, would they have done other than they did. The only objective of the paras was to bring down the chief of staff of the air force.

Q. Why were you forced to resign as prime minister in September 1975?

A. Since May or June of that year, there were movements to try and bring down my government. This was part of a group which eventually became the Group of Nine. The President, Costa Gomes, was under pressure to fire me, but he argued instead that I should resign. I refused to do this. Otelo also wanted my resignation, since he said that I had only 20 per cent of the people behind me. Only eight days after the appointment of my fifth provisional government, in a meeting between the Directorate [this was composed of Otelo, Costa Gomes and Vasco Gonçalves; see chronology, 25 July] and my cabinet, we were told that Otelo had asked his friend Melo Antunes to write a programme for a new government. We saw this as an attempt to dismiss our fifth provisional government and so we decided to accelerate legislation in order to advance the cause of the revolution before we were dismissed.

By the end of August 1975 the navy suggested that I should be made general chief of staff of the armed forces. They also thought that Pinheiro de Azevedo, who was thought to be a left-winger, should be appointed prime minister. I accepted the post as general chief of staff. Meanwhile President Costa Gomes, Otelo and Fabião had blocked any attempts to convene the MFA Assembly, where I might have gained support for my government. When the Tancos assembly, which I consider a *pronunciamento* [revolt], met, on 6 September 1975, it voted against my new appointment as general chief of staff of the armed forces. In the end I was not appointed and my supporters and I were dismissed from the Council of the Revolution.

Q. Were you harmed politically by the public support that you received from the PCP?

A. I do not see things in that way. In fact, throughout the whole process there was in general a convergence in the fundamental lines of action between the more consequential sectors of the MFA and the lines of action of the popular and democratic movements and their political (the PCP) and social organisations (the trade union movement). We could not, either for opportunistic reasons or in order to dissociate ourselves from the PCP, act in a way which was against our awareness of the national interest and the interests of our people. If our image was damaged it was only among the right-wingers.

Q. What are your political beliefs?

A. I fight for the freedom of my people and their economic progress. I have always thought that political activity is one of the noblest activities and has to be morally sound. I think that political freedom cannot exist without economic freedom and a caring society. In order to achieve freedom, we have to build a socialist society, but socialism is a tool and not an end in itself. By socialism I mean the collective ownership of the principal means of production. In this respect Marxism is highly relevant to Portuguese society, because it is both an instrument of social analysis and a guide for action. I remember when I was only twenty years old walking down one of the main streets of Lisbon and saying to myself, 'One day the economic monolith CUF will be nationalised.'

In the most creative period of the revolution, from 11 March until the fall of my fifth government, we were not supported by COPCON, but were supported by the workers. Even though in the latter days of the fifth government we had lost power, we managed to produce a law to nationalise CUF and despite everything CUF was nationalised. It was inevitable.

THE INDEPENDENTS

These were the non-aligned officers. For example Colonel Fabião initially belonged to the Spínolist group and, partly because of this, was put in charge of decolonisation in Guinea-Bissau by Spínola. But, instead of acting on Spínola's behalf, he followed the MFA line. Throughout the revolution he did not appear to belong to any particular faction and frequently acted independently.

Carlos Fabião (CF)

Lieutenant-Colonel Carlos Fabião. Born in 1930 in Lisbon.
Father was a bank employee. Secondary education in a state
school in Lisbon. Entered Military Academy in 1950. In 1954
was promoted to sub-lieutenant and from 1955 until 1958 served
in Guinea-Bissau. During this time was promoted to lieutenant.
Returned to Portugal for four months and in 1959 re-posted to
Guinea-Bissau as a captain. From 1961 until 1963 was a captain
in Angola and from 1963 until 1965 an officer in a Lisbon
infantry regiment. In 1965 was on active service in Guinea-Bissau
until 1967. Returned to Portugal and was promoted to major; in
1968 again posted to Guinea-Bissau, where for two years he
served under General Spínola. Returned to Portugal in 1970.
Then on active service in Guinea-Bissau from 1971 until 1973 by
invitation of General Spínola, where he organised and was in
charge of the African troops (Milicia). In 1973 returned to
Portugal, and attended a course at the General Staff School. Here
he denounced a proposed right-wing coup and as a result was put
under house arrest in Braga, March 1974. After 25 April 1974
was released by Spínola and sent to Guinea-Bissau in May as
governor-general and commander-in-chief of the local armed
forces. On his return became a temporary general, elected chief of
staff of the army and so became a member of the Council of the
Revolution. Resigned from the Council of the Revolution following the 25 November coup and in May 1976 was given an
administrative post and asked to enter the reserves in January
1983. Is currently in publishing.

The interviews

99

Interview

Q. Why did you join the Movement of Captains?
A. I did not formally join the Movement of Captains before 25 April. But I had close contacts with it because I was closely linked with Spínola, and I had worked with him in Guinea-Bissau for some time.

A few weeks before 25 April I publicly denounced at the General Staff School, where I was attending a course, a proposed right-wing coup by General Kaulza de Arriaga. I had been told that there were plans to arrest Spínola and Costa Gomes. Because of my denouncement the Caetano regime put me under house arrest in the north of Portugal where I was until 25 April. Prior to my arrest I had been active in making General Spínola a national and international figure. In the early seventies in Guinea-Bissau, the group working with Spínola had reached the conclusion that there was no military solution to the conflict in Africa. At that time, Spínola could not convince the regime to negotiate with PAIGC. So a group of us decided to build up the image of Spínola to such an extent that he could not be ignored and had to be placed in an important position by the regime. This happened.
Q. What did you do following 25 April?
A. On the 25th I was under house arrest, but I was immediately called by Spínola to work in the CCO [Centro de Coordenação de Operações, Centre of Co-ordination of Operations], a unit which co-ordinated the operations of all the armed forces. It was controlled by Spínola's supporters and I was there along with Baptista, Bruno, Firmino Miguel, Hugo dos Santos, Dias de Lima, Morais, the Durões, Antunes, Azevedo, António Ramos and Otelo. [Some of these people had worked with Spínola in Guinea-Bissau and some had been involved in preparing the book, *Portugal and the Future*; see part 1. It is noteworthy that the military operation which led to the 25 April coup was run by Otelo, Garcia dos Santos, Vitor Crespo, Sanches Osório and Lopes Pires, and at that time none of these people were closely associated with Spínola.]

I was sent to Paris a few days after the coup to talk with President Senghor, the Senegalese President. The aim was to reactivate a project to give Guinea-Bissau its independence. This project had previously been worked out by President Senghor and

Spínola. President Senghor told me that the project was a waste of time, since Guinea-Bissau had already been recognised by eighty countries, and thus was effectively independent. He also said that Senegal and the OUA [Organisation of African Unity] would collaborate with Portugal in the decolonisation of the other colonies, if Portugal, as a gesture of goodwill, would recognise the independence of Guinea-Bissau.

When I returned to Portugal, Spínola sent me to Guinea-Bissau to take charge of decolonisation and I was temporarily promoted to brigadier.

On 16 October I was back in Portugal. Prior to this on 11 October they had elected me to be chief of staff of the army, and so automatically I became a member of the Junta of National Salvation. I became a member of the Council of the Revolution after the 11 March coup and was chief of staff of the army until 27 November 1976 when I resigned. I resigned because the old military hierarchy had regained control of the army.

Q. Do you think 25 April was a revolution?

A. Yes it was, both a political and military revolution. It was initiated by the armed forces and immediately received the full support of the Portuguese people. It was successful because it could rely on the support of Spínola and Costa Gomes. On the day of the coup the power was never in the streets and power passed in an orderly way from Caetano to Spínola. All this blocked any reaction from the right and the higher ranks of the army.

The revolution continued because within the armed forces there arose a group of highly politicised officers who dominated the rest. While this group, the MFA, was united the revolution continued. Within the MFA, there were socialists, social democrats, communists, Maoists, Trotskyites and ultra-left-wing anarcho-populists. Initially, it was easy to work out a programme which was acceptable to all these groups. However, when the armed forces came into contact with the people they became populists, but they were slightly paternal populists. In other words, it was they who tried to solve problems, rather than letting the people solve them themselves. The army populists were essentially COPCON under the leadership of Otelo. COPCON created such a revolutionary momentum that in the end it lost control of it.

The end of COPCON came on 25 November. In the preceding months there were several attempts to work out an agreement between the Group of Nine, COPCON, the Gonçalvists and a number of independent moderates. Ultra-leftists in COPCON blocked any agreement and this precipitated 25 November. The revolution had reached the stage that it could not continue. There was even talk of a Lisbon commune, but this could never have happened, as all that had to be done was to turn off the city's water supply.

Political parties had no interest in revolution since they would have been unable to control it. But the most important factor in stopping the revolution was that decolonisation was completed on 11 November 1975. From that date on the revolution had to be tamed, since most of the armed forces and political parties wanted it stopped. Before 11 November the people had to be mobilised to prevent any right-wing counter-coup from taking place and blocking the decolonisation programme. There were many attempted counter-coups by people connected with UNITA, FNLA, and also with the Church in the north of Portugal. Following the independence of Angola on 11 November, the right was no longer in a hurry.

Q. What happened on 25 November?

A. There were two coups prepared for that time. There was one which might be called from the left under the leadership of the Group of Nine and supported by the PS. There was another group in the north of the country, from the right, under the leadership of Sá Carneiro and Pires Veloso [see Interview].

The American ambassador Carlucci supported the southern group because, unlike Kissinger, he believed that only a centre-left government could stabilise the Portuguese political situation. The plans from the northern group were as follows: COPCON would be provoked into setting up a Lisbon commune. Then Pires Veloso and the air force general Freire would move on Lisbon, take it, and set up a new government under Carneiro. Pires Veloso would then be put in charge of the army. The group in the south, which included Eanes, Firmino Miguel, the Group of Nine and Loureiro dos Santos, had a plan that if a revolution started in Lisbon they would crush it. If they were unsuccessful, they would then withdraw to Rio Maior, a town just north of Lisbon. Working out of this town the PS, with the support of the right, had blocked the roads to the south on 24 November.

The Group of Nine won in Lisbon on 25 November. There was no resistance from the rest of the army against the Nine because we had to choose between the lesser of two evils. Like many of the uncommitted army people we preferred the PS and the Group of Nine to the PPD and the CDS. Since we independents were unable to oppose either the northern or southern groups, we chose the least bad.

Q. What was the influence of COPCON on the revolutionary process?

A. It hoped to create a mass movement, but it had no party affiliations and no political doctrine. In the end it served small political groups, the PRP and the UDP and it transformed itself into a populist organisation. Otelo never controlled COPCON.

Q. When did the revolution finish?

A. It finished when the MFA ceased to function. This was after 25 November. When the MFA was in operation it guaranteed the revolutionary process, but the MFA was composed of many groups, the Spínolists, the Gonçalvists, the Nine, COPCON and the independents. On 11 March 1975 the Spínolists left and in the Tancos assembly on 16 September 1975 the Gonçalvists left and on 25 November COPCON and the independents left. In the end only the Nine remained.

Q. What do you consider to be the achievements of the revolution?

A. It overthrew the previous regime and it brought about decolonisation. It was very successful in enabling the Portuguese to obtain political awareness and to become politicised. It gave the workers a chance to organise trade unions and made them aware of their own individual rights. It demolished the old economic monopolies.

The limitations were that big jumps were made. For example, when we nationalised the banks, we also nationalised all the firms they owned, which included boutiques, tobacconists and night clubs, and so on. We even nationalised firms that were bankrupt, which was equivalent to distributing debts among the Portuguese people.

The revolution went so fast that it did not allow laws to be passed that would legalise those changes. In principle, revolutions and legality seem antagonistic, but if revolutionary changes are not guaranteed by law, they will be lost and things will revert back to the old regime.

In the course of the revolution, the Junta of National Salvation and the Council of the Revolution tried not to frighten large sections of the Portuguese people. There was a constant concern for legality. At the most critical moments when new laws did not exist laws of the old regime were applied. This is why I am not in prison. I was never charged with unlawful action.

THE LINK-MEN

These officers tended to play useful roles but avoided the revolutionary limelight. Captains Marques Júnior and António Ramos played important roles when they acted as the link between groups or important individuals.

Marques Júnior (MJ)
António Ramos (AR)

Captain Marques Júnior. Born in Aveiro in 1946. Father was a forest guard. After a primary education in an isolated part of the Leiria district, was employed in a glass works factory in Marinha Grande. Friend of the family paid for his secondary education. At fifteen became a construction worker. When parents moved to Viana de Castelo, finished secondary education at a state school. Entered the Military Academy in Lisbon in 1966. In 1969 entered the infantry training school at Mafra. In 1971 was posted to Angola as a sub-lieutenant. Returned to Lisbon in 1972 and was sent to the infantry training school at Mafra as a training officer. In 1973 joined a group of officers who were opposed to the Oporto 'Congress of Combatants'. Was secretary at the Évora meeting on 9 September 1973 when the Movement of Captains was formally created. After Évora became the liaison officer between the Movement of Captains and the Mafra. In December 1973 at the Óbidos meeting (see Vasco Lourenço interview) was elected to the Co-ordinating Committee of the Movement of Captains and to the sub-group that was planning the military operation for the coup. Acted as a liaison officer on 25 April coup and Otelo's aid when Otelo became commander of the Lisbon military region. On 11 March was appointed to the Council of the Revolution and became a member of the Group of Nine, although he did not sign the Document of the Nine. Following the 25 November coup, the Council of the Revolution nominated him to lead an enquiry into the events of the coup. Was a member of the Council of the Revolution until it was dissolved. Is currently an officer at Mafra.

Interview

Q. What was your attitude to the previous regime?

A. I was always against the regime, but never politically active. My experience in Angola showed me that there was no military solution to the Colonial War. I also found there that I had a close affinity both with the soldiers and the Angolans who were being treated very badly.

Q. Why did you join the Movement of Captains?

A. I was involved in a protest against the Congress of Combatants and I participated in the Évora meeting as the secretary. I was elected to the first Co-ordinating Committee of the MFA in Obidos. Here Victor Alves, Vasco Lourenço and Otelo were elected to form the directorate of the Co-ordinating Committee of the MFA. The motor behind the whole movement was Vasco Lourenço.

Q. Since you were Otelo's aid, would you like to comment on how COPCON worked?

A. This question is really related to the participation and the active intervention of the armed forces in the political and social events that followed the 25 April coup. The reason why the MFA Co-ordinating Committee was not dissolved after 25 April was because the MFA soon realised that there was a risk that the programme would not be implemented. Although we handed over power to the civilians, within three weeks of the coup the mass movement removed power from the government. The armed forces were fractionated and so power did not rest there.

The biggest problem at COPCON in carrying out government orders occurred when people felt that these orders were against the ideals of the MFA. Everywhere the MFA were called upon by the people to solve their problems, and so power was given to them by the people. There was a point when in the eyes of the people the MFA was identified with COPCON.

COPCON was strictly an operational command without any law-enforcing function, but after the revolution the police force had lost prestige because they had supported the previous regime. Time and time again the police failed to act when told to by the government. The result of this was the COPCON was forced to step in and act both as a policeman and as an arbitrator. COPCON had no choice. Otelo was aware that often when asked to intervene he should not have done. As a member of the MFA and probably its leading member, he felt that he had a moral responsibility to try and solve the people's problems. Frequently it was the civilian government that handed over problems to Otelo. It is difficult to say that he controlled COPCON. Theoretically he gradually lost power, but in practice this was not so. I think that some actions by the units and officers under COPCON were carried out not under his orders.

Q. What were the relationships between Otelo and the Group of Nine?

A. Otelo would like to have been with the Group of Nine, but he could not have been, as this would have meant losing the trust of COPCON. There were many meetings between Otelo and the Group of Nine to try to attempt a reconciliation of their two positions.

Q. Since you were in charge of an enquiry into the events of the 25 November coup, in retrospect do you think the findings were correct?

A. Obviously I am in a delicate position to answer that question, since I supervised the committee of enquiry, although the committee had a brigadier as a president. There are some things that we were not aware of at that time, but which have since become public. This forces us to view 25 November differently from the official version. I refer, for example, to the book written by Paradela de Abreu. [This book describes the involvement of the Church, the MDLP, some right-wing officers, some members of the Group of Nine and some political parties' attempts to build up a counter-revolutionary movement at the time of 25 November. See also Vasco Lourenço's interview.]

Q. Was there any danger that the communists would take over on 25 November?

A. I am sure there was no danger of a communist take-over on 25 November. The danger came from the civilian right supported by officers in the armed forces. The Document of the Nine was against the right. However, some members of the Group of Nine felt that the PCP was controlling the mass movement and had to be stopped. Today I still don't know why the paratroopers occupied the air force bases.

Although the Group of Nine supported the military operations that took place on 25 November under the command of Eanes, they lost power immediately afterwards. Some of the military and civilian forces of the winning side moved their attacks from the PCP to the Council of the Revolution in which the Group of Nine sat.

The military operation of the coup cannot be identified with the political aims of the coup, formulated by the Group of Nine, although there were links between the group that planned and was in charge of the military operations [the operationals] and the Group of Nine. The military group had to gain strength by associating with other forces. These forces after 25 November demanded repayment.

Before the 25 November coup, when the Council of the Revolution was making a decision, they had to know how the ultra-left regiment RAL1 would react to a decision. After the coup, they had to take into account the reactions of the commandos [a right-wing regiment].

Q. Was there any evidence of foreign intervention before and after 25 April 1974?

A. I don't know of any evidence suggesting any foreign intervention before 25 April and directly related to the coup. I think that there is evidence of foreign intervention in several sectors and at different levels of Portuguese society after 25 April. But I will not put forward any further details.

Captain António Ramos. Born in 1942 in Vilares. Parents were farm workers. Secondary education at a state school in Lisbon. Read literature at Lisbon university for three years before being conscripted in 1962 into the army as an officer. From 1963 until 1965 on active service in Angola as a sub-lieutenant. Returned to university and then became a journalist in the state-run news-agency ANI. In 1967 was recalled to serve a second term in Guinea-Bissau as a non-professional army captain. After two years returned to Lisbon and attended the Military Academy for three years. Completed the course to become a professional officer and then on active service in Guinea-Bissau under General Spínola, first as a sub-lieutenant and then as a captain. Was wounded in combat and returned to journalism in Lisbon. Was private secretary to Spínola from the beginning of 1974 until 28 September 1974 when Spínola resigned. Returned to journalism, but was arrested on 11 March 1975 for aiding Spínola to flee the country. Released from prison on the day of the 25 November coup by Eanes. Is currently political adviser to President Eanes.

Interview

Q. Why did you join the Movement of Captains?

A. I signed the document opposing the Oporto Congress of Combatants, and I gathered most of the signatures for this document when I was in Guinea-Bissau. I joined the Movement for political reasons, and to express solidarity with my brother officers, even though by then there was no need for me to do this as I was no longer on active service. I had believed that Marcello Caetano would liberalise Salazar's regime, but when President Thomaz was re-elected, all the officers in Guinea-Bissau, myself included, realised that the regime could not solve the Colonial War. A political solution was needed. The armed forces were frightened of becoming the scapegoats, if they were defeated in the Colonial War, in exactly the same way as they had been in India. [This fear of becoming a scapegoat was known as the 'Indian Syndrome'.]

Because I had been a conscripted officer and because of my relationship with Spínola [private secretary], I was the liaison officer between Spínola, the professional officers and the conscripted [non-professional] officers.

Q. What happened on 25 April 1974?

A. This was not a revolution in the French or Russian style but in a general sense it was a revolution.

The MFA Programme was written by officers who had a revolutionary attitude but, because of the demands of Spínola, their programme was partially diluted. Spínola and Costa Gomes played parallel roles throughout this process. Both had lived very well in the previous regime and their attitudes were largely the result of the 'Indian Syndrome'. Spínola became politicised slightly earlier than Costa Gomes because of his experience in Guinea-Bissau.

The officers who wrote the MFA Programme did not predict the popular movement that followed the coup. The Programme was written in an attempt to please a wide section of the Portuguese people and they wanted the changes to take place in an orderly way. When the mass movement got under way it carried the MFA with it.

On the day of 25 April my job was to keep Spínola calm until he was needed and I was also responsible for his personal security. I was with him when he formally took over from Caetano and on the way to this I saw the people taking to the streets. This was the beginning of the mass movements.

Revolutions don't stop and the Portuguese revolution is slowing and being contained. The risk of containment is that it will lead to a convulsion, and in a reaction against this convulsion the politically inarticulate armed forces that are now being created will take over and install a new dictatorship. The latest generation of officers have been taught that 25 April 1974 was a bad thing!

Q. What was the relationship between 28 September 1974 and 11 March 1975?

A. Spínola tried to gain political control of the country. I was near him and saw that he wanted to control the revolution but not stop it. He was frightened that the outside world would be against us. He failed in this attempt because revolutions cannot be orderly.

The 11 March was the first serious attempt to stop the revolution by well-intentioned and prestigious officers who were frightened of the mass movement. They belonged to the MFA but they wrongly analysed the situation and so acted incorrectly. Spínola was involved because a few of these officers whom he trusted well told him that he was going to be killed. So, like a soldier, he fought back.

In the end 11 March was the result of two campaigns by the public. One from the ultra-right, which opposed independence of the colonies. The other by the PCP, which created political instability. There is no doubt that the right had prepared a coup and then they called in Spínola. The nationalisations which followed 11 March were not the reason for the coup.

I was arrested on 11 March because I had helped Spínola to leave the country. On that day I was critical of his involvement in the coup, but helped him to leave because he was my friend. I did not want to see him humiliated in public and, if I have to choose between an ideology and a friend, I would choose a friend.

Q. Although you were in prison up to 25 November, when Eanes released you, how do you explain his emergence as a political and military leader?

A. From September onwards there was a progressive dissociation between the mass movement and the far left. The Document of the Nine had been a warning about this, and an attempt to regroup the revolution and extend it from Lisbon to the rest of the country. The Nine were an alternative to the ultra right and ultra left.

The military operations of 25 November were a way of getting rid of the far left, which was confined to the Lisbon area. The paras' occupation of the air force bases was an act of desperation by the far left. It is interesting that they did not occupy the Cortegaça base because it was an American base, and they were frightened of the Americans.

Eanes led the military operations on 25 November. He emerged as a leader because he was a respected military man with a good cultural and political background. He was not a revolutionary, but he was accepted by the moderate left, as he is not a conservative. He is a reformist.

There was a hope on 25 November that the masses would catch up and participate in the revolution. The swing to the right that followed was due to the political parties and the civilian right became dominant after the middle of 1976. In the army, 'grey' officers, who had neither been involved in the previous regime nor in the revolutionary process, now [in 1984] occupy the important positions of power. This is due to outside civilian pressure.

THE ORGANISERS

The organisers were officers with strong, often charismatic, personalities. They had special abilities to lead and were often the men of action of the men of action. They were good co-ordinators, usually adept at designing and implementing tactical plans. Politically, they range from populists such as Otelo through to conservatives such as Pires Veloso.

Otelo Saraiva de Carvalho (OSC)
Franco Charais (FC)
Victor Crespo (VC)
Vasco Lourenço (VL)
Pires Veloso (PV)

Lieutenant Colonel Otelo Saraiva de Carvalho. Born in Maputo (Lourenço Marques) in Mozambique in 1936. Father was a civil servant and mother a railway clerk. Secondary education at state school in Maputo. Entered the Military Academy in Lisbon at the age of nineteen. On active service in Angola from 1961 until 1963 as a sub-lieutenant. Then on active service again in Angola, as a captain from 1965 until 1967. Posted to Guinea-Bissau in 1970 as a captain under General Spínola. In charge of civilian affairs and propaganda. During this period became involved in the protest against the Congress of Combatants. In 1973 returned to Portugal and helped set up the Movement of Captains. Planned and commanded military take-over on 25 April 1974. In July 1974, was temporarily promoted to brigadier and became the commander of the Lisbon military region and the head of COPCON. In May 1975, temporarily promoted to general. Following the 25 November coup, demoted to major at his own request. Two months later, was arrested on charges of abuse of power, whilst in charge of COPCON. Released after forty-four days in prison. During 1976 was a presidential candidate. In October 1976 was again arrested. After twenty days in jail, was released and suspended from duty. In 1979 was put into the army reserves. In 1982 recalled to the army, since it was shown that his discharge had been politically motivated. In June 1984 was arrested for his alleged leadership of a terrorist organisation (FP25, Forces of 25 April).

Interview

Q. Why did you join the Movement of Captains?
A. Originally I was apolitical like most army officers. I was first really affected by politics in the Delgado elections in 1958 [see part 1] and was upset by the political repressions that followed these elections. My political awareness was really brought alive by the Colonial War. This was due to the contacts I made with the enemy and with their political propaganda and to my associating with brother army officers, who were not professional men. All of these men had been to universities and many had taken part in anti-regime unrest that occurred in the universities in the early 1960s. Finally, the close associations that existed between the ordinary soldiers and myself made me aware of the social conditions that had existed throughout the country under Salazar.
Q. So you joined the Movement of Captains because you were politically aware?
A. Initially, the Movement of Captains had nothing to do with politics. The Movement was formed to defend the privileges of the professional army officers against the law passed by the regime [see part 1]. However, some of us saw the Movement of Captains as an opportunity to unite the young army officers against this erosion of privileges and then we could show them that the only way to achieve our aim was to overthrow the regime. We thought that the professional problems were a result of the Colonial War. The regime had had thirteen years of Colonial War and had been unable to reach any form of political settlement.
Q. What was your role on 25 April 1974?
A. After the failure of the attempted coup of Caldas de Rainha, the Movement of Captains was in disarray. The coup took place on 16 March and on 24 March, along with Victor Alves, I managed to assemble most of the Co-ordinating Committee of the Movement of Captains. In the meeting I convinced them that the only thing to do was to go forward, otherwise we would all end up being persecuted, like many of our brother officers. As Vasco Lourenço, the third element of the secretariat of the already formed MFA, had been transferred to the Azores, I, in the same meeting, took it upon myself to produce the military plan to

take over the country and to command the corresponding military operation for bringing down the regime. I chose the date for the operation to be between 22 and 29 April.

From 24 March onwards I gathered information about the enemy, i.e. the Portuguese Legion, the PIDE, the Republican Guard, the police and the reactionary part of the armed forces. By 16 April the plan was ready, and for the next four days I allocated tasks to different military units. On 22 April the commandos were given their orders and on the 23rd the passwords were distributed to the liaison officers.

At 9 o'clock at night on 24 April I took charge of the command post which had secretly been set up in an engineering barracks at Pontinha. In the early hours of the morning, we started and everything went as planned. By late morning of 26 April, it was all over. I took off my uniform, I changed into civilian clothing and went home to my family. The mission had been accomplished.

Q. What did you do after 25 April?

A. I worked, somewhat anonymously, at the general staff headquarters until June 1974. Then I was sent to Lusaka, Zambia, with Mário Soares, who had the job of negotiating an unconditional cease-fire with FRELIMO. The mission I was given by General Spínola was to make sure that Soares carried this out.

I saw myself, not as a Spínola man, but as a representative of the MFA. I had signed the Programme of the MFA, which had been written under the leadership of Melo Antunes, which committed the MFA to allow the colonies to have self-rule or total independence, regardless of cost. During the Lusaka negotiations, I collided with Soares, who wanted to carry out Spínola's instructions.

Q. Why were you appointed the commander of COPCON?

A. COPCON was planned by Franco Charais [see interview], as the co-ordinating body for all the military regions. [After the 25 April coup, militarily Portugal was divided into four regions – the north, central, south and Lisbon.] It was also an attempt to establish discipline within the armed forces, especially the army. Spínola's idea was to promote me to a four-star general so that I could act directly under his orders and independently of the general chief of staff of the armed forces, Costa Gomes. Acting on behalf of the MFA I refused, and forced Spínola to make me a temporary brigadier under Costa Gomes. It was Spínola, acting on his own initiative, who appointed me as commander of the Lisbon military region.

I would like to add that on the same day as I was appointed to COPCON, 13 July 1974, Vasco Gonçalves was made prime minister. This was a result of a suggestion of mine that I had made to the Co-ordinating Committee of the MFA. [The power structures that followed the 25 April coup are explained in part 2.] 13 July also marks the beginning of the increased involvement of the MFA in the revolutionary process, since members of the MFA were appointed to positions of power, for example, COPCON, the prime minister, the foreign secretary [Melo Antunes]. This day also marked the coming into the open of the fight between Spínola and the MFA on the best way of solving the colonial problem. The MFA was directly in negotiation with the liberation movements, but Spínola openly supported reactionary groups in the colonies in an attempt to frustrate the MFA plans. In the end, Spínola was defeated and resigned on 28 September 1974.

Q. Do you see any parallels between the coups of 11 March and 25 November?

A. Both coups took place against a background of fear of a communist take-over of the country. On 11 March the fear was almost paranoic.

Q. In reality do you think there was a risk?

A. It is a controversial question. My view is that on 25 November the Communist Party was at its weakest. During the summer of 1975 there had been a popular and spontaneous revolution, which had completely by-passed the Communist Party.

Q. Do you see 25 November as the end of this popular revolutionary process?

A. The MFA was never really a homogeneous body, with a clear political programme. There were a number of groups with different political outlooks who had all worked together in the MFA to bring down the regime. The Spínola group wanted Spínola as President and him to be in charge of any political changes. When the Spínolists left on 28 September 1974, the MFA was united for a short period, until disagreements arose about the economic policies of the Gonçalves government. These disagreements were about the nationalisations that were taking place on 11 March

1975. They were a rejection of the Melo Antunes plan [see Gonçalves interview].

The turning point of the political situation occurred after the elections of 25 April 1975. These elections were part of the MFA Programme, where the people were asked to elect an Assembly to draw up the new Constitution. The elections showed that the PS and the PPD had a large following [see chronology]. On the other hand, the PCP had a much smaller following than had been expected. However, the MFA had obtained a written agreement with the parties that the results of these elections would not influence the power structure in the post-25 April coup non-elected government. But the political parties claimed power, based upon election results.

Since the 25 April coup the PCP had been the only organised party and had eased itself into positions of power within the media, the local authorities and the civil service. The popular revolutionary process had created amongst officers and civilians alike a fear of the PCP. The election results, coupled with this fear, enabled the PS and the PPD to demand that they should have and hold positions of power. Most members of the Council of the Revolution felt this pressure from the PS and the PPD.

Q. Are you referring to the Group of Nine as those who felt the pressure within the Council of the Revolution?

A. Yes. The Group of Nine actually appeared as a group on 8 August 1975, when they produced a document fiercely critical of the PCP and the Vasco Gonçalves government. By not producing any alternative solution, it implicitly supported the PS and the right. And so a tactical alliance was established between the Group of Nine, the PS and all the right. COPCON was not directly criticised by the Document of the Nine but indirectly as it (the document) criticised the prevailing political anarchism.

In reply to the Group of Nine's document, COPCON, under my direction, produced a document in which the ideological position of the revolutionary left was presented. But the Council of the Revolution, driven by the Group of Nine, and with the support of the MFA officers, dismissed Gonçalves as prime minister. There was large popular support for our document, which was also critical of the PCP, and, because of this, the Group of Nine attempted a reconciliation. They produced another document written by Melo Antunes, which was supposed to be a fusion of the two documents. However, when it was presented to members of my staff at COPCON by Victor Crespo and Vasco Lourenço, my staff realised that a new government had already been appointed on the basis of this new document. Thus, in reality, it was not open for discussion.

Q. Was it only Melo Antunes who wrote this new document?

A. I don't know. I was in a meeting in the house of Gomes Mota, along with Eanes, Garcia dos Santos and Loureiro dos Santos when the new document was read out. Later on, I read it again, when it was carried by Victor Crespo and Vasco Lourenço across to the COPCON staff for discussions. [Mota, Eanes, Garcia dos Santos and Loureiro dos Santos were all important figures in the military planning and execution of 25 November coup.]

Q. Did you control the COPCON?

A. COPCON, although it only had a few members of staff [about twenty, at its peak] was always under pressure from the outside political groups. The same thing was happening through all of the MFA. COPCON controlled the military units under its command, provided that the officers were in agreement with my decisions. In the 'hot summer' of 1975 some marine and paratroop units which had been assigned to COPCON were removed from my command and thus from COPCON, so that we became less powerful. At the same time, because of the revolutionary changes that were taking place in the army, many of the officers became frightened of losing their officer status and so sided with the Group of Nine. The real loss of power came about in September 1975, as most officers supported the Group of Nine, and were anti-COPCON, which they saw as a revolutionary force.

Q. Were you aware that there was a military group planning the operation that came into effect on 25 November?

A. Yes. I knew that Eanes and Loureiro dos Santos were involved. In September 1975, Vasco Lourenço came to warn me that these officers were planning a military operation and that, if anything happened to oppose them, they would clamp down heavily on the left. This meant that Vasco Lourenço was aware that he himself was siding with the right. In COPCON we then knew we had lost power and our plans were involved with the eradication of illiteracy! We were not planning any political coup. It makes me laugh that we were accused of that after 25 November.

Q. What was the coup of 25 November?
A. Since the Group of Nine were under pressure from the PS and PPD, and unable to reach an agreement with COPCON, they decided to act and stop the revolutionary process.

The main object of 25 November, as stated by Loureiro dos Santos, was to abolish COPCON. To do this, Eanes needed a pretext. I tried by all possible means not to give him one.

The PCP were losing power and in despair and decided to play their cards. They chose a place where they had power – the paratroopers. The overwhelming majority of the officers [123 of them] of the paratroop regiment stationed at Tancos had left with the support of the chief of staff of the air force. These officers had left in protest against the unrest amongst the soldiers and sergeants that had been caused by the Council of Revolution ordering the paratroopers to bomb Rádio Renascença [see chronology]. The chief of staff of the air force had threatened to disband the paratroop regiments, but, as the operational commander of Portugal, I publicly supported the Tancos para regiments and allowed the personnel still remaining in the base to requisition for arms for defence. A tremendous tension built up, as the air force was continually flying over the Tancos base. Once the PCP saw I supported the paras, they told them to leave Tancos and occupy all the air force bases in the south and centre of the country.

The PCP's aims were to force the resignation of the chief of staff of the air force and get General Rangel de Lima appointed to this post, and to place Costa Martins once again in the Council of the Revolution. General Rangel de Lima would automatically become a member of the Council of the Revolution and so increase PCP influence there. I am sure that there was a well-organised plan to occupy the air force bases, since the operations took place in the early hours of the morning (05.30) and only lasted for three-quarters of an hour.

The paratroopers occupying the bases was the pretext Eanes needed. I could have called out paratroopers and marines loyal to me and Eanes would have been in trouble. This would have meant a civil war, so I decided not to resist. Eanes and the commandos of Jaime Neves had no opposition.

President Costa Gomes had attempted to solve the problem of the Tancos paratroopers occupying those air force bases by telling them that he and I would go to Tancos on the following day, 26 November. We would discuss putting them all under my command and thus the paratroopers would be moved from the air force and into the army. Meanwhile Costa Gomes had asked Costa Martins to talk to the paratroopers to get them to return to Tancos, but Costa Martins vanished. Again, I laugh when it is said that 25 November was a great military victory for Eanes and his commandos. Against whom?

Q. What is your political outlook?

A. I am a man who fights for the principles of human dignity and social justice. I want to raise the standards of living, education and health for the less well-off. I don't agree with the present party-controlled democracy. I believe in direct democracy. I defend base socialism [meaning from the base, that is, the people – a direct democracy] and I consider that only socialism can bring dignity, happiness and well-being to the workers and place economic and political power in the hands of their direct representatives. Marxism is relevant to Portugal, but we do not have to import ready-made regimes. We should profit from the good experiences of other revolutions. For example, I refer to the early stages of the Cuban and Russian revolutions, before they became stratified into dictatorial regimes with a new class structure, and a privileged and single party, and so on. We should harness the spontaneity and creativity of the masses, which gives them the ability to solve their own problems. I saw, during the Portuguese revolution, the power of this creativity in the streets and the towns and in the fields.

Q. What do you think of the recently formed Association of 25 April?

A. I am afraid that within a few years the Association will become an institution which only remembers. Jokingly, and rightly, the less kind say that it is an Association of 25 November. In fact, the leaders of the Association were actively involved in stopping the revolution, while most of its members had nothing to do with 25 April. I confess that my hope that it survives is not great.

General Franco Charais. Born in 1931 in Oporto. Father was a
bank employee and mother a school teacher. Secondary education at a state school and one year at university in Oporto.
Entered the Military Academy and trained to be an artillery
officer. Conventional military career in Portugal until the outbreak of the Colonial War and then two years' active service in
Mozambique. Returned to Lisbon and attended a course at the
General Staff School. 1971–3 in Angola, first as a major, then as a
lieutenant-colonel in supplies and logistics. Returned to Lisbon
and worked on the general staff; was posted abroad to France,
South Africa, England, Cape Verde and Guinea-Bissau. Was
involved on the day of the 25 April coup, as a member of the
group that wrote the Programme of the MFA. While in the
general staff of the armed forces, set about restructuring the
armed forces (for example, amongst other things, was involved in
the formulation of COPCON and the Fifth Division of the
general staff of the armed forces). At the 13 June 1974 Manutenção Militar assembly of the MFA was elected to the Co-ordinating Committee and thus became a member of the Council of
State. On 11 March 1975 became a member of the Council of the
Revolution until it was abolished in 1982. In May 1975 temporarily appointed to brigadier and became commander of the
central military region, during the period that he was a member of
the Council of the Revolution. Is currently a general presiding
over the Committee for Accounts and Responsibilities of the
Army.

Interview

Q. Why did you join the Movement of Captains?
A. Like most civilians and officers, my political background before the revolution was very narrow. I became more politically aware after attending the general staff course, and also during my tours of duty in Mozambique and Angola, where I had close contacts with the social problems in the colonies. At the end of 1973, as a member of the general staff of the army, I was put in charge of a section which dealt with arms supplies and here I became aware of both political and technical perspectives of the Colonial War.

The political perspective became clear to me when I made an official visit to South Africa. The South Africans wanted to create, by any available means, an independent Angola and Mozambique under the control of the white settlers. They wanted this so that South Africa would be protected by a belt of white-dominated countries and at the same time they would have access to the Angolan oil. If this had happened, it would have broken connections between the peoples of Angola and Mozambique and Portugal.

The technical perspective became clear to me when I realised that we could not afford to fight the Colonial War; the financial resources available would not cover more than 20 per cent of its needs. Even if we had had the money, there was an embargo on the supply of arms for the Colonial War by the NATO countries. Only South Africa and Israel would have sold us the necessary war supplies, but even these countries could not have met our demands.

For these reasons I joined the Movement of Captains for a few months before 25 April. I was invited to join by Major Victor Alves, who was one of my subordinate officers. I was in the group which wrote the MFA Programme. This group included Victor Alves, Victor Crespo, Vasco Gonçalves, Hugo dos Santos, Sanches Osório, and Contreiras, and two other naval officers. We worked on a draft that was written by Melo Antunes, who at that time was in the Azores.

Q. Do you think 25 April 1974 was a revolution?
A. It was not planned to be a revolution, as the MFA wanted to install a democracy. When we planned the coup, we debated as to

whether the armed forces should hand over power as soon as possible or whether to hang on for a while. We decided to draw up a new Constitution through a National Constitutional Assembly, as soon as possible, so that the politicians could take over. Even during the period before formal democracy was established, civilians were brought into the institutions created for the pre-Constitution transition period. For example, the Council of State had seven civilians and in the first provisional government the Prime Minister Palma Carlos was a civilian. In this, and future provisional governments, military officers were appointed to ministerial posts, because the civilians could not agree as to which civilian should fill the post. In the end, the civilians preferred officers in these posts. For a long time, the minister of home affairs [home secretary] was an officer, since no civilian would take that job, because of the power struggles between the developing civilian, political forces.

A few days after 25 April there was an explosive mass movement. All the underground political groups became active in the streets, the schools, the factories, everywhere. This created a clash between two groups in the MFA: one under the leadership of the Co-ordinating Committee and the other led by General Spínola. The first provisional government was powerless, since it did not control either the army or the police force. As a result, Prime Minister Carlos demanded more power. He wanted to control the police and the armed forces and so he would control the MFA. This would have meant loss of autonomy within the MFA.

Q. Was this the background to the so-called Palma Carlos crisis?

A. Yes. The implications of Palma Carlos's demands were that the MFA would be dissolved and that there would be an immediate reinstatement of Spínola as President of the Republic, through a referendum. This would have removed the legitimacy of the political involvement by the MFA. Spínola would then give special powers to the prime minister. This led to the convening of the MFA assembly at Manutenção Militar [see interviews of Sanches Osório and Vasco Lourenço for further details of this meeting]. At this meeting, the MFA insisted that Spínola carry out their programme.

The Council of State blocked the proposals of Palma Carlos

and he resigned. The Co-ordinating Committee still wanted a civilian as prime minister, but the divisions between the civilian parties were then so wide that they could not agree on a civilian. That was why Vasco Gonçalves was selected as prime minister.

The underlying problem in the Palma Carlos crisis was the mass movement and the Colonial War. The MFA wanted at all costs to avoid any solution that would clamp down the revolution. But there were many sections of Portuguese society that were afraid of this revolution and they exerted pressure on President Spínola.

Q. What brought about President Spínola's resignation on 28 September?

A. On 28 September sections of Portuguese society, the so-called 'silent majority', which included the very powerful economic groups under Salazar, attempted to reinforce Spínola's powers to such an extent that he would be able to control the political situation. Spínola wanted a democratic system based upon a Constitution that would be written by a group of people and not by an elected National Constitutional Assembly. In the end, the 'silent majority' did not materialise as a powerful political force, and this led to Spínola's resignation. The 11 March was the third attempt to let Spínola take over, this time by military means, but by then he was unable to gather sufficient military support.

After 11 March the revolution gained momentum under the strong influence of the far left. The far left was made up of young inexperienced political activists. The PCP was left behind. The PCP has a deep understanding of the Portuguese and the economic and social conditions of the country. Although disagreeing with the far left, it was forced to follow it, in order not to lose its popular support. In the end, it was prevented from political suicide by the intervention of President Costa Gomes [see Costa Gomes interview].

Q. Was there any danger of a PCP take-over on 25 November 1975?

A. My knowledge of the military and civilian situation at that time was that neither the PCP nor the far left could have taken over. The civilian far left dreamt of a military take-over by the military far left, which meant Otelo. They were anti-communists and so would not unite with the PCP. But Otelo was not strong, he did not control COPCON. The military commanders of the military regions outside Lisbon (I was in charge of the central military region and Pezarat Correia commanded the southern military region), although formally under the control of COPCON, would not obey orders that would lead to a political take-over by Otelo. Even in the Lisbon area, only two regiments were loyal to him (RAL1 and the military police) and then, only if they agreed with his orders. The situation in Lisbon was similar to the Paris Commune. Everything was happening in Lisbon and its surrounding industrial belt, and the rest of the country watched and waited.

Except for providing, along with Pezarat Correia, a rearguard support for President Costa Gomes, I don't place any importance on any of the events that took place on 25 November. The paratroopers occupied the bases for professional reasons. They wanted the resignation of the chief of staff of the air force and their reinstatement as paratroopers. The 25 November showed that the MFA was completely fractionated and the emergence of General Eanes was an attempt to stabilise these fractions within the armed forces.

On the actual day of the 25th, I returned to the headquarters of the military region I commanded at Coimbra. I was alone in my car, after a meeting of the previous night at the Council of the Revolution. As far as I was concerned, it was just another day in the life of a country seeking its identity. My only actions were to control the Portuguese television (RTP) aerial at Lousã and to give support to the cavalry-training regiment of Santarem, from which armoured cars were to be used under Salgueiro Maia's command.

Q. How do you assess the political role of the Council of the Revolution after the institutionalisation of formal democracy?

A. The Council of the Revolution acted as a political cushion between the different sectors of the armed forces and the President of the Republic and the government. We tried to pacify the armed forces and we brought to the attention of the military chiefs any undercurrents of opinion that had not reached them by the normal channels.

Today, the armed forces are not involved in politics and I agree with this. Many of the officers that have left the armed forces since 1976 had been very politically active. They would not feel fulfilled within the armed forces. Some left by themselves, others were slightly pushed, but I am sure that all of them feel freer on the outside.

Admiral Victor Crespo. Born in Porto de Mós in 1932. Father was a lawyer. Secondary education and one year at university in Coimbra. Entered the Naval Academy in Lisbon in 1952. In 1957 attended a naval artillery course. From 1958 to 1961 worked with NATO naval forces. In 1961 was sent to Mozambique and stayed there until 1963. From 1963 to 1969 was professor of naval ballistics at the Naval Academy. From 1970 until 1973 was commander of a light frigate in Mozambique. Was a member of the Co-ordinating Committee of the MFA. Was governor-general to Mozambique from 1974 to 1975 and from 1975 to 1976 a minister in the sixth provisional government. Became a member of the Council of the Revolution in 1975 until it was dissolved in 1982. Is currently an admiral in the navy.

Interview

Q. Why did you join the Movement of Captains?
A. Although my father had been a supporter of the previous regime, I was always against it. I was not politically active whilst in the navy, but as a professor in the Naval Academy, and in charge of the cadets' cultural activities, I managed to organise groups where social, economic and political matters were discussed. This explains why some of my previous students approached me and asked me to join the Movement of Captains. But I only joined after the Cascais meeting [see part 1] because only then the solution of the colonial problem, the implementation of a democratic regime and the will to develop were definitely fixed as the main aims of the Movement. I was elected by the navy as a representative to both the political and military sub-groups of the Co-ordinating Committee of the MFA. I should say that the military participation by the navy in the 25 April coup was, on the whole, modest.

On that day I was in the Pontinha headquarters, along with Otelo and the others. At that time, there were twenty-six NATO ships in the Lisbon harbour, a huge force, which was larger than all the forces involved in the coup. The presence of these NATO ships would dissuade Spain from sending troops to support the Portuguese regime, under the Iberian pact. I involved myself in military action to control the naval forces. The NATO ships were sailing when the coup started and among them were Portuguese vessels. In control of naval operations, I could prevent a Portuguese frigate, sent back from the NATO forces, from firing on our troops.

I joined the Movement to participate in a revolution, whose final goal was to transform Portugal into a modern and progressive country. In retrospect, the final result was revolutionary in many ways – socially, politically and economically. Although all the roots of the previous regime have not been erased, Portugal is today internally and internationally much different from how it was in 1973. Nowadays, the revolution has been completely stopped by the action of the last two governments [PS/PSD coalition and AD coalition], but the potentialities of the old regime still exist.
Q. How do you interpret the events that occurred on 28 September and 11 March?

A. The 28 September and 11 March were the result of a split within the MFA. On the one hand, there were the Spínolists, who wanted to liberalise, but not drastically change, the country from what it had been under the previous regime. Their way of ending the Colonial War was to give only a certain degree of independence to the colonies, which meant not finishing the war. They were backed by the old economic groups of the previous regime. They failed as they were incompetent in both analysing the political situation and militarily organising the counter-coup. You can see this on 16 March 1974, 28 September 1974 and again on 11 March 1975.

Following 11 March, many supporters of Spínola left the country with much of their wealth. The nationalisations that followed were an attempt to gain control of the economy. These nationalisations were even advocated by moderates, such as Dr Silvo Lopes, and were determined much more by technical reasons than by a pre-planned policy.

On the other hand, there were those in the MFA who wanted to stop the war and bring about radical changes within Portugal in order to ensure that the colonies gained full independence.

Q. Do you think the 25 November coup was a reaction to the events of 11 March?

A. No. The 25 November took place as a reaction against the anarchy that had developed in the country. Power was dissipated throughout a number of groups. Many thought that the PCP, through its influence on the government, the President of the Republic and the media, had too much power and I think that this was not an accurate reflection of the following it had in the country. There was a general feeling that Portugal was becoming something people did not want. But this does not mean that the communists were the only ones responsible for the anarchy, even though they had a strong influence in the Lisbon industrial belt and the Alentejo region. In fact, I think that by that time the PCP had no chance of taking over the country, even if it was their intention, which I do not know.

The 25 November was not only an attempt to stop the spread of anarchy, but the main reason for part of the MFA planning it was to create national support for the return to a coherent line of an already started economic and social revolution, that was necessary for the country. If you examine the Document of the Nine, you will see it is a left-wing document.

Q. How do you explain that the Group of Nine, who produced the document that led to the 25 November, rapidly lost power after the coup, yet this did not happen with the military who brought about the coup?

A. The Group of Nine was a political group and the accepted leader of a military group, which, along with others, included Eanes, Garcia dos Santos, Tomé Pinto, Rocha Vieira, and Loureiro dos Santos. The military action that took place on 25 November was under the control of Eanes and the military group. However, one of the members of this group was Vasco Lourenço, who also belonged to the political group.

The political outcome of the military operations was not what the Group of Nine wanted. There was common ground between the military and political groups, but this did not mean that there were not differences of opinion. However, the Group of Nine could have done nothing without the support of the military. The Group of Nine also had to get political and other support from those who had nothing to do with them. In the end, the Group of Nine lost military support because the leaders of the military group became political leaders, and, as a result, they [the Group of Nine] lost political power.

Q. What was the relationship between Otelo and the Group of Nine?

A. I never understood Otelo, nor could I see any logical reasons for his actions.

Q. Did the Tancos paratroopers' occupations of the air force bases give the Group of Nine the chance they needed to act?

A. Yes. The paratroopers' occupations were militarily inconsequential. They occurred because their officers had left and some radical sergeants, probably under pressure from outside, decided to act.

Q. What do you think of the decolonisation process?

A. The decolonisation process had been marked by both thirteen years of Colonial War and the political crisis that arose in Portugal, with the dispute over the methods of decolonisation.

The transitional period required much more time and a greater co-operative effort to minimise the difficulties experienced by the countries, at the beginning of their independence. This would also have reduced the settlers' problems, which in many situations required them to leave.

The decolonisation process did not go the way we dreamed,

when we drew up the MFA Programme, but it was an honourable settlement for both parties. The greatest merit of the process was to create conditions for future special relationships between Portugal and its former colonies.

Lieutenant-Colonel Vasco Lourenço. Born in 1942 in a small village near Castelo Branco. Father was a shop-keeper and a small farm owner. Secondary education at a state school in Castelo Branco. In 1960 entered the Military Academy in Lisbon and graduated as an infantry officer. Was promoted to a sub-lieutenant in 1964, captain in 1968, and then major in 1978. Saw active service in Guinea-Bissau 1969–71, where he was in charge of an infantry company. Military governor of Lisbon (commander of the Lisbon military region) from November 1975 to April 1978. Was promoted temporary brigadier on 27 November 1975 and temporary general on 11 August 1976. Returned to his rank in 1978 and then promoted to lieutenant-colonel in 1984. Is currently still serving in the army.

Interview

Q. What was your involvement in the revolutionary process?
A. I was involved in everything. I participated in the organisation of the opposition to the Oporto Congress of Combatants in the spring of 1973. Afterwards, I organised the first meeting of the Movement of Captains in Evora on 9 September 1973. I am the only member of the MFA who belonged to all of the different Co-ordinating Committees of the Movement of Captains and the MFA. I was the moderator and spokesman of the Council of State, the Committee of Twenty, the MFA Assemblies and the army Assemblies. I was the spokesman for the Council of the Revolution, until I was appointed military governor of Lisbon. I was also the president of the organising committee of the Association of 25 April and I am now its current president.

I was in charge of organising the military operations of the MFA and of all the links between the members of the Movement of Captains, before I was arrested and sent to the Azores. Along with Otelo and Victor Alves, I belonged to the Directorate of the Movement. After my arrest, Otelo took my place. I was in the Council of the Revolution from its creation on 14 March 1975 until it was dissolved in 1982. I was the first person to sign the Document of the Nine. I was a military commander of the Lisbon military region. During the 25 November coup I was second in command of the military operation. First, there was the President of the Republic, then me, then Eanes.

Q. What were the causes of the revolution?
A. There were two different causes. One cause was the political, social and economic situation of the country, in which the Colonial War had played an important part. The other cause was the unrest in the army. Army people were tired of the war and were frightened of the occurrence of a similar disaster to that which had occurred in India. In Portuguese India the military were made scapegoats for a defeat that was political and not military. Army officers also felt that they had lost prestige with the Portuguese people, for they were seen to be supporters of both the regime and the Colonial War. The oposição had managed to convince people that the officers gained from the war in terms of salaries, etc. Also, as a result of their close contacts with non-

professional officers and the people in Africa, the regular army officers were becoming increasingly politicised.

The first opportunity for the army to register its disapproval against the regime was the Oporto Congress of Combatants [see part 1]. The second chance came when the law was passed reducing the time spent at the Military Academy from three years to one year. This enabled non-professional officers to become professional army officers by attending this shortened course and, at the same time, they were allowed to keep their seniority [see part 1]. The protest movement that materialised from the passing of this law was known as the Movement of Captains.

The majority of officers involved in the Movement were apolitical, but, right from the start, I realised that by exploiting a professional protest it could be made to become a political protest. The strategy was to convince my fellow officers that the regime was degrading the army, and only by bringing it down could we solve our problems.

The regime was brought down on 25 April by a military coup. But, because Portuguese society was ripe for a large upheaval, it became a revolution that was helped along by active revolutionaries. The revolutionary process went on for a year and a half and finished on 25 November 1975. It finished because the revolutionary forces were never well-organised and they forgot the cultural traditions of the Portuguese. They violated their feelings. Because of the excesses of the revolution, a progressive move towards democracy was not possible. The reactionary forces were strengthened by these excesses.

Q. Had there been any attempts to halt the revolutionary process?

A. There were several before 25 November. The first was in June 1974, when Spínola tried to take over and throw out the MFA Programme.

The second was on 28 September 1974, which led to his resignation, and the third was on 11 March, when Spínola was militarily defeated. As a result of 11 March, the left, and in particular the PCP, speeded up the revolutionary process. This created a split within the Council of the Revolution and the armed forces. Within the MFA, there were two groups: both wanted a revolution and democracy, but they had different concepts of democracy.

This crisis led to the Document of the Nine and, after that, the political situation began to change. The first result in response to the Document was that in September 1975 Vasco Gonçalves was dismissed at the Tancos assembly [see chronology]. The political situation then became complex and the result was the 25 November coup. If 25 November had not taken place, the right would have taken over some time in the next few months.

Q. What were the disagreements between the Group of Nine and COPCON?

A. The Document of the Nine defended a democratic process, which would take into account both the Portuguese culture and experience. The Document of COPCON defended the existence of a revolutionary vanguard, even if there was only 10 per cent of the population behind it.

Q. On 25 November was there a danger of a communist take-over?

A. In my opinion, the democrats, of whom I am one, always had more power than the communists. The PCP was well-organised in areas where we had no influence, such as the industrial belts of the big towns and the Alentejo region, but I was never afraid that the PCP would take over. The PCP was aware of its own weaknesses, and the proof of this is that on 25 November the communists avoided confrontation and pulled back. The PCP was always trapped between two attitudes: one was its desire to control large sections of Portuguese society, such as local government, the media, etc., with its own methods; the other was that it had to deal with the ultra left and not appear reactionary, and this sometimes made the PCP act in a cavalier-like way.

The big danger at the time of 25 November was that the right would react against the prevailing anarchy and take over the country. Although I was at the centre of events that took place on 25 November, I cannot say what took place on that day. Things were happening all over the country. Later, I was to find out that many of my collaborators had been involved in other conspiracies and that there had been several groups all plotting at the same time. Pinheiro de Azevedo stated later that another coup was under way which, had it been successful, would have outlawed the PCP. President Eanes is often accused of having connections other than with the Group of Nine. I was not aware that this was the case at that time.

Q. Do you think the revolution was a success?
A. No, but the coup d'état was. The regular army made a coup d'état. It brought down a regime, it decolonised, it democratised the country and finally handed over power to the civilians. We were unlucky that 25 April took place at the beginning of an international economic crisis. This made it difficult to introduce successful economic measures and stimulate the economic development of the country. At the moment, we have a conventional democracy, but I think this is not enough. I believe people should be able to participate more directly in the political life of the country. This could take the form of workers' committees in factories, neighbourhood committees, and a wider role for local government.

It was also not a success, because we did not attempt a gradual political evolution, and, at the same time, respect the culture and the way of life of the Portuguese people. For example, in the cultural dynamisation programme of the Fifth Division, they attacked the Church and this often shocked villagers, who have a strong religious tradition. The Agrarian Reform also shocked the northern farm owners, who worked their own land, and who were not absentee landlords. Because the Agrarian Reform in the Alentejo region was carried out in a revolutionary way, it frightened many people in the country and created opposition to changes that were really needed. After 25 April, in the industrial belts, because the workers were well-organised and powerful, they were able to obtain conditions that the country, as a whole, could not really afford. Other less powerful sections were unable to obtain similar conditions and this further divided the country. Finally, the political parties themselves blocked any evolution towards a direct democracy in conjunction with formal democracy.

Brigadier Pires Veloso. Born in 1926 in the small village of Folgozinho in the Serra da Estrela mountains in the centre of the country. Parents were school teachers. Initially had a strict education at home, but finished secondary education in a state school in 1944. Entered the Military Academy in 1946, where he graduated as an infantry officer. After a year's training at Mafra, was posted to Macau in China in 1949. Returned to Portugal in 1951 and was posted to a frontier infantry regiment. Six months later became a teacher at the Sintra air base. In 1958 was placed in a military technical institute (secondary education level) until 1968. During this period was on active service in Angola (1961–4) and Mozambique (1965–7), serving both times as a captain.

In 1968, now as a major, was on active service in Mozambique. Returned to Portugal in 1970 and was posted to the ministry of the army. In 1972 returned to Mozambique as a lieutenant-colonel and soon joined the Movement of Captains. In July 1974 was posted to São Tomé and Príncipe, first as governor-general, then as a high commissioner and commander-in-chief. After these islands became independent, returned to Portugal and became commander of the northern military region from September 1975 to October 1977. His proposed promotion to general by the superior council of the army was blocked by the Council of the Revolution. At his own request, was put into the reserves in order to stand as a candidate in the presidential elections of 1980. Is currently a farmer.

Interview

Q. What was your attitude towards the previous regime?

A. I was against the previous regime, especially after the 1958 Delgado elections. The hypocritical attitude of the regime then became clear. It pretended that we had elections 'as free as in Britain' and yet it did everything to prevent the oposição's candidate, General Humberto Delgado, from having any chance of being elected. Although I lived, as did all the military then, in a very closed environment, I became aware of what was happening to Delgado. From then on, I voiced my opposition to the regime which although provided an apparently peaceful social climate, suppressed freedom of thought and expression and blocked the creativity of the Portuguese people. As a result, Portugal fell behind the European nations, especially in the fields of education, health and scientific research.

Q. What was your involvement in the Movement of Captains?

A. When I was on active service in Mozambique (1972–4) and, through the aide-de-camp of General Kaulza de Arriaga, Captain Mário Tomé, I became aware of the Movement of Captains which I immediately joined. I saw in the movement the possibility of bringing down the regime, of establishing a democracy and of solving the Colonial War by dialogue and not by military means. I contributed to the movement, by chairing meetings and bringing into it officers from the three branches of the armed forces.

Q. How do you see 25 April?

A. It was a revolution, since it brought with it a new Constitution and deep changes in our institutions, economic conditions, ideas and way of living. However, in the short term, the revolution failed. Not every promise was fulfilled, and furthermore, it did not change the legacy of the previous regime, and in some cases, it reinforced it. In the long term the revolution did not fail, since we had to bring down the old regime which had placed us in the tail of Europe. Unfortunately, the revolution was not properly exe-cuted and led us along a path which resulted in an enormous foreign debt, to further delays in our development and to a profound moral crisis, which endangers our national identity. If the economic decline continues, there is the danger that a Stalin or a Hitler will emerge as our national saviour. If we can avoid that, then the goals of 25 April will be achieved in the long term.

Q. Could you comment on the key events of the revolution?
A. From 1 May 1974, the PCP took charge of the revolutionary process. It began to strongly influence the MFA, from which Spínola was moving away. Since Spínola and his followers were the main obstacles to the PCP, they had to be removed from power. That was done on 28 September. Once the moderates of the MFA were removed, and in order for the PCP to control the decolonisation, it needed to control the economic and the political power. For that purpose the PCP carefully prepared and triggered 11 March.

25 November was a military coup; that is, it was an event where the military had the dominant role. The military were then divided into two large groups: those who were true soldiers, who cherished military virtues, who wanted a true democratic regime with the return to the ideals of 25 April, and those with close connections with the civilian parties who had personal ambitions and who were prepared to walk over their own comrades. People who belonged to this second group had convinced themselves that they were the heroes of the revolution.

25 November had two aims: to project Ramalho Eanes as President of the Republic, and to save the PCP by defeating the far left, which was not controlled by the PCP any more. There was the need to keep the left in order. The far left was always a minority, incoherent and lacking organisation. It served the PCP until the last months of 1975, when it went ahead of the PCP. The far left could never have taken over the country.

On the other hand, I am prepared to admit that COPCON was created to serve the PCP. Through COPCON, the PCP could control all the armed forces and convert them into popular revolutionary forces. Also, we know today, that members of the Group of Nine had regular meetings with representatives of the PCP and had meetings with the main officers of COPCON. People from COPCON and the Group of Nine often served interests that were against the nation, without being aware of it. This applies in general to the left-wing military, which, both consciously and unconsciously, served the civilian left.

Q. What was the role of the Church before and after 25 April?
A. Before 25 April the Church ignored the prevailing social injustices and passively accepted that human beings could be put in prison or deported for political reasons. Thus, in the eyes of the

people, the Church collaborated with the previous regime. After 25 April the Church recognised its past mistakes and saw its members being attacked, sometimes physically. So, either because of this or because it felt threatened as an institution, the Church reacted in the right way, denouncing affronts to morality, social misery, the dangers of demagogy and the opportunism of pseudo-revolutionaries.

Q. What do you think of the decolonisation process?

A. In my opinion, the decolonisation process was carried out in the wrong way: it did not serve Portugal or the Portuguese ex-colonies. It was hasty and anarchic, but it is the old regime which should be held responsible. The old regime made the mistake of not recognising the right to autonomy of our colonial territories and embarked on a long war, during which a methodical and persistent subversion of the armed forces took place. In the end, the Portuguese forces were inoperational.

To carry out decolonisation, when the armed forces both in Africa and in Portugal were disintegrating, was, in practice, to abandon simple and good people who, despite everything, believed in Portugal and in the Portuguese. They saw (and see) us as tolerant, friendly, human and anti-racist, even as brothers. Under the circumstances, we handed over our colonies to other colonisers, less human and with completely different languages and customs from those they had absorbed from us. People from our ex-colonies had become used through centuries to our flag and to us. I saw this in São Tomé and Príncipe.

When I arrived, three months after 25 April, everybody was demanding immediate and total independence. The people had been 'drugged'. Immediately after 25 April some local people organised a political movement against this craziness, but were defeated by young politicians, who convinced the population to demand immediate independence, with the help of some members of the MFA posted there. These officers received orders from Portugal. A referendum at the time would have been useless.

São Tomé and Príncipe became independent after a year. After independence, the São Tomé government sought co-operation from Portugal and, when it saw that this was not forthcoming, established links with the eastern-bloc countries. But the worst events took place in Timor. Our decolonisation in Timor almost erases our past glories, which had taken place during the Portuguese discoveries of the fourteenth and fifteenth centuries. What happened in São Tomé and Príncipe was a pale image of those events in Angola, Mozambique, Guinea and Cape Verde.

Q. What were the achievements of the revolution?

A. It brought down fascism: the fascist regime had blocked progress in the country. It increased social security, it gave greater autonomy to local authorities (which has allowed a relative increase in local development and created better conditions in the country), it made the country aware of the need for a democracy and a rejection of obscurantism. It also showed the need to improve education, agriculture, health and social justice.

But the revolution is not yet over and it will only finish when the democratic institutions are in full operation. The Constitution which was written in the middle of an emotional climate has to be changed to fit better the personality and the traditions of the Portuguese people.

There is still the danger of a dictatorship. People who live under the shadow of 'robot-like' President Ramalho Eanes and who owe their present privileges to the PCP are interested in a dictatorship. The military cannot be good revolutionaries, since they are trained to obey, to discipline and to follow regulations. Portugal is still going to suffer the consequences of a deep moral crisis. Ten years after the revolution, and, as a result of mistakes that were made at all levels, and of the unfulfilled promises of President Eanes, Portugal is in a crisis. President Eanes never refrained from negotiating with the parties in order to consolidate his position. On the other hand, he has opposed practically every government since his election, and he has surrounded himself with people of doubtful morality and has rejected those who are competent and loyal to him, either from fear of competition or because he did not want to hear their criticisms. Through his ambiguous and divisionist behaviour, he has contributed towards instilling in Portuguese society mistrust and disloyalty. By sponsoring a party while speaking against the other parties, he shows that he wants to become the president of a single party, which will create a socialist republic even against the wishes of the people.

I am hoping that, when he leaves, the present moral and economic crisis will be attenuated and that the Portuguese people, benefiting from the experience gained in the revolution, will rise again, as they did in the past. I also think that entering the EEC will decrease the danger of a dictatorship, because it will force the Portuguese to work, in order to compete. Entering the EEC will also create better links between the universities and the country, stimulate research, and force the politicians to revise the Constitution.

Q. What is your opinion of the Association of 25 April?

A. It is an extension of the extinct Council of the Revolution and will decrease in importance as soon as Eanes leaves the presidency, unless another president, similar to Eanes, comes along, who also wants a transition to a socialism that is like that of Russia and other eastern-bloc countries.

THE POPULISTS

The populists were, in general, young officers who were politically immature at the onset of the revolution. During the course of the revolution, they had to deal with a large number of practical problems that were created by the fall of the previous regime. Because they were called upon to arbitrate in a variety of conflicts, their decisions had frequently to be made on the spot and so their politics were learnt on the streets of Lisbon. The political position they took up was often idealistic and similar to the philosophy of populism. They often played important roles in the mass movement that followed the coup d'état.

Arlindo Ferreira (AF)
Lourenço Marques (LM)
Mário Tomé (MT)

Major Arlindo Ferreira. Born in 1940 in Mesão Frio, Vila Real, in the north of Portugal. Father was a shopkeeper. Primary and secondary education in state schools in Vila Real, Guimarães and Braga. Left school in 1957 and worked one year as a clerk in a ceramics factory in Oporto and another year as a civil servant in Mesão Frio. In 1959 entered Military Academy and in 1963 began training as a helicopter pilot. Was promoted to sub-lieutenant in 1964 and then from 1965 to 1967 on active service as a helicopter pilot in Guinea-Bissau. Was promoted to lieutenant in 1966. In 1967 returned to Portugal and trained pilots at the Tancos air force base until 1970. Became a captain in 1968. From 1970 to 1972 on active service as a helicopter pilot in Angola. Returned to Lisbon and joined the Movement of Captains in its early stages. Signed the document opposing the Congress of Combatants and became a representative for the air force in the Movement of Captains. In 1974 was promoted to major. During the coup of 25 April 1974 acted as a liaison officer, was then placed in CCO and then into COPCON until it was dissolved. Was arrested on 27 November 1975, imprisoned and then released on 25 February 1976. Was placed under house arrest for a year and not allowed to leave the country until 1978. Was suspended from duties until 1978 and in the same year accused of taking part in a left-wing coup during 1975. In 1982, was put in the air force reserves, and lodged a successful appeal to the supreme military court to be reinstated as a pilot. In 1984 was yet to be reinstated. Is currently involved in publishing.

Interview

Q. Why did you join the Movement of Captains?
A. I had had a divalent attitude towards the previous regime. When on active service in Angola, during the day I was committed to the war, but at night I was against it. This was the attitude of most of my fellow pilots. For example, when the new French Puma helicopters arrived, we became obsessed with designing things to make them more efficient. When I returned to Portugal, my attitude changed, for, by then, I had been to France twice during general elections and I had become fascinated by the democratic process. But I did not have any ideological problems; I was more worried about my actions in society and with the social implications of the war. As a helicopter pilot, I was in and out of the fighting zone and also in close contact with the local people. I was frequently ordered to move people out of the fighting zone to a safe zone, but I eventually realised that something was going wrong. I kept moving the same people to the same place. Obviously they were returning back to where I had taken them from.

These and other facts made us understand that the inefficiency of the armed forces was due to the regime. In general, the regime was authoritarian and incompetent and provided cover for many 'wheeler-dealers'. In 1974, after fifteen years of active service, I wanted to go into the reserves. I was influenced then by a member of my family, who belonged to the oposição, and is today a member of the PS. I could not continue to belong to a corrupt institution (the army) which supported the regime I hated. The Movement of Captains (which then existed only in the army) seemed to me to be a way out and through the Movement I could fight the regime from within. However, I did not then think in global political terms and did not think of possible political alternatives. I just wanted to bring down the regime and with that stop the war, corruption and social misery. My struggle was with individuals, such as Caetano, and I was not fighting against a political system. It was my experience in COPCON which gave me my political awareness. It was in COPCON that I understood many things which I had read about before.
Q. What did you do on 28 September 1974?
A. Three days before, on 25 September, I was on holiday,

relaxing in the north of Portugal, but on that day I was recalled to Lisbon. We knew something was up and on my way back I found the roads blocked by barricades. It was Spínola who triggered the events on 28 September, when he detained Otelo at the presidential palace. At COPCON we were ready to act, if he was arrested. We all thought that Spínola's attempted coup was closely linked to the unrest in Mozambique and Angola. In fact, it was a desperate attempt by Spínola to stop decolonisation and democratisation, but we knew what he was about and we were ready.

Q. What was the 11 March 1975?

A. This was an attempted coup which aimed at halting the mass movement. By then it was clear that the MFA and the armed forces in general controlled the political situation. The light artillery regiment RAL1 was attacked by the Spínolists. It was chosen for the attack as to them it symbolised disorder.

The support for Spínola on 11 March was wider than is generally known. In fact, the political implications of 11 March and 25 November were the same. At the time of 11 March, the discussion of the Melo Antunes plan was going on, but the plan was generally ambiguous and opposed by most of the MFA. Many honest officers ended up by giving their support to Spínola because of the black list. This list had supposedly been circulated by the left and threatened to kill Spínola and a number of right-wing officers.

Many regiments withdrew their support on 11 March at the last moment: regiments such as the commandos, the Estremoz and the Braga regiments. In COPCON we knew what was going on; we discussed it openly in order to dissuade people from embarking on it. We knew what Spínola wanted, but we did not know when and where things were going to happen.

Q. What was COPCON?

A. A big fire station! When Otelo was appointed, he was practically unknown and he only came into the limelight as a result of this appointment. Spínola chose him for the appointment; he trusted him as did the Co-ordinating Committee. He was placed in COPCON in order to discipline the army. He was seen as a political lightweight and it was only after 28 September that he emerged politically.

COPCON was a structured organisation. There was Baptista

as chief of staff and a number of sections such as operations, information, and so on. There was a group of political advisers to Otelo and I was one of them. When Otelo wanted to make decisions, he would call the chief of staff, the vice chief of staff and the advisers.

COPCON was called for everything. Militarily and politically, it co-ordinated the armed forces, it was responsible for people's safety on the streets, it was a police station, a co-ordinator of national security for air space and frontiers, a gatherer of information, a fire station for industrial and union problems and it was even a legislator! There are many accusations made against COPCON. None of them is consistent and COPCON was never accused of running away from its responsibilities. Sometimes, it did more than it should have, from a legal point of view, but when this happened it was because the other institutions were inoperative or were afraid to act.

Q. Did Otelo control COPCON?

A. Yes, he could have, but he did not have time. If we had wanted, we could have done anything. He trusted the people under him.

Q. Why do people talk of the influence of the political parties on COPCON?

A. Because it existed and because it was encouraged; we encouraged contacts with civilians, mainly those who were members of the parties. Otelo had his contacts and, after having made them, he would come to us. The advisers would analyse the political part, and Baptista the technical part. We encouraged contacts with all parties and when it happened they were always recorded in reports. Whenever there were contacts with a civilian party, Otelo always knew about it. The most influential parties on Otelo were the MES [Movimento da Esquerda Socialista, Movement of the Socialist Left], through a conscripted officer, who was working in COPCON, and the PCP. Of course, there was also a large influence by the PS. Then there was the PRP and the UDP. I think one of the reasons why Otelo talked to the PRP and the UDP was because they were small, sincere and direct. The PRP provided Otelo with a lot of useful information. UDP's influence was quite small. In the end, the influence by the parties stopped, as we all became saturated. Things were changing all the time, but not their speeches.

Q. Were you involved in the house occupations?
A. Yes, I was involved in the second wave of occupations. It was a highly organised operation and had the support of the MRPP, the MES, the UDP, the PRP, the PCP, and the PS. On the first night, three hundred flats were occupied in an orderly, well-planned way. I was astonished to find that, in the Campo do Ourique area alone, there were thousands of empty flats. I initially negotiated with the landlords and then Lourenço Marques took over [see LM interview]. Most landlords ended up by signing rent agreements.
Q. What were the relationships between COPCON and the Group of Nine?
A. I was involved in the contacts made between COPCON and the Group of Nine. Otelo read the Document of the Nine before it was published and he agreed with part of it, in particular, with its criticisms of the PCP. However, he also considered that the document took a social democratic line and so he asked his political advisers to write an alternative document that stated COPCON's political philosophy. When the Group of Nine went ahead and published their document, Otelo, without informing his advisors, went and asked another group to write COPCON's document. This group included some junior people from COPCON. This document was the one that was published. At that time, there were meetings between Otelo, Vasco Lourenço, Melo Antunes and Marques Júnior, which Otelo attended without advisers. Whenever he came from these meetings, he was depressed. My impression was that he gave his agreement at the meetings, but when he came out he realised that he had been taken for a ride. He had difficulty in absorbing the political implications of what was going on. Some of us at COPCON thought that the Nine were right on several accounts, but we did not agree with the alliances they made.

In the end, it became apparent that the Group of Nine was powerful and that there was a need for us to negotiate. They wanted to impose a second document, the so-called Group of Nine–COPCON Document [in April 1984 this was still a classified document] which had been written by Melo Antunes and Gomes Mota. Negotiations were carried out by Victor Crespo and Vasco Lourenço with some of the officers of COPCON. In Crespo's view, COPCON should have simply signed the joint document, because we were inarticulate and weak. The joint document contained many things acceptable to us at COPCON, for example, it legalised the Agrarian Reform. But we could not accept it, as it would have led to the persecution of the Gonçalvists and the PCP. If it wasn't for the intolerant attitude of Victor Crespo and some COPCON officers, we might have reached an agreement.

Q. What was 25 November 1975?

A. It was clear that it had been planned for some time. On 30 September 1975 COPCON received information about troop movements that we were able to confirm. On 29 September the sixth provisional government had taken refuge in the Monsanto regiment. At that time there were rumours about that Tomé was at RAL1 plotting a left-wing coup, but this wasn't true, because we knew he wasn't there. These three pieces of information told us that a coup was being planned, well before 25 November. I have further proof of this. In my possession I have a document, written by Melo Antunes in September, in his own hand-writing, with details of the plan. On 25 November, about 4 o'clock in the morning, the paratroopers moved and took over the air force bases. They were not expecting any opposition from COPCON. The paratroopers were pushed by their own chief of staff to move from their corner and occupy the bases. This was the sign to start the counter-coup.

There is something that puzzled me. On 24 November, at 11 o'clock at night, Costa Martins presented himself at COPCON with a transit order [a document that has to be carried, when personnel are transferred between military establishments] signed by the chief of staff of the air force. This was unusual for a chief of staff to sign orders, and also for them to be carried out at night. I had no idea what he was doing at COPCON.

There was no doubt that the coup was being planned in November, since a few days before the 25, air force planes, helicopters and ammunition were being flown into the Cortegaça air base. Yet, when we in COPCON received this information and tried to confirm it with all the air force bases and also with the general staff of the air force, we always received the same answer, 'No movements were taking place'.

Captain Lourenço Marques. Born in 1945 in Beja in the Alentejo. Father was a shopkeeper who went bankrupt. Secondary education at a state school in Lisbon. In 1965 entered the Military Academy and trained as an air force pilot. From 1971 to 1973 was on active service as a fighter pilot in Guinea-Bissau. On his return to Lisbon became an air force delegate to the Movement of Captains, while stationed at the Monte Real air force base. In January 1975 became a member of COPCON until the 25 November 1975 coup. Was arrested after the coup and later expelled from the air force. Is currently studying engineering and running a small business.

Interview

Q. What did you do in COPCON?

A. During the first few months, I did nothing at the head-quarters, as there were no aeroplanes in COPCON. Then I was moved to operations. February and March 1975 saw a wave of house occupations in Lisbon in the suburb of Campo de Ourique, and I was sent there to see what was happening. I found it very confusing, for in my mind at that time private property was sacred. But I also had seen tremendous social injustices. There was a large number of empty dwellings and, at the same time, an even larger number of people without homes or houses. Prior to 25 April we had complained about everything but, after the successful coup, when we had the power, we did not know what to do. The people took the initiative and we were caught by surprise.

It was a shame to see buildings that could be inhabited left to rot so that the owners could knock them down in order to build larger blocks with more apartments. When the people occupied the houses, the police intervened, thumped them up and threw them out. When we in COPCON were confronted with the situation of having to choose between the owners and the needy, we chose the needy and so we stopped the police from intervening. Between 25 April 1974 and 25 November 1975 some 80,000 people occupied houses in the Lisbon area.

Q. Why did COPCON get involved in civilian problems?

A. At that time we were asked to solve nearly every problem. The civilian ministers pushed the problems on to us and yet, today, we are accused of having meddled with civilian affairs. By the middle of 1975, we were all exhausted and planning to hold on until the decolonisation programme had been completed. (This happened on 11 November with the independence of Angola.) By then, the COPCON staff was reduced to between seven and ten. Many people had left, mostly because they did not agree with the role of COPCON.

Although, in principle, COPCON controlled the whole country, because Otelo was also the military governor of Lisbon, it acted mainly in the Lisbon area. Outside this region, COPCON's orders were frequently ignored.

Q. What were your views on 25 November?

A. It still remains a bit of a mystery to me. The coup was aimed at eliminating the left wing of the MFA and the influence the left-wing politicial parties, especially the PCP, had on the armed forces in general. This does not mean that there was any danger of a PCP take-over at that time. The 25 November was effectively against COPCON and it was a project of the PS. But there was no danger of COPCON taking over the country. We simply did not want to.

I think that COPCON did not reach an agreement with the Group of Nine because the politicians were frightened that the MFA would become strong again, if an agreement were reached.

Major Mário Tomé. Born in 1940 in Alentejo. Father owned a small tool-making business. Moved to Guinea-Bissau in 1951. In 1956 returned to Lisbon and entered Military Academy in 1959. In 1963 was posted to Guinea-Bissau on active service as a sub-lieutenant in the cavalry. Here he was assigned to the military police. Frequent requests to be transferred to the fighting zone were refused. In 1966 was posted to Mozambique in charge of a company. Was decorated with the war cross. From 1970 to 1972 on active service in Guinea-Bissau. Repeated attempts to resign were refused. In 1972 returned to Mozambique as an aide-de-camp to the commander in chief of the army, Kaulza de Arriaga. From 1973 to 1974 organised the Movement of Captains in Mozambique. In July 1974 returned to Portugal in a cavalry unit in Santarém. Was later transferred to a cavalry regiment in Lisbon. In 1975, was transferred as a major to the Lisbon military police. Delegate of the MFA until his expulsion from the army in April 1976. On 5 October 1980 became a Member of Parliament, representing the UDP in the third Legislative Assembly. Four years in Parliament. Failed to get re-elected in the 1984 elections. Is currently in the army reserves and one of the leaders of the UDP.

Interview

Q. Why did you join the Movement of Captains?

A. Although there had been a complete change in my political attitude towards the war and thus the regime, during my three commissions, my political outlook was somewhat blurred when I arrived in Mozambique in 1972. Nevertheless, in the parliamentary elections in 1969, I had voted for CDE and was anti-regime by then.

Looking back, the main reason I joined the Movement of Captains was because of the Colonial War. People now give other reasons for the politicisation of the army: the class origins of the officers, the political influence of the non-professional officers and the contacts with the local population. But the fact that political unrest started in Guinea-Bissau, where the military situation was at its worst, shows that the war was the most important factor.

In Mozambique, the politicisation of myself and other officers was helped by the anti-army attitudes of the white settlers. They accused us of being inefficient in not winning the Colonial War for them.

My position in the army headquarters in Mozambique allowed me to use all its facilities for broadcasting pro-MFA propaganda. I was also able to establish contacts with officers in the fighting zones, but the organisation we set up was only a loose one.

Q. What occurred after the 25 April coup in Mozambique?

A. We were so confident that the movement would be successful that we had not thought what to do with the old military hierarchy and the PIDE network, after the coup. In the end, the MFA recalled the military hierarchy and by the time we started to arrest the PIDE agents, the senior agents were by then in South Africa or Rhodesia.

The other difficulty which arose was the result of our attitude towards decolonisation. After 25 April, we said that we were now a democracy and so the liberation movement FRELIMO should also be a democratic organisation, and thus there should be no need to continue the war. But, if FRELIMO did not stop the war, then, by definition, they had to be terrorists. It was only later we realised that, of course, FRELIMO would only stop the war after they had gained full independence.

Fortunately, we had brought into the MFA non-professional officers and soldiers and so our political attitudes changed. We started to make plans for troop withdrawals, we fraternised with FRELIMO and we even stopped playing the Portuguese national anthem on the radio. The higher-ranking officers within the MFA reacted against these measures.

Q. What role did you play in the revolutionary process on your return to Portugal?

A. On my return, I entered the cavalry training school at Santarém as an MFA delegate. Political problems were beginning to emerge at this time because of two different perspectives within the MFA. There were the idealists, who saw the MFA as the motor of the revolution, and there were the reactionaries. The way in which the cleansing of the fascist elements (*saneamentos*) was going showed what the MFA was. Initially, people were expelled from the army for political reasons. But, as the conservatives gradually took over, they allegedly applied professional competence as the criterion for the Saneamentos of the armed forces.

When the 28 September counter-coup came, it was clear that the sympathies of the commander of my unit lay with Spínola. On 28 September he sent us to examine some fresh-water dams; that was his way of compromising. He kept his position safe and sent somebody who was sympathetic to the MFA away from the regiment – that way no problems arose.

After 28 September I was transferred to the second cavalry regiment in Lisbon and became involved in the cultural dynamisation programme of the Fifth Division. I was, by then, a delegate to the MFA Assembly and also a delegate to the regimental assembly.

In the meantime, the opening-up of the MFA to officers, who had not been actively involved in the Movement of Captains, resulted in the influence of the civilian left and the PCP being felt within the MFA. The objectives of the PCP were to 'revolutionise the armed forces from within', without changing their institutions. It wanted to reform, but not revolutionise. They felt that, if they called the armed forces progressive often enough, they would act and feel progressive.

The cultural dynamisation programme had similar objectives. On the surface, its aims were to bring culture to the uncultured and to aid people at a local level with physical tasks, such as road-building. The main objective, however, was really to control the local population. Since the repressive forces – the police, the Republican Guard, etc. – were in total disarray and the armed forces were falling apart, there was a danger that in certain regions there would be a class struggle, for example, between employer and employees. The message of the cultural dynamisation programme was, 'Keep calm, because the MFA has everything under control.'

Q. Who controlled the cultural dynamisation programme?

A. It was CODICE [Central Committee for Dynamisation], a branch of the Fifth Division. They provided the guidelines and we translated them into actions at a local level. The whole programme was based upon the Fifth Division politically trusting its delegates in the field.

The programme was very useful for the officers and soldiers involved in it, for they were exposed to all the problems of the local population and they gained political experience. It was also useful, because some worthwhile work, such as road-building, was done. The programme effectively mobilised some intellectuals and artists and it brought them into contact with the people when they performed. From a political point of view, it was patronising. It eroded local initiative and inhibited the oppressed people from rising up.

Q. What did you do on 11 March?

A. Although my participation was small, it was interesting. On 10 March myself and three other MFA delegates from three other Lisbon regiments were ordered by COPCON to visit the Liceu Gil Vicente [a Lisbon secondary school], as a student strike was scheduled to take place. At that time the only 'authorised' strikes in the country were those that were simultaneously authorised by the PCP and the MFA. Whilst in the high school, a student told us that the RAL1 regiment was under air attack. Quickly, I returned to my regiment and there I found my commander calmly talking to a Spínolist. I told him that the coup had failed, though I did not know whether it had or not, and I asked him if the regiment was on the alert. He said that all was under control.

I went to the parade ground and saw that the armoured cars were inoperational, and the soldiers were having ammunition handed out to them, bullet by bullet. I asked the major in charge if he had seen the planes in the air and if he knew whether they were friend or foe. I ordered him to get moving.

My impression was that the Spínolists' plan was to attack one regiment to give an impression of strength. At the same time, to inactivate all the other regiments with the knowledge that the regimental commanders would have supported the coup.

Q. What was your impression of what happened between 11 March and 25 November?

A. The weakness of the revolution movement under way then was that it was under the joint leadership of the PCP and the MFA. The MFA was a heterogeneous body and so was conciliatory towards imperialism and the reactionary forces. In that period, whatever was done was done despite the MFA and PCP. This especially applies to the house and land occupations.

The PCP said it was they who brought about the Agrarian Reform and they were accused of doing so by the right. Neither is true. The first occupations were done despite the PCP; they were spontaneous and supported by the more radical elements of the MFA and especially by COPCON.

The end result of the revolutionary movement was a series of reformatory measures, such as the increase in salaries, wider strike laws and the creation of workers' committees in the factories. The provisional governments and the MFA always legislated, after the events had taken place. The legislation they passed was always less than what had happened. Likewise, the PCP recognised less than what had taken place. The PCP's strategy was to enter any revolutionary changes that were taking place and then bring them to a halt. The PS was fighting the PCP everywhere and at the same time opening itself up to the right.

Within the MFA, the revolutionary movement, brought in by the ordinary soldiers, was tearing the army to shreds. In the regimental assemblies I felt uneasy. Although I thought of myself as a democrat, I realised I wanted to be a democrat-in-command. Accepting majority decisions was, in general, difficult, so that in the end I just had to side with the ordinary soldiers.

Q. Do you think Otelo controlled COPCON?

A. Otelo did not control COPCON as I, even as second in command, did not control my regiment. This was all characteristic of the times.

Q. Do you think the Group of Nine tried to stop the revolution-
ary process?
A. Yes. But the two main forces that tried to stop the revolution
were the PCP and the PS. The PS and the PCP used the spell of 25
April and the support of the right which was regrouping to stop
the revolution. The PCP was committed to the petite bourgeoisie.
The PS pushed the Group of Nine, along with support from the
PSD and CDS. Although there was a disagreement between the
Group of Nine and COPCON, there were many attempts at
conciliation by Otelo. On the other side, there were attempts on
the part of the fifth provisional government and the PCP to
control Otelo.
Q. In the months before 25 November were you aware that a
coup was approaching?
A. We were aware that there was something in the air, but we
were intoxicated by the achievements of the revolution. But I now
see these achievements as reformist.

On the eve of the coup, I was warned by some non-professional
officers that the regiment should prepare its defences. I said, 'Yes',
to be polite. Although there was a split in the armed forces, I
always felt that my comrades in arms would never attack me.
Inside me there was a conciliatory attitude based upon class
solidarity. When people say we lost 25 November because the
left-wing regiments were not disciplined, they were wrong. We
did not have a strict discipline, but we had one based upon
consensus. We realised the only way the mass movement could
continue was with the support of the ordinary soldiers within the
army. This movement of privates would be risky – there would be
a weakening of the traditional military discipline, and this new
army would be less effective in any confrontation with a more
traditionally disciplined military force. Militarily, we were
defeated, before 25 November took place.

On the night of 25 November, we were asked from the
Presidency if the regiment was with the President – I think it was
Vasco Lourenço who asked us. We replied that there was no
reason not to be. At 8 o'clock in the morning of 26 November, we
were asked to go to the presidential palace in Belem. We
assembled the regiment to inform them of the situation but,
whilst we were on parade, unarmed, gun-fire broke out outside
and hand grenades were thrown at us. A sub-lieutenant was

killed. I went to the gates, which had been pushed down by an armoured car, and ordered the driver to stop. The regimental commander joined me, and we went straight to the presidential palace. On arrival, we were offered lunch!

I was furious and wanted to talk to the Council of the Revolution, but they refused and we waited at the palace for the rest of the day. At night, we were taken to the air force base at Sintra and from there we were flown to Oporto. I was kept under arrest until April 1976, initially without any charges being made. Then the gossip was that we were to be charged for our involvement in the coup. In the end, we were never charged.

The political situation on 25 November was very complicated. When the people wanted to go to the streets, the trade unions persuaded them not to go. Then there was a state of emergency declared for no reason. To me it was all very puzzling.

THE STRATEGISTS

These men often acted within a wide political context. They were practical officers, who tended not to be obsessed with their own political positions, and they often showed remarkable degrees of flexibility in order to achieve their political aims. Colonel Melo Antunes was always able to produce relevant political documents at critical moments. Marshal Costa Gomes gave continuity to the revolutionary process. Admiral Rosa Coutinho successfully presided over the decolonisation of Angola; a difficult task, since he had to contend, not only with the dissatisfied white settlers, but also with three warring liberation movements.

Melo Antunes (MA)
Rosa Coutinho (RC)
Costa Gomes (CG).

Lieutenant-Colonel Melo Antunes. Born in 1933. Father was an army officer. Attended a state school, and in 1950 entered the Military Academy, where he trained to be an artillery officer. In 1953 was posted to the Azores and remained there until 1961 and the outbreak of the Colonial War. Saw active service three times in Angola, the first of which was in 1972. Joined the Movement of Captains in 1974 and was one of the main authors of the critical Programme of the MFA. After 25 April 1974 was a member of the Co-ordinating Committee of the MFA Pro-gramme. He was minister without portfolio in the second and third provisional governments and negotiated with the independence movements of Guinea-Bissau. Minister of foreign affairs in the fourth and sixth provisional governments. He was the main author of the Document of the Nine and the (still classified) joint Group of Nine/COPCON Document. He became a member of the Council of Twenty after 28 September 1974 and the Council of the Revolution after 11 March 1975. Remained a member of the Council of the Revolution until it was dissolved. Was president of the Constitutional Commission, following the implementation of the new Portuguese Constitution. After the constitutional revision, became a member of the Council of State. Currently a member of this body, which is an advisory group to the President.

Interview

Q. What was your attitude to the Salazar and Caetano regimes?

A. I was a parliamentary candidate for the CDE Movement in the last elections of the Caetano regime. I became involved with the CDE, but I was not aligned to any political party. My opinion, at that time, was that the Portuguese political situation had reached a dead end, and the only way out would be active intervention by the armed forces into politics. The political alternatives presented by the different parties in the oposição had all failed. The PCP party line at that time was 'mass insurrection', but I thought this was a dogmatic formula far removed from reality. So, I associated myself with the CDE, as it provided me with a platform, which I would not have otherwise had.

Q. Why did you join the Movement of Captains?

A. The Movement started in the middle of 1973 with purely professional objectives, and, because of this, I had reservations about it. I only joined when I was sure that it could be transformed into a political movement. This was in January 1974, when it was decided to produce a document which stated the political objectives of the Movement. This document, 'The MFA and the Nation', was written by me and some officers and approved by the MFA in March 1974, at the Cascais meeting. From then on, my role in the MFA was to give it an increasingly political content. This content was expressed in the Programme of the MFA, of which I was the main author. I believed that the regime would only fall by direct military intervention, but this intervention had to be based upon a clearly defined political programme. If this was not the case, we would have a coup and a real danger that a military dictatorship would end up replacing a fascist one.

Q. Do you think 25 April was a revolution?

A. Yes, because a few hours after the start of the coup, on that same day, the mass movements began. This immediately transformed it into a revolution. When I wrote the Programme of the MFA, I had not predicted this, but the fact that it happened showed that the military were in tune with the Portuguese people.

Q. How do you interpret 28 September?

A. This was the end of a contradictory period within the MFA. Those who supported total independence of the colonies against those who supported a neo-colonial solution. There were other important events that forced Spínola and his followers to propose political solutions that resulted in a confrontation between the Spínolists and the Co-ordinating Committee of the MFA. At that time, there was a powerful popular movement that gave political content to the social changes that were taking place. The Spínolists were frightened of this movement, because they did not have adequate political backgrounds to interpret the situation.

Q. Was 11 March a result of 28 September?

A. 11 March was the climax of the process that was already under way in September. The mass movement was gaining momentum right up to 11 March, and, in retrospect, 11 March was also an attempt by the PCP to gain control over the Portuguese political process. The PCP had a strong influence over the political situation right up to the 'hot summer' of August 1975.

On 11 March the Spínolists tried to remove the influence of the PCP and to recreate the conditions that existed on 25 April 1974. They lost and their influence shrank. The outcome of 11 March was a victory to the civilian and military sections, who were very closely linked together. The PCP had forced through such social changes that there was a massive reaction against this party. This reaction was from both the civilians and from the MFA. The PCP and its supporters in the armed forces thought that the conditions were right for the establishment of a regime modelled on Soviet Russia, and they did everything possible to achieve this end. They carried out massive nationalisations, the Agrarian Reform, and they attempted to control the whole of the political apparatus. This led to a confrontation between the PCP (and its supporters) and a large fraction of the armed forces and civilians.

Q. Was 25 November a coup aimed at bringing down the communists?

A. Yes. But we shouldn't forget the fight that went on from August 1975, for it was then that the Document of the Nine, also known as the Melo Antunes Document, was published. This document mobilised large sections of Portuguese society, who were opposed to the formation of a communist state. The fight against communism starts there, and reaches its climax on 25 November. The communists had a good hold in the Alentejo and Lisbon regions and in various other pockets scattered throughout the country.

The power structure on 25 November did not necessarily favour the communists, but the popular movement and the corresponding social changes that were taking place could have been easily controlled by the PCP. However, they were not going to wait. After the Second World War, several communist parties in Europe attained power from minority positions. Although I was aware that the Red Army was not backing the PCP, the PCP thought that a Cuba-like situation could be created in Portugal.

After publication of the Document of the Nine, we discovered that the majority of the armed forces were against the communists. But the PCP had managed to infiltrate the armed forces to such an extent that it could mobilise very active minorities within the armed forces, especially in the Lisbon area. Active minorities may under certain political situations gain the upper hand.

On 25 November the forces that got together were a wide political spectrum within the civilians and the armed forces. There were groups on the extreme right who wanted a counter-revolution followed by a witch-hunt. The Group of Nine was aware of this pressure from the right, and that is why on 26 November I went on television and said that the PCP still had an important role to play in Portuguese politics. This statement blocked a right-wing counter-coup that was planned to follow the 25 November coup, and, in this way, we prevented the PCP from being smashed.

Q. What were the differences between the Group of Nine and COPCON?

A. The differences arose because COPCON's position was often similar to that of the extreme left, but there were channels of communication open between the Group of Nine and COPCON. The two groups were unable to reach an agreement on a common document [see Otelo interview] because of the intransigence of some radical COPCON officers and some civilians who surrounded Otelo. Although he was formally in command of COPCON, I have to admit that he frequently changed his position, as a result of pressure from his own officers and the civilian extreme left.

Q. Why did the Group of Nine lose power following the coup of 25 November, and Eanes, who was in charge of military operations, gain power?

A. It was inevitable that the power of the Group of Nine should wither away, since we brought about the coup in order to achieve a western parliamentary democracy. It is clear that we controlled the events of 25 November, since the right was unable to take over. We created the conditions for agreements between politicians and the armed forces, and for the Constitution [see chronology, 2 June 1975] to be set up and approved.

General Eanes participated in all the meetings of the Group of Nine. As he was a prestigious military man, it was only natural that he should be given control of the military operations. He agreed with me that the PCP should not be destroyed. 25 November was a tactical success. It is undeniable that it stopped the revolutionary process, but we should not be held responsible for this. The responsibility falls upon the sectarianism of the PCP and the adventurism of the far left. The revolution stopped once formal democracy was established.

This does not mean that democracy cannot bring about revolutionary changes. Unfortunately, our democracy did not change the country as much as it should have done, and over the last few years, we have seen regressive changes in social and political conditions.

Q. Would you like to describe the present political attitudes of the armed forces?

A. The armed forces do not want to get involved in politics, but we in the armed forces think that formal democracy is not enough for Portugal. We are not like the developed countries of Europe and we need special strategies for development that are adapted to our historical and social roots. The present political structure of the country is too rigid and we need to open new forums outside the present political parties, forums where the military and civilians can debate. Following 25 April 1974, the active involvement of many officers in a political life eroded their image, and this explains why so many left after 25 November. The result of this is that there is now a reasonable balance between the different political tendencies within the armed forces. The number of politically articulate officers, faithful to the ideals of 25 April 1974, who are still in the army, are enough to ensure that these ideals will continue to be upheld. I also think that the actions of the Council of the Revolution showed that the armed forces can play a political role without necessarily holding power.

Q. What is the role of the Association of 25 April?

A. The Association is a witness to an important moment in Portuguese history. It keeps alive a number of ideals that were the basis of the MFA. These ideals may generate a certain political and civic awareness among both the military and civilians. It may lead the Portuguese to discover that there are democratic ways of developing their country. It should not have the role of a political association. It should be a forum for political discussion, otherwise people will be right in thinking that it is a conspiratorial organisation.

Admiral Rosa Coutinho. Born in 1926 in Lisbon. Father was a shopkeeper, mother a school teacher. Secondary education at a state school in Lisbon. At eighteen entered the Naval Academy and spent a year at Lisbon university as part of the course. Normal naval career until twenty-eight years old and then spent three years training to be a hydrographic engineer at Lisbon university. From 1957 to 1958 was in the USA on a civilian course in hydrographics. Was posted to Angola and to São Tomé as a hydrographic engineer until 1961. Then posted to the Far East as a first lieutenant on a sloop. Returned to Lisbon before being sent to Mozambique as a director of the dredging operations taking place all along the Mozambique coast. After serving there for nine years returned to Portugal in 1972. Commander of a frigate and worked with NATO forces until 25 April 1974. Then became a member of the Junta of National Salvation and was promoted to admiral. In July 1974 was appointed president of the governing junta of Angola and later, when the post was created, the high commissioner to Angola and commander-in-chief of all the armed forces in Angola. Member of the Council of the Revolution until 25 November 1975 when he resigned. In 1977 was tried by the superior council of the armed forces but was acquitted. Despite this the chief of staff of the navy transferred him to the reserves, but he was quickly reinstated by the supreme military court. Remained in the navy as an admiral until December 1982, when he asked to go into the reserves. Is currently a businessman.

Interview

Q. What was your attitude to the political structure before 25 April 1974?

A. Although I did not agree with the previous regime, I was never politically active.

Q. What was your role on 25 April?

A. On 25 April I ended up being selected by the navy to become a member of the Junta of National Salvation. On that day I was on normal duty in the NATO headquarters in Lisbon, as NATO exercises were planned, and took place, for the week starting on 25 April.

Q. Was 25 April a revolution? If so, why?

A. I see 25 April as a coup d'état because it was a military take-over. It was when the people came on to the streets, disobeying orders broadcast over the radio by the MFA, that the revolution started.

Q. What was the MFA Programme?

A. The original MFA Programme did not advocate simply transferring power from one regime to a similar one. It contained proposals to give full independence to the colonies, to democratise Portugal by removing censorship and to destroy the secret police. The coup d'état became a revolution as the people overwhelmingly supported these proposals.

Q. What were the key events throughout the course of the revolution?

A. Although the revolution stopped on 25 November 1975, prior to this it went through crises every two to three months. The first crisis was 13 June 1974 in the MFA Assembly (the second Manutenção Militar meeting) when Spínola demanded the dissolution of the CCP [Co-ordinating Committee of the Programme]. Basically there was a fight between the Spínolists, who wanted a federative solution for the colonies in which defence, foreign affairs etc. would remain in the hands of the Portuguese, and the rest of the MFA who wanted to give the colonies full independence. All the crises up to 25 November had, as a background, the decolonisation problem.

The 28 September 1974 coup was very likely planned by engineer Jorge Jardim. It was an international plot scheduled to start in Mozambique on 16 September, to be followed by an uprising in Angola on 21 September. Then on 28 September the armed forces of the two colonies would demand that Spínola be made the leader of Portugal and that the MFA be dismantled. By accident the planned uprising in Mozambique started earlier and because of this Angola was not prepared. Since I was commander-in-chief in Angola I was able to order the jamming of the radio broadcasts from Mozambique and arrest some of the conspirators. When 28 September came about in Lisbon Spínola had no support in the colonies.

The next crisis came in December 1974. Although specifically about the legalisation of the CGTP as the sole representative of the trade union movement, it was in reality about the independence of the colonies. The crisis was averted because of the negotiations which led to the Alvor agreement [see chronology 15 January 1975].

The next crisis was the 11 March 1975 coup and everyone knows what happened then. It is interesting that the document Spínola would have read out, had he been successful on 11 March, had actually been written for the December crisis. The attempted coup on 11 March took place just before the colonies, with the exception of Angola, were given independence and the Spínolists were against giving all the colonies full independence.

The 25 November 1975 coup started on 8 September 1975 when Vasco Gonçalves, as a result of the Tancos assembly, was not appointed general chief of staff of the armed forces. Angola became independent on 11 November and so the path was clear for the Group of Nine to act on 25 November. They gradually lost power after this as they were no longer useful. The main aims of the MFA were to give independence to the colonies and to finish the Colonial War.

Q. Was there any danger of a communist take-over on 25 November 1975?

A. Throughout the course of the revolution there were mutual and direct influences between the armed forces and all the civilian political groups, which is what you would expect. Although western propaganda said there was a danger of a communist take-over on 25 November, this was not so. The PCP was never strong enough. On 25 April 1974 they had about 5,000 members, mostly workers. At the peak of the revolution they had less than

50,000. After the revolution stopped it grew to more than 100,000 members.

Q. Why were you appointed as high commissioner to Angola?

A. This was a bit peculiar. Spínola chose me because he thought I could not handle the potentially explosive situation that existed there, and so I would be burnt in the process. The left supported my appointment, so I accepted. It was during my stay in Angola that my political outlook matured.

Q. What were the relationships between COPCON and the Group of Nine?

A. COPCON always maintained a populist far-left stance while the Group of Nine were strongly influenced by the Socialist Party, but, because of the friendships that existed between Otelo (who was commander of COPCON) and those in the Group of Nine, COPCON was often paralysed. This friendship was based upon loyalty to brother officers and the fact that they were all about the same age. But that did not mean that they shared the same political ideology. The Group of Nine wanted a parliamentary democracy, COPCON was for popular democracy through the mass movements. Initially, the Group of Nine was under the influence of a splinter group the MES [Movimento de Esquarda Socialista, Movement of the Socialist Left]. Melo Antunes, who was a leading figure of the Group of Nine, was a member of the MES.

Once the anti-revolutionary movement started it was clear that the Socialist Party was with it. This was a disaster because for the revolution to continue we had to have the support of the PS and the PCP. The revolution was supported only by the PCP and the MFA, and so a fight broke out between the PCP and the MFA on one side and the PS on the other. The PS won by breaking the MFA through the Group of Nine.

Q. Did Otelo control COPCON?

A. COPCON was not easy to control. It was a well-intentioned, generous, but indisciplined body. The only man with common sense in COPCON was Colonel Artur Baptista. He was not powerful in the usual sense, because he was not known to the public. COPCON was sucked in by the mass movement, but it also acted in a disturbing way in certain areas such as the occupations of houses. It did not oppose the house occupations and, in fact, it often indicated houses that could be occupied.

Q. Do you see any parallel between the house occupations and the land occupations that occurred in the Alentejo region and were the basis for the Agrarian Reform?
A. These house occupations should not be seen in the same light as the Agrarian Reform. In the Agrarian Reform the fight was against a well-defined enemy – the absentee landlords. The house occupations were against people belonging to several strata of society. This created bad feeling against the revolution from many different sectors of Portuguese society. When you fight a war you need to know who the enemy is and in the case of the house occupations it became undefined. The big landowners were the enemies of the revolution from the start, the house owners became enemies after the occupations. There were more people who became frightened of the revolution as a result of the house occupations than those who benefited from finding a home.
Q. What were the achievements of the revolution?
A. Firstly, the awakening of the political conscience of the Portuguese. Secondly, decolonisation and this meant profound economic changes for Portugal, since the colonies had previously been the most important factor in the accumulation of capital, although most of this went abroad. The foreign powers got the cream of the colonial milk and Portugal got what was left. Thirdly, the development of a powerful trade union movement, which is more politically articulate than in most other countries in Europe. The percentage of unionised workers is extremely high. Fourthly, the development of autonomy of the local authorities. These authorities, even the right-wing ones, have made an important contribution to progress in this country. There has been an enormous increase in the electricity and water supply, there have been great improvements in sanitation and cultural activities are forever growing. Fifthly, formal democracy was established and is now in operation. Although not ideal, this is important. We have come from a pre-25 April situation where the poor accepted their status quo to one now where they want to be rich. We have yet to evolve to the situation where the people revolt against a system which allows poverty.
Q. What evidence is there of any outside influence applied to Portugal before and after 25 April 1974?
A. There was no foreign interference in the Movement of Captains. Some countries, like the USA, were surprised by the

revolution. Prior to the revolution the USA never paid us much attention and that might explain why Dr Kissinger wrote in his report on Southern Africa, that the end result of the Colonial War would be that Portugal would manage to hold on to Angola and Mozambique for some years, after they had lost Guinea-Bissau.

After 25 April, and on several occasions, there was a US aircraft carrier off the coast of Portugal, supposedly there to protect US citizens. During the revolution there was a systematic anti-Portugal campaign from the west. This campaign was fuelled by the Portuguese Socialist Party, who gave the outside world a distorted view of events that were taking place during the revolution – events such as the Republican newspaper affair. Whenever I went abroad during the 'hot summer' the first question I was always asked was, 'What happened at the *Republica*?'

During the 'hot summer' of 1975 there was an economic boycott of Portugal. For instance, West Germany stopped importing port wine.

I know that the CIA mounted an undercover operation in Portugal acting mainly through the Brazilian embassy. It was under the control of the then newly-appointed US ambassador, Carlucci, who, after 25 November 1975, returned to the States to take up a post as second in command of the CIA.

Q. What are your views on the decolonisation process?

A. The process was unique because it took place during a left-wing revolution so the outcome is that the new countries are anti-imperialist. It was also the only decolonisation process that I know of where moral imperatives were paramount. We should not forget that it was the colonial problem that triggered the Portuguese revolution.

In the end decolonisation did not go exactly as we wanted. For example, we did not want the white exodus from the colonies to Portugal. This exodus damaged the future of Angola and Mozambique and fathered counter-revolutionary activity in Portugal.

Q. What are your political beliefs?

A. In 1984 I am a left-winger and an internationalist and of course these two positions are related. Left-wingers are characterised by the way they look at freedom. For me freedom is lack of fear, for example not to fear hunger, disease, and being allowed to express yourself.

The world is in a state of change and is unstable. It is shrinking as a result of technology and the poor countries are even more aware of the prevailing injustices. We are witnessing the fall of Pax Americana, which reigned supreme between 1945 and 1975. The year 1975 was an important transition year because of a large number of events: the Portuguese revolution, the end of the Vietnam War, the Portuguese decolonisation in Africa, the change of the political situation in Southern Africa, the Ethiopian revolution, the strategical parity between the USA and the USSR and the Helsinki agreement. Since then other events have taken place which reveal the weakening of the American empire: the Iranian revolution, the fall of Somoza in Nicaragua, the revolution in El Salvador, the political changes in Upper Volta and Ghana and even the Falklands War. The poor countries no longer admire the Americans. Very soon they will discover that they have to fight the whole system. Present distribution of wealth in the world and, in particular, the distribution of the world's non-recoverable resources, is shocking. Three-quarters of humanity has 10 per cent of the resources. This is the real pressure for change and it has nothing to do with the military rivalry between the USA and the USSR.

Q. What do you think of the Association of 25 April?

A. Its main role is to keep the armed forces politically alert, so that they do not get used as a repressive political instrument against their own people. At the moment there is a political witch-hunt going on instigated from outside and against the left and the armed forces. In the navy we were promised frigates, but only if we cleaned up our act first.

Marshal Costa Gomes. Born in Chaves in 1914. Father was an army officer. At eleven entered the Military College and in 1933, entered the Military Academy in Lisbon. While still in the army obtained a mathematics degree from Oporto university. In 1944 was promoted to captain and then spent five years studying to become an officer of the general staff. Then appointed general chief of staff of Macau in China. Returned to Lisbon and spent the next two years in the General Staff and planned the training of a Portuguese NATO division. In 1943 was stationed as a NATO officer at Sacland. In 1956 worked with the Chief of Staff Botelho Moniz in the reorganisation of the Portuguese armed forces. In 1958 was appointed as a cabinet minister, secretary of the army. In 1961 was removed from power because he supported some senior officers, among them Botelho Moniz, who had attempted to remove Salazar from power. From 1961 to 1963 commanded a number of military regiments. From 1963 to 1964 attended a course to be promoted to the rank of general. The following year became a professor of this course. From 1965 to 1967 was second-in-command of the army in Mozambique. In 1969 returned to Portugal and was appointed quarter-master general of the army. After seven months sent as commander-in-chief of the armed forces in Angola and remained there until 1972. Then returned to Lisbon and was appointed as general chief of staff of the armed forces of Portugal. On 14 March 1974 Caetano removed him from his post. On 25 April 1974 became a member of the Junta of National Salvation and reinstated as general chief of staff of the armed forces. Following Spínola's resignation, became President of the Republic in September 1974. In April 1976 stepped down to Eanes who was the newly-elected President. Is currently marshal of all the armed forces.

Interview

Q. Why were you involved in the Movement of Captains?

A. Of all the generals, I was the only one who objected to the law passed by the Caetano regime which gave rise to the Movement of Captains. After the Movement's meeting in Evora [see part 1], I prevented any disicplinary action being taken against the Movement, even though the other generals were in favour of it.

I was frequently consulted by the members of the Movement of Captains. Whilst in command of military operations in Mozambique and Angola, I had been able to stabilise the military situation and create necessary conditions for a negotiated solution, so that was why I was respected by the MFA and probably why they consulted me. Eight days before the 25 April coup, Vasco Gonçalves, and before him Spínola, had asked my opinion of the Programme of the MFA. On 25 April I was called in to the Junta of National Salvation.

Q. Why did you not take the Presidency of the Republic, since the MFA had chosen you as its leader?

A. Because I did not want to be a politican, neither had I a political following in Portugal. I considered myself an able general and better fitted to the post of general chief of staff. At that time, I thought that Spínola was more politically experienced than I was.

Q. Why was Vasco Gonçalves selected as prime minister, following the resignation of Palma Carlos in July 1974?

A. President Spínola wanted Palma Carlos to remain as prime minister, but he would not keep the post. Spínola then invited the commander of the southern military region, Fontes Pereira de Melo, to accept the post, but he refused. He then chose Brigadier Freire, who did accept. But Spínola found out that this man had pledged allegiance to Caetano's government in March 1974, so he withdrew that invitation. To my surprise, he then chose Vasco Gonçalves. I thought Melo Antunes, who had written the MFA Programme, was more politically experienced. Later on, I realised that Vasco Gonçalves was more politically aware than I had first thought.

Q. How do you see the attempted Spínolist coup that took place on 11 March 1975?

A. Politically, it was an attempt to reverse the changes that were taking place. Already the Spínolists had attempted to stop them in September 1974. Militarily, it was a poorly prepared operation, doomed to failure from the start. Prior to this, Spínola had usually had good and numerous staff to prepare his briefs and from these he usually chose well. On 11 March he did not have the staff.

Q. Was the revolution that was going on in the streets at that time led by the PCP?

A. No. A number of parties had popular support. The PPD had support in the north, the PS had large support in most towns, the MRPP was strong in certain Lisbon areas. The PCP was strongest in Lisbon, Setubal and the Alentejo and was probably the best organised of all the parties.

Throughout the whole course of the revolution, there was never a danger of a communist take-over. Although the PCP was well-organised and a recognisable political force, it would never have attempted a take-over. It knew the country very well and was well aware that it lacked the necessary popular support.

Q. The failed coup of 11 March probably allowed a number of important radical political changes to take place. Were there any plans for nationalisations, for example, before 11 March?

A. No. But Silva Lopes, who was minister of finance in March 1975, was of the opinion that the banks and insurance companies should be nationalised, as they were in the hands of a few powerful families who controlled the economy of the country. The MFA were also arguing politically through their Assembly for nationalisations.

The nationalisations were not an ad hoc response to the mass movements, even though there was a public demand for them. Although many economists advocated nationalisations, they were not really aware that nationalising the banks and insurance companies would also nationalise large numbers of firms that were owned by them.

The nationalisations that took place were an attempt by the newly-formed Council of the Revolution to introduce irreversible political and economic changes, so that any right-wing counter-coup would be prevented. The Council of the Revolution was able to do this, because it had the support of the masses.

Q. These nationalisations occurred, as a result of legislations passed by the Council of the Revolution. But, in other areas, such as the farm occupations in the Alentejo region, for example, is it fair to say that some laws were passed after the events had happened?

A. Yes, in some cases the Council of the Revolution was carried by events, rather than being the leader. But the Alentejo region is a special region. In 1936 I saw 10,000 people demonstrate and they were carrying black flags, as symbols of their hunger. During the previous regime, the Alentejo was a depressed area, owned largely by absentee landlords, who were uninterested in cultivating the land. After 25 April 1974, things started to happen quickly. When the workers asked for guidance as to what to do, the officers of the local regiments said, 'Do what you want.' The conventional forces of law and order, the police, the Republican Guard, had been supporters of the fallen regime. They were afraid to act. So the workers occupied the land and the Council of the Revolution was forced to legislate.

Q. Why did the Council of the Revolution never pass legislation, similar to that for the land occupations, for the house occupations that occurred in the urban areas?

A. There were similarities between house and farm occupations. Two short documents regulating house occupations were produced: one by COPCON and one by the Council of the Revolution, but legislation was never as complete as the Agrarian Reform. Some of the house occupations resulted in abuse. For example, house owners occupied other houses and then sub-let them! Also, in order to carry out laws, you need to have the power to enforce them.

Q. Does this mean that there was a lack of discipline in the Lisbon military units under the control of COPCON?

A. Yes, COPCON allowed considerable erosion of discipline in the units under its control in the Lisbon area. Although COPCON was under the control of Otelo, the military units were out of control. They had undergone an explosion of freedom. On a number of occasions, Otelo tried to resign his command of COPCON.

Q. Was there any disagreement between the Group of Nine in the Council of the Revolution and COPCON?

A. Yes. The Nine thought that COPCON had gone too far in promoting some social measures. But this was due, in part, to the fact that the Group of Nine was not directly involved with the civilian or the military disciplinary problems that COPCON had to deal with. But Otelo frequently did not implement the decisions that had been taken by the Council of the Revolution, and that he had voted for. It was not that he could not carry them out. He was easily swayed by the people, and the only person who could control him was Lieutenant-Colonel Artur Baptista, the chief of staff of COPCON.

Q. Do you think that there were any lines of communication between Otelo and the Group of Nine?

A. No. By then, the Group of Nine had become withdrawn and had established contacts outside the Council of the Revolution with people such as Eanes, Rocha Vieira and Loureiro dos Santos. As far as I knew, Otelo was unaware of the military plans being formulated by Eanes and others which ended in the 25 November coup. After August, the 'hot summer' of 1975, I think that Otelo realised that he could no longer control the units in the Lisbon area.

Q. On 25 November paratroopers from Tancos invaded three air force bases. Did they act on their own initiative?

A. No. A few days before 25 November, most of the paratroop officers had left. I think there were elements to the left of the PCP which triggered that action and they were convinced that some of the left-wing regiments in the Lisbon area [RAL 1 and ALMADA] would follow them.

As a military action, it did not make sense, and, as soon as I knew about it, I tried to get the paratroopers to return to their base at Tancos. Their action was used as a pretext for the counter-military action that was brought about by the Group of Nine and associated military officers.

Q. Do you think the action of the paratroopers was set up by the Group of Nine?

A. I don't think so. I always assume that military officers are honourable people. Even if it was convenient for the events to happen, I, as an officer, would never set them in motion.

Q. Were there any military plans, drawn up by the associates of the Group of Nine, which could be put into operation following an event such as the invasion of the air force bases that occurred on 25 November?

A. There were plans, but not detailed ones, which were immediately put into operation. The only military units that they could rely on were the well-trained and disciplined commando regiments. Any military actions would have to be based on them. There were no plans for a political take-over.

The solution of the occupation of the air force bases by the paratroopers could have been achieved by negotiation. I tried to do this, but I had no one with whom I could talk.

Q. Since the Group of Nine had popular support, and the support of the north, south and central military regions, why was it necessary to use the commandos?

A. Because some people thought that the marines would be loyal to the paratroopers. Also, the paratroopers thought they could count on the support of the marines.

Q. But the marines did not support the paras, so why was there a military operation?

A. There was not one. The commandos surrounded the air bases and the paras surrendered.

Q. Why did the commandos attack the military police?

A. This was an unnecessary action.

Q. Who sent the commandos to attack the military police?

A. There were two command posts. One near me, under the control of Vasco Lourenço, and the other in the commando regiment headquarters at Amadora, under Eanes. The order came from the Amadora headquarters. When we in Belem tried to stop the commandos, their commander, Jaime Neves, demanded a written note from Eanes and then continued. So three people died unnecessarily, since the commander of the military police had said that he would not offer any resistance.

Q. So unnecessary military action leads to profound political changes?

A. The political changes were already taking place, following the appointment of the sixth provisional government. One can see 25 November as a reversal of 11 March in that the government was able to undo some of the changes introduced by Gonçalves's government. 25 November did not stop the revolution, but it slowed it. It also resulted in the control of the Lisbon military and paramilitary units, especially the Republican Guard and the police force. I think the revolution stopped when the AD coalition was elected. And now, in some areas, it is returning to the old order.

Q. It is often said that 25 November was a reaction against an attempted PCP take-over. If this is so, how do you explain the speech of Melo Antunes on 26 November in which he said that the PCP still had a role to play in Portuguese politics?

A. We have to thank the PCP for not letting 25 November end up in civil war. On that day, the PCP supporters were intending to block the barracks of the commandos with bulldozers and excavators. They invaded and surrounded the naval unit at Almada and the Alfeite arsenal. These communists withdrew when I asked the CGTP to do so. [The CGTP was the Portuguese trade union confederation; the English equivalent is the TUC. The CGTP was under the influence of the PCP.] The communist supporters were armed and, if they had not withdrawn, there would have been a civil war. In his speech, Melo Antunes was acknowledging the collaboration of the PCP.

Q. Why do you think that all of the Group of Nine later lost power, even though they were successful on 25 November?

A. This is because of the way in which they behaved in the Council of the Revolution, from 1976 until its dissolution in 1982. The Council was meant to be the watchdog of the Legislative Assembly [Parliament]. They failed in this role. Also, some councillors suffered an erosion of their public image through over-exposure. The army has not changed much since the revolution. The young officers between 1974 and 1984 were, on the whole, progressive. It is the new intake that worries me.

Q. Was there a danger of a right-wing coup following 25 November?

A. No, because the majority of the officers up to the rank of major are not right-wingers and these are the ones you see at the commemorations of 25 April 1974. There were some associations between the Group of Nine and the right, of which at the time I was not aware. I consider these associations to have been a mistake.

Q. Were you happy with the way decolonisation went?

A. No, but I am happy we decolonised. The process, if anything, went too slowly and it was disturbed by the events that took place in Portugal between 11 March and 28 September. Under my command, conditions had been created in Angola and Mozambique which would have allowed negotiations to have taken place with the liberation movements. I don't mean to say that we had won the war, because the enemy was regrouping for a new offensive.

Q. What is the role of the newly-formed Association of 25 April?

A. If it acts as a meeting place for the progressive officers of the armed forces, it could be important, provided it does not get involved in politics. It is dangerous to keep the discussion of politics outside the armed forces, because in the end the soldiers will get their politics from outside.

Q. How do you see yourself politically?

A. I am an independent and I do not belong to any political party. I am a progressive Catholic, although I do not agree with some of the policies of the present Pope, especially, for example, on abortion and divorce.

Analysis

INTRODUCTION

The coup d'état on 25 April opened up the path that was to lead to Portuguese democracy. It is clear from the interviews that the events that followed the coup were not expected either by the officers or by the outside world, which anyway had largely ignored Portugal during the previous fifty years. On the day that Caetano handed over power to Spínola, the people spontaneously took to the streets. This was the beginning of the mass movement so often talked about in the interviews, which give an intimate account of the feelings and actions of those young officers. The aims of this section are twofold: firstly, to use the interviews to analyse, examine and explain the officers' feelings and actions throughout the course of the revolution; secondly, to use the interviews to deal in greater depth with the events that were given factually in the chronology above. As the interviews are used, they are referred to by the officers' initials. (The initials were given on the introductory page of each group of interviews.)

The mass movement that immediately followed the coup was the result of fifty years of frustration. Demonstrations occurred simultaneously throughout all large and small towns in Portugal. People took to the streets, stopped traffic, embraced one another, threw flowers in the air and overnight became intoxicated with their new-found freedom. For forty-eight years there had been no spontaneous demonstrations in Portugal: it was as if the captains had removed a dam. The power and strength of this mass movement took everyone by surprise.

The captains had not expected it, nor did they want it. As army men they preferred a more controlled situation. The MFA Programme (see appendix 1) even stated that the change of regime should take place 'without internal social upheaval which would affect the peace, progress, and well-being of the nation' (third paragraph, opening section of the MFA Programme). Neither did the MFA see itself as a revolutionary force, since its Programme stated that any 'major reforms can only be adopted within the framework of the future National Constitutional Assembly' (section B5, MFA Programme). Thus changes were only to be made after the new Constitution had been written, defining what changes should take place. The Programme also stated that the new President would appoint a civilian government composed only of those in tune with the aims of the MFA. Interestingly enough, the Programme did not immediately foresee the formation of civilian political parties, since it only mentions 'political associations' which might be the 'embryos of future political parties' (section B5b).

Like the captains, the Communist Party did not predict or expect the strength and power of the mass movement. From almost all the interviews it was clear that the PCP was taken aback. Hoping to see a gradual, controlled evolution to a communist Portugal, it witnessed a mass movement with a revolutionary fervour that it had trouble keeping up with. The communists' relationship with the mass movement caused them problems throughout the whole post-coup d'état period.

THE POST-COUP PERIOD, 25 APRIL – 31 DECEMBER 1974

The pressure of the mass movement played a decisive role in the immediate post-coup d'état period. The old regime was clearly frightened by it. Intimidated, it offered no resistance to the MFA and quietly handed over power. The movement was important in maintaining the course of the revolution, since most of the armed forces on the day of 25 April were passive. The navy and air force were hardly involved (VC), and it was only a small number of army units that took over Lisbon and Oporto. It was the force of the public demonstrations that made the uncommitted sections of the armed forces follow this lead. Often they followed in a half-hearted way. This probably explains why there were such a number of counter-coups. The Spínolists always hoped they could swing these uncommitted sections of the armed forces to their point of view. However, the ending of the Colonial War was something that united most of the military and kept them backing the MFA Programme until the last colony became independent.

In the days that followed the coup the mass movement affected not only the armed forces, but also the local civilian authorities. The mayors of most towns voluntarily resigned and handed over their local councils, in many instances, to the supporters of the communist-backed CDE. This transfer of power was usually done in the presence of military authorities, by a request of the local councils. Almost overnight the military were assumed to be arbitrators in most civilian matters and so in a way, contrary to the MFA Programme, the MFA had power thrust upon it. In essence, the MFA wanted to hand over power to the politicians and act only as a watchdog to the implementation of the MFA Programme. Thus the Political Committee of the MFA was renamed, following the coup, the Co-ordinating Committee of the MFA Programme (CCP, see chronology). The CCP acted only as a consultative body, but nevertheless, by being active and near the centre of power it was able to influence events (see chronology, block diagrams 1 to 4). A significant episode which illuminates the MFA's intention of not clinging to power can be seen in Lieutenant-Colonel Otelo Saraiva de Carvalho's interview. He says, 'By late morning of 26 April, it was all over. I took off my uniform, I changed into civilian clothing and went home to my family. The mission had been accomplished.'

Further evidence comes from an examination of the composition of the JSN (table 1). The Junta did not include any members of the MFA, even though it was still the centre of power, following the coup d'état. Nevertheless, Costa Gomes and Spínola had had connections with the Movement before the coup (CG). Costa Gomes was chosen by the MFA to be its leader. He refused to accept the post and offered it to Spínola, with the argument that Spínola had more political experience than he had and that he was better suited as general chief of staff of the armed forces. It is, however, tempting to speculate that Costa Gomes's decision to give the presidency to Spínola was politically a very astute move; as a strategist, he was probably aware that, by being in charge of the armed forces at that time, he would be in control of the political situation. The result of his decision and appointment of Spínola as leader of the MFA was that, in the early stages of the revolution, power was theoretically in the hands of the Spínolists (CF). As President, Spínola chose the composition of the first provisional government. However, subsequent events were to show that the government was not always going to follow him. For example, Fabião presided over the decolonisation of Guinea-Bissau in accord with the aims of the MFA, which were in opposition to the gradual decolonisation programme proposed by Spínola and his supporters (CF).

One of the important findings from the interviews is the constant obsession of the officers and the MFA with 'legality'. As soon as the JSN was in power, it decided that Salazar's 1933 constitution should remain in force. Only under certain specific cases, when the need arose, and whenever the Constitution contradicted the Programme of the MFA, was the 1933 Constitution to be disregarded. From the Programme of the MFA, from most of the interviews, especially from Lieutenant-Colonel Carlos Fabião's, it is clear that law and order were important and that the anarchy of the mass movement was really anathema to those well-disciplined officers.

In the weeks that followed the coup there was a power struggle within the armed forces. Spínola wanted to dissolve the MFA in an attempt to control the armed forces, but this was to prove difficult, as the MFA was beginning to emerge as a powerful political and military force, in parallel with the normal military structure. This power struggle had started even before 25 April. In the first draft of the MFA Programme decolonisation had been one of the major issues, but in the final MFA Programme decolonisation is not even mentioned. Spínola wanted a gradual decolonisation and was able to persuade the MFA to accept, at least implicitly, his point of view. An examination of the final MFA Programme in appendix 1 infers that the Colonial War is expected to continue, notwithstanding that there should be a policy of ending the war through political negotiation. Thus section A2c of the Programme states that the secret police

(PIDE/DGS) should be disbanded in Portugal, but they should continue to exist in the colonies in order to police the gathering of information 'while the military operation so demands it'.

The MFA grew as a powerful force because power was given to it by the people. Also the police force and other bodies, who had been active supporters of the previous regime, and responsible for the maintenance of law and order, were in disarray. They were apprehensive of the mass movement and unable to act.

As the power struggle continued within the armed forces, the mass movement gathered momentum. There were enormous public demonstrations, and purges (*saneamentos*) of those who had supported the old regime in government and private institutions. Official buildings of the previous regime were taken over, such as those of the grémios and sindicatos. In addition, house occupations started to take place (AF, LM), strikes for the implementation of wage agreements that had been made under the Caetano regime occurred, businesses were taken over in the absence of the management who had fled the country, or after struggles of the workers with the existing management, and a number of different trade unions were set up. At this time, the first populist structures emerged: the neighbourhood committees, workers' committees and assemblies in schools, universities and most institutions.

These drastic social changes were too much for the first provisional government under Prime Minister Palma Carlos and this led to the second meeting at the Manutenção Militar. Here, members of the Palma Carlos government tried to convince the MFA that giving in to the workers' demands and letting things run as they were would result in the economic collapse of the country. In the same Manutenção Militar meeting Spínola attempted to take control of the political situation, by demanding that the MFA give him its full support. The MFA refused (SO). Spínola continued his attempts and asked the Council of State to allow presidential elections to be held early and to reinforce the powers of the prime minister. The Council of State refused the first request, but allowed the second. However, Professor Palma Carlos resigned, arguing that, without Spínola being in a strong presidential position, he would be unable to govern.

The Palma Carlos crisis had two effects: one was that the MFA was seen to be a really powerful political force and the other was the emergence of Otelo as a national figure. After the coup, Otelo vanished from the public eye. However, he was a good organiser and, as Spínola did not see him as a political threat, he was appointed as commander of COPCON and the Lisbon military region (OSC, AF). COPCON was to play an important role in the revolutionary process. It was the centre of operations for all the armed forces and was a loosely based structure with representatives from all three branches of the services. Under its direct command, it had a few military units, but operationally, at least in theory, COPCON could order the commanders of the four military regions (north, central, Lisbon and south: see block diagrams) to act. The number of people involved in COPCON was small: twenty officers at the height of its powers, which reduced to seven in the later stages (LM). Because of its special role as arbitrator and the maintainer of law and order in the Lisbon area, COPCON developed close contacts with the civilian parties (AF).

Lisbon tended to be the centre of political activity following the 25 April coup. Otelo's appointment as commander of the Lisbon military region, allowed him to use these military units in the service of COPCON. His joint appointment as commander of COPCON and head of the Lisbon military region was indeed a powerful one. The appointment of Vasco Gonçalves as prime minister of the second provisional government by Spínola can also be seen in the same light as Otelo's appointment to COPCON (VG). Spínola probably thought that, like Otelo, Gonçalves was not a threat to him (VG).

Supported by the mass movement, the MFA pushed ahead with its original intention of giving independence to the colonies. Rosa Coutinho was appointed high commissioner to Angola and a short while later Victor Crespo took up the same post in Mozambique (RC, VC). Both these men set about implementing a full and rapid independence for the colonies (RC, VC). Spínola, having failed to win over the MFA from within, tried elsewhere and, in a series of speeches made in military units and broadcast throughout the country, he criticised the spread of anarchy and bemoaned the loss of military effort that had been expended during the Colonial War. He increased his contact with the right, especially with the white settlers in the colonies. A civilian organisation emerged, pro-Spínola and representing the so-called 'silent majority'. The organisation set up demonstrations and on 28 September attempted to march on Lisbon demanding, amongst other things, that Spínola should be given special powers. The march was frustrated by road-blocks set up by left-wing elements and the demonstration was later cancelled by Spínola (FC). When the JSN refused to give him special powers, he resigned as President and the 28 September crisis was over. It showed that the Spínolists were not well organised and that Spínola had made a poor analysis of the political situation (CG, VC). It was the beginning of the fall of the Spínolists and the rise of the left-wing parties, especially the PCP, which had played an important role in setting up the road-blocks and preventing the march on Lisbon.

The other political parties, such as the PS and the PPD, were nowhere near as well organised as the PCP (OSC), nor did they command the popular support from the mass movement, as did the PCP and the ultra-left-wing parties. In general, the more moderate political parties were overshadowed by the left and the MFA. Throughout the course of the revolution, the PCP was seen to support the MFA and always projected the image of being its civilian ally. Even in 1984, it spoke out for the alliance between the people and the MFA (Povo/MFA)and claims that it was the true representative of the Portuguese people. The PCP was not only well run and organised, but it also had respect from a large number of people for having a clean political past. The party had always opposed the previous regime and most of the members of its central committee had spent years in and out of Salazar's prisons. It is not surprising that the other parties were not well organised. The PS was only formed in April 1973, the PPD on 3 May 1974 and the CDS on 19 July 1974. The PCP had been started in 1921.

Once Spínola had resigned as President the natural choice for the new President by the JSN was Costa Gomes. All along he had been the MFA's choice for leader (CG). The resignation was a victory for the MFA, as Spínola had wanted their dissolution. With this victory, the MFA formally restructured (see table 2) and created the Committee of Twenty (Superior Council of the Revolution).

The end of 1974 saw the MFA as the main political force in Portugal. By then they had given full independence to Guinea-

Bissau and, in principle, to São Tomé and Príncipe. In December the Melo Antunes plan for the economic recovery of the country was being discussed by the MFA. The plan was later to play a key role in the progress of the revolution. Although opposed by large sections of the MFA, it was, however, approved by the MFA Assembly and received the public support of Prime Minister Vasco Gonçalves (VG).

In the next year, as a result of the failure of the 11 March coup, the Melo Antunes plan would not be implemented. Supporters and opponents of the plan were to be the cause of a split in the MFA that eventually led to the formation of the Group of Nine and the 25 November coup in 1975.

POLITICAL TURMOIL AND THE 'HOT SUMMER',
I JANUARY–31 DECEMBER 1975

1975 started with the Committee of Twenty defending the principle of Unicidade Sindical. This principle was a proposal of the second provisional Gonçalves government, where each trade was represented by one trade union. If the principle was accepted it would mean a recognition of the trade union federation CGTP/Intersindical as the federation which represents the workers. Intersindical had close links with the PCP (see chronology). The debate around this principle marked the emergence of the PS as a political force. The PS needed an issue with which to challenge the supremacy of the PCP, and it took up the cause of the Unicidade Sindical. The Socialist Party argued that, if the principle was accepted, the PCP would control and dominate the whole trade union movement and they were able to mobilise considerable public support on this issue.

The spring of 1975 saw the final confrontation between the Spínolists and the MFA. On 11 March Spínola and his supporters attempted a coup by taking over Lisbon airport, the Republican National Guard barracks at Carmo and they bombed and then surrounded the barracks of the left-wing light artillery regiment (RAL1). The coup had been known about in advance, but it had not been pre-empted (CF), for within the MFA there were divisions and Spínola had support, especially from the older generals and the higher-ranking officers. Once the Spínolists had moved on 11 March and accomplished their initial objectives, they waited for the rest of the armed forces to join them. This did not happen; most of the military units preferred to remain passive (MT).

The public did not give the attempted coup much support either and, in fact, the Spínolist troops surrounding the RAL1 barracks were almost attacked by a hostile crowd. Finally, there was no clear support from within the MFA, since the problems of the Colonial War had yet to be completely solved and the colonies had not been given their independence. The coup was probably prematurely triggered (SO) and it was suggested that the appearance of Spínola's name on a 'death list', put out by the ultra-left, forced him to act. It was clear that Spínola misjudged the mood of the country (VC), and in the end he fled the country to Spain with his wife and a number of officers (SO).

The removal of Spínolists from the MFA opened the way for the Gonçalves government to push ahead with left-wing legislation (CG), which was mostly concerned with nationalisation (see chronology). There was support for this from most of the MFA and some of the political parties, including the PS. However, disagreement arose over the extent of nationalisation. Some of the MFA argued that it was not necessary to nationalise all the old economic monopolies, as this would mean massive nationalisation and the taking over of large numbers of often bankrupt firms (CF); others in the MFA argued that the country was not yet ready for it, since formal democracy had yet to be established (SO). Spínola's departure from Portugal was the signal for a massive outflow of capital from the banks. Gonçalves and his finance minister argued that massive nationalisation was essential, if the economy was to be controlled. This view won the day. Melo Antunes was not appointed finance minister by Vasco Gonçalves, since the Melo Antunes plan did not propose this degree of state intervention into the economy (VG). The second provisional government also intervened in the national economy by appointing government delegates into a large number of non-nationalised firms: often these firms were suffering economic difficulties. In order to allow the Gonçalves government to pursue these radical policies, the MFA proposed an MFA–Parties Pact (see Appendix 2 and chronology). The pact intended to pre-empt any claim that the political parties might have through the results of the elections for the Constitutional

Assembly. The MFA specifically wanted to prevent the different political parties from demanding power in proportion to the number of votes gained at this election: they were frightened that the civilian parties would gain control and reverse the progress of the revolution (OSC).

From the beginning of 1975 the mass movement had continued to grow. The 11 March coup added further impetus to this growth. February and March saw a massive wave of house occupations in Lisbon (LM) and after March the path was open for land occupations to take place in the Alentejo region. The land occupations were the final stage of political action in the Alentejo region that had started immediately after the 25 April coup. Since then agricultural workers had continuously demanded better wages and fuller employment in the region (see appendix 8). The result was a confrontation between farm workers, who had organised themselves into a union, and the farm owners who likewise had organised an association. The agricultural workers were often supported by the local councils and military units and the pressure they exerted on the farm owners resulted in a backlash. The landowners tried to make the farms unworkable by a number of means: decapitalisation, slaughtering and disposal of cattle and the selling of farm machinery (PC). In reply, the workers started occupying the farms. The involvement of the Communist Party in the early stages of the land occupations was small (MT). Initially, the workers organised themselves with the help of the ultra-left-wing parties such as the UDP, but later the PCP was to be the most active party in pushing for legislation to implement a structured Agrarian Reform. In July 1975 legislation was passed by the Council of the Revolution which established the rules of land distribution (Appendix 6). This is a good example of how the MFA legislated after an event had taken place.

Because of its intervention in both these land occupations and also in the house occupations that were taking place in the towns, COPCON became politically identified with the mass movement – an identification that was compounded, since COPCON was often called upon and seen to arbitrate in industrial disputes. The officers in COPCON were also influenced by some of the ultra-left-wing political parties of the mass movement (AF). This growing link and interchange between COPCON and the mass movement resulted in a conflict between COPCON and both the Gonçalves government and Melo Antunes and his supporters. The Gonçalves government wanted to carry out far-reaching reforms, that generally were in tune with the aims and ideals of the PCP (VG), by a legislative procedure. While Melo Antunes and his supporters, who were gradually aligning themselves with the PS, wanted gradual reforms based upon a social democracy, COPCON opposed both groups since they supported the radical populists. Both the Gonçalvists and the social democrats were concerned that COPCON was alienating the lower middle classes, which constituted a large section of the Portuguese and whose support was essential for any political party to hold power (RC, CG, VG).

It was during the period after 11 March that the officers of COPCON became radically politicised through having to deal with the practical problems that resulted from the 25 April coup (AF). This politicisation started a fight between COPCON and the social democrats that was to end in the 25 November coup. The social democrats were to organise themselves into the Group of Nine and, although Otelo never severed his links with his brother officers in the group (OSC, AF, VG), the Group of Nine was to become increasingly dissatisfied with the way COPCON acted. They resented the way COPCON behaved as an extra-parliamentary political force (VG, PC), and thought it wrong that a military organisation should be outside the control of the military. COPCON was meant to be the co-ordinating body of the armed forces. Instead, they considered that it acted as an 'anarchic policeman' (VG, PC).

A further outcome of 11 March was the formation of right-wing groups: in Paris, Spínola set up MDLP (SO) and in the north of Portugal, under the protection of the Church, the Maria de Fonte movement was formed (CF, MJ, VL, see chronology).

The elections for the Constitutional Assembly were held on 25 April. The results were important, for they showed that the party with the largest following was not, as had been expected, the PCP, but the PS (see chronology for results). The importance that the PCP and MDP/CDE had gained in the political arena was not in proportion to the results and led the PS to demand a greater role for itself in Portuguese politics. The first clash between the two parties took place on 1 May during the May Day demonstration and the second clash occurred when the *República* newspaper was closed by COPCON (see chronology for details). Although the socialists accused the communists of shutting down one of the few non-PCP controlled newspapers, it is probably fair to say that the PCP was not involved (OSC, RC). The PS effectively used the *República* incident to gain internal and international support for its fight against the PCP and also against the Gonçalvists and COPCON.

The political turmoil created by the mass movement and the radical legislation of the Gonçalves government was further heightened by the propaganda produced by the Fifth Division. In September 1974 Costa Gomes had created the Fifth Division and included within its structure a well-known communist, Colonel Varela Gomes. The initial function of the Fifth Division was to raise the political consciousness of the Portuguese. Following 11 March, and driven by Varela Gomes, the Fifth Division exalted the aims of the Gonçalves government. Its activities were carried out through a number of regiments which received guidelines for action from the Fifth Division headquarters. Political turmoil reached a peak in August 1975, the so-called 'hot summer', with the publication in the national papers of the Document of the Nine. This attacked the PCP, the Gonçalves government, and, by drawing attention to the anarchy of the mass movement, criticised COPCON (OSC, CG, MA).

Along with the Group of Nine, another group emerged, the operationals (*operacionais*), under the leadership of Colonel Eanes (PC, CG, VL). The group had originally been formed after the 11 March coup in order to study alternative strategies and operational plans (in case of emergencies during the post-coup period), and was part of the general chief of staff of the army. The operationals led and planned the military operations that were carried out during the 25 November coup (MA, OSC, AF, VL).

On 25 August the Fifth Division was closed down by the Council of the Revolution, as it was considered to be disobeying orders: this was the first sign of the downfall of the Gonçalvists. Three days later the Council of the Revolution removed Vasco Gonçalves as prime minister of the fifth provisional government. They appointed Admiral Pinheiro de Azevedo in his place and Gonçalves was given the post of general chief of staff of the army.

However, Vasco Gonçalves's appointment was not ratified by the army assembly at Tancos and so he was removed from power (see chronology). The Gonçalvists had become increasingly isolated and the PCP had sensed this and quietly withdrawn its support for Vasco Gonçalves and his fifth provisional government. Their final defeat came on 11 September when nearly all the Gonçalvists in the Council of the Revolution were replaced. The following day Pires Veloso, a member of the Group of Nine with close links with the PS, was appointed military commander of the northern region. This appointment meant that the three military regions outside Lisbon were now in the hands of the Group of Nine (PC, SO).

The Group of Nine was now in a position to take power; what it needed was a pretext (OSC); this came when the paratroopers occupied the air force bases around Lisbon (see chronology). To understand this occupation it is necessary to return to the events of 18 June 1975. In June, the Church, which owned a national radio station, Rádio Renascença, tried to close it down because it had been taken over and had been broadcasting left-wing anticlerical propaganda. The Council of the Revolution vacillated, unable to decide if it should leave Rádio Renascença in the hands of the workers or if it should protect the rights of the Church. The Gonçalves government, wary of the power of the Church, wanted to return it. This resulted in a series of contradictory decisions (see chronology). Finally, on 7 November, the Council of the Revolution ordered the chief of staff of the air force to bring the dispute to an end, by sending paratroopers to blow up the broadcasting equipment of Rádio Renascença. The public outrage that followed upset the paratroopers and they accused the chief of staff of the air force of having misled them a second time (see chronology). The lower ranks of the paratroopers questioned their officers' authority with the result that the chief of staff of the air force threatened to disband the Tancos unit. The officers left the base and formed a separate company at the Cortegaça air force base (AF, see chronology). Otelo publicly supported the lower ranks. When the Tancos base was harassed by fighters he allowed the lower-ranking paratroopers to requisition arms (OSC). With this act, he was the only powerful figure giving them support, but on 24 November the Council of the Revolution decided to replace Otelo as commander of the mili-

tary region and, at the same time, they disbanded the paratroopers. The paratroopers, thinking that COPCON would not
intervene, planned the operation to occupy the air force bases.
The reason why they moved is still not exactly clear (FC, PC,
OSC, CG). It is argued that the paratroopers were making a
professional statement about their efficiency and discipline. The
occupations were carried out in the early hours of the morning at
lightning speed and were completely successful: it was a show-
case operation. It has also been argued that the occupations were
a protest aimed at bringing about the dismissal of the chief of staff
and the vice chief of staff of the air force in an attempt to get
themselves reinstated as paratroopers. The relationship between
the paratroopers' actions and the left-wing civilian unrest that
occurred at that time has yet to be established. The PCP was
probably involved at first when the construction workers moved
to besiege the right-wing commando regiment with heavy
machinery (CG), but the construction workers withdrew and the
PCP did nothing else (CG). The operationals waited a few hours
before moving (AF). When they did move, they met virtually no
resistance from either the paratroopers or the left-wing regiments
(CG, MT). This could explain Franco Charais's comment that
'25 November was just another day' (FC).

The Group of Nine gave the operationals a political dimension;
in return the operationals gave the Nine military strength and
carried with them support from many non-committed and right-
wing army officers (VC). Members of the Group of Nine argued
that the coup pre-empted a possible right-wing coup, coming
from the north of the country (CF). Today, there is little evidence
to support this claim. At that time, the Group of Nine's stated aim
was to suppress a left-wing take-over of the country and prevent
any right-wing counter-coup (PC, FC, VC, PV and VL; see
appendix 4). The immediate effect of the coup was the closure of
COPCON and the end of the MFA as a political force, the
removal from the army of the politically active officers (including
those who belonged to the Group of Nine), the gradual take-over
of the armed forces by the non-aligned and right-wing officers
and the emergence of the operationals as important military and
political figures (AR).

The coup could not have been held much earlier, since the
military above all else, wanted to end its commitment to the

colonies. On 11 November, Angola, the last colony, became independent (RC, AF, CF, LM). In the days that followed the coup members of the Council of the Revolution who were not members of the Group of Nine were forced to leave (RC). The fear of a right-wing backlash led Melo Antunes to defend the participation of the PCP in the political life of Portugal (MA). The 25 November coup was essentially a military affair in that there was no immediate change of government as had happened after 28 September and 11 March. Its immediate effect was the removal of the involvement of the armed forces in Portuguese politics. From that date on, there was a progressive reinforcement of the power of civilian governments and the growth of the three mainstream political parties, the PS, PPD/PSD and the CDS. The 25 November coup is generally considered to be the end of the Portuguese revolution (RC, LM, MT, etc.) and saw the collapse of the ultra-left wing and the mass movement. The collapse of this populist movement was partly due to the urban middle classes becoming frightened of the communist-backed Gonçalves government, to the house occupations and to the left-wing purges that were taking place throughout the whole of Portuguese society. The collapse was also partly due to the small landowners in the north and central rural areas of the country becoming frightened of losing their land through an extension of the Agrarian Reform. These small landowners were also subject to effective anti-communist propaganda from the Church (PC). Its collapse in the Lisbon area, where it had been most effective, was helped by the abolition of COPCON and the imprisonment of many of the left-wing populist officers who had been supporters, leaders and guardians of the movement.

The Gonçalves government, although MFA controlled, had throughout the year progressively become weaker. On 22 May 1975 the socialist ministers and the PPD/PSD ministers joined forces and left the fourth provisional government in protest over the closure of the *República* newspaper and the meddling in government affairs by the PCP. Although in July there was an attempt to bring Otelo into government and reinforce Gonçalves's position, it failed. The MFA created the Directório in an attempt to hang on to power, but its three members failed to meet and were unable to work together. The fifth provisional government was only half-heartedly supported by the PCP and the

MDP/CDE and was easy prey to the power of the Group of Nine. The sixth provisional government, which had members from the three main parties, the PS, the PSD and the PCP, was unable to govern because of the mass movement. The government was even put under siege by the construction workers during their demands for an increase in wages. Finally, it went 'on strike', saying that because of the public anarchy it was unable to govern (see chronology). After the 25 November coup, the sixth provisional government returned to work, and the country set about electing the first constitutional parliament.

THE TRANSITION TO DEMOCRACY, I JANUARY–
31 DECEMBER 1976

In February 1976, in an attempt to prevent the gradual erosion of their powers, the MFA organised a second MFA–Parties Pact (see Appendix 3). The MFA wanted to make sure that the MFA Programme would be implemented. The pact created a transitional period after which the military would no longer play any further political role, and relationships between the military and government would be similar to those found in the Western European democracies. During the transition period the Council of the Revolution would play an important role in disciplining the armed forces and gradually bringing them under civilian control. The pact also contained provisions forbidding any changes in the new Constitution which would end up reversing the achievements of the revolution, such as the nationalisations and the Agrarian Reform. To avoid any bypass of the new Constitution, the pact ruled that public referenda were to be considered unconstitutional. The effect of this pact was that a reversal of any pre-revolutionary situation by constitutional means would be impossible, and also that some of the major changes brought about by the revolution could not be undone.

On 2 April 1976 the new Constitution was finally proclaimed. On 25 April elections were held for the first Legislative Assembly (or the Portuguese parliament). Once again, the PS emerged as the major party and the more right-wing party, the CDS, doubled the vote it had obtained in the previous elections for the Constitutional Assembly (see chronology). Portugal formally became a democratic nation on 14 July 1976, when General Eanes was sworn in as President of the Second Portuguese Republic. He asked Mário Soares to be prime minister in a minority PS government. The first constitutional government was sworn in on 23 July 1976.

By the end of 1976 Otelo had been arrested for participating in political meetings and Spínola had returned to Portugal without being arrested. The socialist government had abolished the Unicidade Sindical in an attempt to break the PCP's hold on the trade union movement. The government also produced legislation to hand back substantial portions of land to the original landowners, thus reversing some of the effects of the Agrarian Reform. Prime Minister Soares dedicated his government to set the Portuguese economy right using a more free-market economy. In December 1976 the first elections for local authorities were held. These results were similar to those obtained during the elections for the Constitutional Assembly (see chronology), with the PS obtaining the largest number of votes.

AN OVERVIEW OF THE CAPTAINS

The interviews give, in general, an overall impression of the Movement of Captains and, in particular, of those officers who translated its aims into action. The officers interviewed played extremely important roles in bringing about the 25 April coup d'état and affecting the course of the following revolution.

They were the leaders, but not necessarily because of their social and political background. Table 3 summarises their background at the time of the coup, and it was probably not markedly different from that of hundreds of other young officers involved in the Movement of Captains. Although they did not always think and act in unison, the drive of the officers to rid themselves of the old regime came across strongly. Table 3 shows that only two had publicly declared their opposition to the previous regime. In a short while, all the officers became extremely politicised with ideologies ranging from the ultra left to the right. It is remarkable that such diverse political opinion was able to unite, bring about decolonisation and create democracy in Portugal.

Problems arose when the officers came to define democracy. A reading of the interviews shows that many wanted some form of

Table 3. *The captains*

	Number of times on active service	Father's profession	Attitudes towards previous regime*	Age on 25 April 1974	Rank on 25 April 1974
Melo Antunes	3	army officer	+ +	41	major
Otelo Saraiva de Carvalho	2	civil servant	–	38	major
Franco Charais	2	bank employee	–	43	lieutenant-colonel
Pezarat Correia	4	army officer	–	42	major
Rosa Coutinho	2	shopkeeper	–	48	frigate commander
Victor Crespo	2	lawyer	–	42	light-frigate commander
Carlos Fabião	4	bank employee	+	44	lieutenant-colonel
Arlindo Ferreira	2	shopkeeper	–	34	major
Costa Gomes	3	army officer	+	60	general
Vasco Gonçalves	3	accountant	–	53	colonel
Marques Júnior	1	forest guard	–	28	captain
Vasco Lourenço	1	shopkeeper	–	32	captain
Lourenço Marques	1	shopkeeper	–	29	captain
Sanches Osório	1	civil servant	–	34	major
António Ramos	3	farm worker	–	32	captain
Mário Tomé	4	toolmaker	–	34	captain
Pires Veloso	4	school teacher	–	48	lieutenant-colonel

* + indicate degree of anti-regime political activity

'direct democracy'. The nature of this democracy ranged from the anarcho-populists' view of people taking power, creating their own revolution and radically changing society, through a Marxist–Leninist vision to a direct democracy, based upon autonomy of the local authorities in a mixed economy. All the officers felt that the conditions in Portugal prior to the coup d'état needed radically changing, and that, sooner or later, this would involve nationalisations and an Agrarian Reform of some kind.

Opinions differed as to the method, timing and extent of these changes.

The title of this sub-section includes the rank of captain. Although a number of important officers were above this rank at the time of the coup (see table 3), many of their actions embodied the spirit of the Movement of Captains. There was an esprit de corps of young men working together, often idealistically, in attempts to bring about changes in society. The Movement of Captains soon changed from a body of men making professional protests to one making political protests. The spirit often appeared at critical moments in the revolution when ties of comradeship amongst the young officers would often override different ideological positions.

The military's love of order and discipline also influenced the behaviour of the captains. This is seen in the interviews time and time again as they complain about the anarchy in the country and the lack of orderly progression of the revolution. Even political parties were often anathema to these men of action. They seemed unaware that, in a country without any democratic experience, the civilian parties would take time to develop and create their own political identity. The newly formed political parties were in a way overshadowed at the beginning by the political importance of the MFA. Before they could emerge as independent parties, they realised that they had to limit and control the involvement of the military in Portuguese politics. The officers felt they had an important job on their hands, which was the democratisation of the country along the lines of the MFA Programme. They wanted to carry this out as quickly as possible, but were often frustrated by what they saw as devious tactics being used by the civilian parties, as the parties fought amongst themselves and with the military in attempts to gain power. Apart from the PCP, the civilian parties would often use the prestige of the MFA amongst the people to gain popular support. Initially, all the parties avoided dealing with any controversial social problems, pre-ferring to leave these to COPCON. Later, as they grew stronger and more self-assured, they deliberately set about curbing the powers of the military. (Appendix 9 plots the rise and fall of the military in government: by the time of the second constitutional government there was only one member of the armed forces in Soares's government.)

The special role that the PCP had with the officers is apparent from the interviews. Many officers were frightened of the communists infiltrating the armed forces (see Pires Veloso interview) and exerting their influence upon the lower ranks and sympathetic officers. They imagined that the PCP might attempt to take over the country through the army. The communists were very much in evidence since they controlled the media. There was a strong pro-PCP line taken by the Gonçalves governments and the propaganda machinery of the Fifth Division at one stage was very pro-communist. The communists held positions of power in trade unions, local authorities and a variety of bodies, such as neighbourhood committees, workers' assemblies and so on. The officers were further apprehensive of the PCP, since, following the coup d'état, the number of party members increased tenfold. The party became less disciplined and was often blamed by the military for actions carried out by its members who, through enthusiasm or other motives, were not always following the communist party line.

The interviews also show that the officers were taken aback by the mass movement that followed the coup d'état. Although in sympathy with the demands of the mass movement, they nearly all wanted a 'programmed revolution' carried out in an orderly way so that their positions within it were well-defined. This was also the PCP's position. Both the military and the PCP often found themselves chasing the mass movement. For the military, this meant that sometimes they produced a wave of legislation following changes that had already taken place, such as the laws covering house occupations and the Agrarian Reform. The PCP was concerned, as it did not want to be seen trailing after the ultra left, but at the same time it did not want to lose support from the substantial middle-class sector of Portuguese society, which was often alienated by the mass movement. The PCP quickly realised that whoever controlled this sector had power within Portuguese politics. In the end, they were unable to gain support from this sector. The PS emerged as the victor, and the PCP became the scapegoat.

The way in which the officers answered the questions about 25 November was crucial in understanding the officers' current political positions. For the populists and those committed to the idea of the mass movement, 25 November represented the end of the revolution. For the Group of Nine this was the coup that pre-empted a right-wing take-over and stopped the spread of anarchy throughout the country. The Group wanted to extend the revolution to the rest of the people by regaining the confidence of the middle classes. Their vision was of a true social democracy. The results of their coup were not to their liking, however. After the coup, all the Group of Nine lost power and their dreams of direct democracy were never realised. In their replies to the questions on 25 November, the officers were not as forthcoming as they might have been. Perhaps this was due to their present dissatisfaction with the outcome of the coup they had brought about.

The officers were also not as open as they might have been in replies to questions about the role of the Church in the revolution. From recently published material the Church was strongly involved in the setting up of the Maria de Fonte Movement, which blew up several of the local headquarters of the PCP and the MDP/CDE. Only a few officers mentioned this, although probably most of them were aware of it. Furthermore, in the north of the country, the Church played a political role by stating that certain political parties should not be voted for. Few officers drew attention to this.

There was a reluctance by some officers to discuss the degree of foreign intervention in the revolution, even though there was circumstantial evidence that suggested it had occurred. For example, there was the economic boycott of the country by other western powers that suddenly stopped after the 25 November coup, when money began to flow back into Portugal. There was the US ambassador in Portugal during the revolution who, on his return to America, was appointed second in command of the CIA. There were also close links between Nixon and Spínola. The PS had ties with the SDP of West Germany and the PCP with the Soviet Union. None of those interviewed offered specific information which substantiated or denied this evidence.

The truthfulness of the captains' replies to the questionnaire can be assessed, since all of them were, more or less, answering the same set of questions. There were few contradictions and all appeared to answer sincerely. The interviews also show that interpretations of the key events of the revolution were, on the whole, similar. Where there were differences in interpretation, this was usually due to the ideological position of the officer. Overall, the interviews gave a coherent story of the Portuguese revolution carried out by the MFA and the Portuguese people.

THE AFTERMATH: RESULTS OF THE THREE YEARS OF POLITICAL UPHEAVAL

In almost three years major changes had occurred in Portugal. Some of these changes have been referred to as the 'three d's': decolonisation, democratic freedom, and dismantling of the old economic monopolies. There were other important changes such as the Agrarian Reform and, perhaps most important of all, the birth of political awareness amongst the majority of the Portuguese people.

Decolonisation caused the MFA and the Portuguese people a number of problems. Because of the indiscipline that occurred within the armed forces immediately after the 25 April coup the army was effectively in disarray. This meant that the policing role of the army was virtually non-existent: the soldiers wanted to leave Africa and return home as quickly as possible. Thus, the transition to colonial independence was brought about in the absence of a strong Portuguese military presence.

There were different problems in different colonies. In the colonies where there were few white settlers, as in Guinea-Bissau, São Tomé and the Cape Verde Islands, decolonisation went smoothly. However, in Mozambique and Angola it was a different story. Mozambique had only one liberation movement and negotiations with this movement were reasonably straightforward. Nevertheless, the white settlers continuously tried to hamper the emergence of Mozambique as an independent nation: when they saw that independence was inevitable, they left the country in their thousands for Portugal. Angola had three liberation movements and the situation was made even worse in that all three movements had outside help with troops, ammunition and supplies. The movements all had strong internal followings and there was no common political ground. They all wanted decolonisation, but the result was a complicated civil war amongst the three liberation movements. Owing to outside intervention in the three liberation movements, Portugal came under a lot of international pressure and the MFA and the provisional governments were not really free to pursue their own policy. This explains why Portugal did not recognise Angola's independence until the end of February 1976, although Angola had declared itself an independent nation on 11 November 1975 in accord with the Alvor agreement (see chronology). The white settlers in Angola also tried to oppose the independence of Angola. As in Mozambique, once independence became certain, the settlers poured back to Portugal. From both countries hundreds of thousands of settlers returned to the cities and towns in Portugal, swelling them almost to bursting point. Most of them had left everything they owned behind. Not surprisingly these *retornados*, as they were known, resented the MFA and its decolonisation programme and felt that they had been betrayed by Portugal. On arrival, they were often placed in huge, makeshift refugee camps that were created on the outskirts of all the big cities. There was an intense housing shortage, and the new provisional governments had yet to organise the social services. There was also an economic crisis and high unemployment. Most of the retornados found themselves living in overcrowded settlements without money, work and homes. There was a scheme for accommodating some of them in tourist hotels inside the resorts and certain amounts of money were handed out by the governments for social subsistence and also to help them set up small businesses. They experienced tremendous hardship and it is remarkable that the retornados did not form an effective anti-revolutionary political force. Indeed their effect on the political evolution of Portugal was small. By 1984, most of them have been absorbed into Portuguese society and they now represent an important sector of the economy, especially in the area of small businesses.

At the end of three years, democratic freedom was firmly established in Portugal. Of this there is no doubt. The MFA had succeeded in implementing one of the main aims of its programme (see appendix 1, A2a, MFA Programme). The new Constitution established that everyone over the age of eighteen has the vote; there should be no discrimination on the basis of race, sex or religion; that there should be freedom of speech; right of assembly and a totally free media. The participation of the Portuguese in the political and social life of the country was ensured by their having free access to parliament and the setting up of collective, elected bodies in schools, universities and most other institutions. These bodies have either executive or consultative or deliberative powers. Moreover, the giving of autonomy to the local authorities made possible the participation of citizens in local government. Free trade unions represent the workers and the right to strike is guaranteed by the Constitution, as is the right to receive free education, free medical care and an old age pension.

Democracy also meant the establishment of a number of new political parties. These parties, as is often the case in the other western democracies, tend to represent different sectors of society and different regions of the country. The four main political parties, the PCP, PS, PPD/PSD and CDS, are discussed in some detail in part 3. Some of the other minor parties were, for example, the MDP/CDE and the UDP. The MDP/CDE was initially established as an electoral front in Salazar's time and included supporters amongst socialists and communists. Following the 25 April coup, the MDP/CDE became a political party. Most of the socialists and communists left and in 1984 it was a Marxist party with a following in the Algarve and in the main towns amongst students and intellectuals. The UDP has a Marxist–Leninist philosophy with a following from university students, and workers in the cities of Lisbon and Setubal. With the exception of the PCP, all the other parties are centred in Lisbon. Party supporters outside Lisbon have little or no say as to how their parties are run.

The dismantling of the old economic empires was an inevitable result of the nationalisations carried out by the Gonçalves government and the introduction of government employees into a large number of Portuguese institutions. The Soares government in 1976 started a policy later followed by other governments of appointing technocrats to manage the public sector. Many of these technocrats had had important positions in the old regime. The purging of the national institutions was one of the main aims of the MFA Programme (see appendix 1, A2h; Final Considerations, C2). *Saneamentos*, as it is known, meant that many people were expelled or suspended from their posts on the basis of being either corrupt, incompetent or supporters of the old regime. The number of purges, however, was not sufficient to change the main institutions. For example, the armed forces, the universities, the judiciary, the police force and the civil service were not drastically changed. When the climate was right, following the 25 November coup, most of those who had been purged were reinstated. Reinstatement was often made easier because purging had been carried out in a random and arbitrary manner. It often reflected personal grudges and political infighting rather than an attempt to restructure the whole of Portuguese society.

The Agrarian Reform caused a clear redistribution of land in a specific zone. This zone, known as the ZIRA (Zona de Intervenção da Reforma Agrária, Zone of Intervention of the Agrarian Reform), started south of the river Tagus and reached down to the Algarve. It represented about 40 per cent of the total land area of Portugal and was just over half of the arable land. At the peak of the land occupations, one-third of the land in this zone was expropriated by the workers. By the end of 1976, the employment of agricultural workers had trebled in this area (see appendix 8) when compared to the pre-25 April 1974 coup figure. In 1976 the Soares government passed the so-called 'Barreto's law', which reduced by half the expropriated land in the ZIRA. The effects of this law were not really felt in 1976 and its repercussions were only to occur in more recent periods.

3 The post-revolutionary period, 1977–84

Part 3 offers an analysis of the major socio-political changes that have occurred since the revolution up to 1984. This is followed by a chronology which acts as a signpost and a point of reference for that period. The chronology ends at the official celebration that marked ten years on from the 25 April 1974 coup d'état.

Revolutionary transformations

The economic, social and political changes of the post-revolutionary period have to be understood within the context of the transformations that took place during the revolution. It was unfortunate for the Portuguese that their revolution occurred during an intense world-wide recession. The revolution ended on 23 July 1976 with the formation of the first constitutional parliament, that followed democratic elections that had taken place on 25 April 1976. By then, Portugal had undergone intense economic, social and political changes.

In terms of the economy, one of the major changes was that the old economic monoliths had been dismantled and large sectors of the economy nationalised (about a quarter of the GNP). Further, the workers had become more organised, powerful and politically aware, forming trade unions. With the support of the MFA, they had brought about a real distribution of wealth. They had also brought about an increase in the total income of the labour force (from 51 per cent of the total national income in 1973 to 66 per cent in 1976). By expropriating farms in southern Portugal, they had achieved some redistribution of land. However, by 1975, the wage increases obtained just after the coup d'état in 1974 were almost cancelled out by inflation, and, by the time the first constitutional government was in operation in 1976, real wages were falling.

The balance of payments took a sharp dip from a surplus in

1972 to a negative value in the latter part of 1973. By the end of 1974, it was out of balance by 823 million US dollars, and by 1976, this had increased to one and a quarter billion US dollars. This rapid fall in the balance of payments was partly due to a reduction in the capital sent back to Portugal by the immigrant workers, frightened by the 1974 coup d'état, partly due to the increased international price of oil and the world-wide recession, and partly due to reduced exports and tourism. Austerity measures were introduced by the sixth provisional government in an attempt to redress the balance. These measures included a wage freeze, new regulations to encourage foreign investment and increases in taxation.

In the short term, the negative balance of payments could have been paid for with Portugal's huge gold reserves, since, under Salazar, reserves of some 865 tons had been accrued. But, in 1976, reluctant to spend gold, Soares's first constitutional government applied to a consortium for a loan. (As we shall see later, in the following years up to 1984 IMF loans were to be applied for. With the application of a number of austerity measures, the country was able, by 1979, to redress its balance of payments. However, by 1980, the balance of payments became negative again and, by 1982, it was negative by some 3.2 thousand million US dollars.)

Extensive social changes had occurred following the revolution, largely as a result of the purging of the old institutions (saneamento; see part 2). Although many of these changes were to be reversed by the end of 1976, those which remained, and still persisted in 1984, were legislated mainly by the first and second constitutional governments. These changes especially occurred in the laws governing education and health.

By 1976, the political changes were without doubt far-reaching. A new democratic constitution had been produced and enacted; political power was now firmly in the hands of the civilians and four major parties emerged. These were, from left to right: the PCP, the PS, the PPD/PSD and the CDS. Subsequent attempts to create other parties, either to the left or to the right of these, generally failed. The UDP, a Marxist–Leninist party to the left of the PCP, managed to have one member of parliament up to the 1983 elections and the PPM managed to obtain a few members of parliament, only by forming an alliance with the CDS and the PPD/PSD. The trade union movement by 1976 had also emerged as a powerful political force.

The parties, 1976–84

Only the first constitutional government was a one-party government and then the PS was in the minority. Since 1976, all governments have been either coalition governments or governments of presidential initiative. A brief analysis of the four main political parties that emerged after the revolution is necessary, if the political alignments and coalitions are to be understood. Moreover, the political parties are the corner-stones of the country's new democracy, so a review of the history and ideology of the parties is essential for an understanding of contemporary Portuguese political life. The order of presenting the parties is from the left of the political spectrum through to the right.

THE PCP

The PCP was a party that had always been the recognised opposition to the old regime and, as such, enjoyed special status after the coup. It is by far the oldest party, founded on 6 March 1921. Its present leader, Álvaro Cunhal, was appointed general secretary in 1961, when the party was reorganised. It then grew and became an increasingly powerful political force, especially among the industrial working class and the agricultural workers in the Alentejo region. Under Salazar, Cunhal spent a total of thirteen years in prison, eight of these in solitary confinement. Most of the other members of the central committee are of working-class origin and, like Cunhal, spent long periods in prison. Throughout the 1960s, 1970s and 1980s, the PCP argued that Portugal lacked a sufficiently large, alienated working class in order to bring about any effective change along the party's own ideological lines. To win over the middle classes to its cause was the background of party political strategy. This was one of the main reasons why it clashed with the far left and explains much of its behaviour during the course of the revolution.

Until 1974, the PCP was an underground party, but, from 1960 onwards, it played a progressively more dominant role in organising working-class protest and influencing student politics.

Since the 1940s, the PCP has also been important in organising occasional electoral fronts that were created whenever Salazar or Caetano called an 'election'. Of these electoral fronts, the CDE, which fought the elections of 1969 and 1973, was probably the most important, since it united a large section of the Portuguese left, which included communists, socialists, independents and left-wing Catholics. As the CDE had fought elections prior to 1974, following the coup there already existed a political infra-structure which meant that, in the post-coup period, the CDE was immediately ready to play a key political role, particularly when it came to obtaining power at the local government level.

Following the 25 April 1974 coup, the membership of the PCP grew rapidly. By May 1974, it had 32 local branch headquarters. By August 1974, it had 74 and, by September 1974, the number had risen to 136 local headquarters, which were to be found throughout the whole country. It is claimed that, during the eight-month post-coup period, PCP membership grew ten-fold so that, by the end of 1976, it stood at 115,000. Many of the leading members of the other left-of-centre parties have, at one time or another, been members of the PCP, for example, Mário Soares, the current leader of the PS.

The position of the PCP amongst the working class grew when, as a result of Marcello Caetano's appointment as prime minister, a certain degree of liberalisation took place in Portuguese politics. In the 1960s the Caetano regime allowed trade union representa-tives to be freely elected with the result that communists openly became trade union leaders. In 1970 the communist-influenced trade unions set up an association called the Intersindical, to which each union elected representatives. However, the liberali-sation by Caetano's regime was only short-lived and Intersindical had to go underground. It emerged again after the 1974 coup and claimed to be the only legitimate representative of the trade union movement. In the weeks that followed the 25 April coup, Intersindical opened branches in practically every district in the country, claiming to be the successor to CGT; it called itself CGTP/Inter.

The CGT had originally been formed in 1919 from the anarcho-sindicalist UON (União Operária Nacional, National Workers' Union). Salazar was quick to ban the CGT and organise the trade union movement around the *sindicatos* (see part 1). In

April 1975 (see part 1, chronology) the Council of the Revolution passed a law, Unicidade Sindical, which established the principle of one trade, one trade union and created the communist-dominated CGTP/Inter. as the sole representative of the Portuguese trade union movement. This privileged position of CGTP/Inter. was immediately challenged by the PS even before the law was passed and, as a result of this challenge, the new Constitution which came into effect in 1976 contained provisions for setting up of trade unions outside the CGTP/Inter. umbrella. The new Constitution allowed the organisation of trade unions based upon political affiliations and, in 1979, a trade union confederation which had clear associations with the PS and the PSD was created. This was the UGT (União Geral dos Trabalhadores, General Union of Workers).

In the post-coup period, the PCP openly aligned itself with the MFA until its demise, and was a supporter of the Council of the Revolution until it was dissolved. In the period from the first constitutional government in 1976 until 1984, lacking support in the air force, army and navy, and with only about a 20 per cent following among the Portuguese people, the PCP tended to play a defensive role. It opposed amendments to the Constitution and was against changes in the Agrarian Reform laws and denationalisation. It opposed negotiations with the IMF and was against application for entry into the EEC. It argued for a closed economy and an economic and political association with Portugal's former African colonies.

In 1984 the PCP was a highly organised party with a strong hierarchy that was systematically persecuted under Salazar. It followed the Moscow line, was against the extreme left and actively expelled any dissenting members. In addition to its traditional following among the industrial working class and the farm workers in the Alentejo region, the communists had a lot of power at local government level and a strong following among middle-class intellectuals. The party played a leading role in the cultural life of the country.

THE PS

The Socialist Party was formally created in West Germany in April 1973 with Mário Soares as its general secretary. Its origins were the ASP (Acção Socialista Portuguesa, Socialist Portuguese Action), which was formed in Geneva in April 1964, and which enrolled in the Socialist International in 1972. The PS did not have a following in Portugal until after the 1974 coup, but then grew rapidly. Soares returned to Portugal on 27 April 1974 and, on 2 May, was sent by Spínola to the western democratic countries in an attempt to obtain official recognition of the new regime. By the end of 1974, Soares had dramatically increased the PS following, mainly by bringing into the party, by clever negotiations, many prominent figures of the opposition. Some of them were leaders of political groups. For example, Manuel Serra, leader of the MSP (Movimento Socialista Popular, Popular Socialist Movement), was absorbed into the PS, along with many of his supporters. The party membership further increased in the early part of 1975 when the PS opposed the Unicidade Sindical law and, from then onwards, the PS was to be seen as one of the main opponents of the PCP.

Because the party has absorbed many different factions of the opposition to the Salazar/Caetano regime, it has been heterogeneous and has also lacked a strong party organisation. Its supporters have not always been loyal (see chronology for marked variations of the PS vote) and its following has been very much greater than its party membership, as it appealed to a wide section of left of centre votes. In April 1975, when the results of the elections for the Constitutional Assembly were made known, the PS realised that it had greater electoral support among the people than had the PCP. (It has always polled more votes than the PCP, although its percentages were less consistent than those obtained by the communists.)

During the decade following the 1974 coup, the PS became strongly anti-communist as it made a bid for power. It moved from its original 'no coalition' stance (the first two constitutional governments) to become a party that would form coalitions in order to stay in power. In 1984 the PS was a member of the Socialist International, the Confederation of European Social Democrats and Socialists and had strong links with the German Social Democratic Party. It could be likened to the right wing of the British Labour Party. Its following came from all sectors of Portuguese society, mainly within the urban areas, and its popularity often reflected the degree of popularity of the other political parties, in that it often received large numbers of tactical votes.

THE PPD/PSD

The PPD was formed on 3 May 1974. Its founders were Sá Carneiro, Francisco Pinto Balsemão, Magalhães Mota and Correia da Cunha and it had from the start the support of members of the SEDES group. All had been members of the liberal wing of parliament in Caetano's regime, and they formed the party in order to fill the centre/right vacuum, created in Portuguese politics after the 1974 coup. In October 1976 the PPD changed its name to the PSD, but continued to represent itself as the PPD/PSD. Until the formation of the AD (Aliança Democrática, Democratic Alliance) in 1979, it was a party split by internal wranglings. Its leader, Sá Carneiro, resigned first in mid-1974 owing to ill health, and, after resigning again because of internal disputes, he returned in June 1978 to take the leadership of the party. A charismatic figure, he led the PPD/PSD into an alliance (AD) with the CDS and PPM, correctly predicting that the alliance would win a majority in parliament. He was elected prime minister in 1979 and again, with an increased majority, in 1980. Under his leadership, the PPD moved more to the right and tried to bring about a revision of the Constitution in order to reverse the political and social changes that had occurred during the revolution. He died in an aeroplane crash in December 1980, just before the presidential elections in which the AD candidate, Soares Carneiro, lost to Ramalho Eanes. After Sá Carneiro's death, the PPD/PSD elected Francisco Pinto Balsemão as its leader and he managed to revise the Constitution after negotiations with the PS. However, Balsemão was unable to keep the PSD united. He resigned twice from government. Since no clear leader emerged, following his resignation, President Eanes called a general election in 1983. The AD collapsed just before these elections. Following the elections, the PPD/PSD was able to stay in power by forming a new coalition with the PS which was known informally as the 'centre-block alliance'.

In the post-1974 coup decade, the party was even more anti-communist than the PS. It received its support from the professional and managerial sectors of Portuguese society, as well as from small farm owners, shopkeepers and owners of small businesses. It had a strong following among the Catholics in the north and centre of Portugal and the off-shore islands of the Azores and Madeira. The party tried and failed to join the Socialist International and the Confederation of European Social Democrats and Socialists. In 1980 it developed ties with the German Liberal Party and could be likened to the British Liberal/ SDP alliance.

The CDS was founded in July 1974 under the leadership of Freitas do Amaral at the instigation of General Spínola, who was alarmed by the lack of non-socialist parties in Portugal. From that date onwards, it grew, but with its following restricted to the religious north of the country. The party voted against the first Constitution and did not sign the second MFA–Parties Pact (see part 2). Although having a smaller following than the PCP, it was in government for a long period, first as a partner of the PS in the second constitutional government, and then as a member of the AD. Its leader, Freitas do Amaral, resigned in 1983, possibly with the intention of competing in the presidential elections, and his departure was one of the causes of the fall of the AD.

The CDS policies were conservative and aimed at dismantling the socialist policies, brought into effect by the 1974 coup and the Gonçalvist governments. It was a party of the property-owning, professional middle and upper classes and drew additional support from right-wing Catholics. It had a strong influence among many managers in the private and public sector, since many of these appointments were political and made when the CDS was in power. The party had links with the European Democratic Union, the Federation of Conservative and Christian Democratic Parties of Western Europe and a strong association with the Confederation of Portuguese Farmers (CAP). Its political outlook was similar to the right-wing of the British Conservative Party of the early 1980s.

The economy: an overview, 1974–6

Any analysis of the rise and fall of the governments that took place between 1976 and 1984 should include a study of the

Portuguese economy. For, one of the main concerns of all the governments was to attempt to set the economy in order. However, post-revolutionary economic events cannot be considered in isolation, so the economic changes that took place prior to 1976 need first to be described.

The year 1974 saw the world in recession and Portugal in revolution. It is probable that this recession would have created an economic slump in Portugal, regardless of any revolution. Following the 1974 coup, many employers and owners became afraid and fled the country with their capital, often leaving behind their factories without any effective management. In 1974 cash inflow from abroad from both emigrants and tourism abruptly ceased, foreign investment was markedly reduced (four-fifths down on the pre-revolutionary figure), and some countries even actively boycotted Portuguese exports. These factors, coupled with the political upheaval, and considerable unrest among the workers, created a dramatic disruption in the industrial activity of the country. Essentially, the first five provisional governments attempted to meet the demands of the workers and, at the same time, implement conventional anti-inflationary economic policies.

In the last days of May 1974 a minimum wage of 3,300 escudos a month was introduced for all wage earners, except farm and rail workers, while prices, rents and wages were frozen until the end of July. During July, the freeze was partially relaxed, but limits on prices and profits were imposed. In September, new measures were introduced to increase the availability of accommodation and to freeze rents, and in the same month the three central banks were nationalised. In October, the previous regime's laws controlling restrictive industrial investment were abolished (see part 1) and, in November, state intervention in private firms was introduced with the aim of giving aid to companies in financial difficulties. In December 1974 a law was passed allowing employers to form associations like the CIP, but regulations were also passed protecting workers' rights against dismissal.

By the middle of 1975 all the banks, insurance companies and transport systems had been nationalised, the Agrarian Reform laws passed, unemployment benefit had been introduced for everyone and the minimum wage increased to 4,000 escudos a month. By the end of the year, the petrochemical industry, the brewing industry and the old economic monolith, CUF, had all been nationalised. But, following 25 November 1975, collective bargaining was suspended which resulted in a wage freeze, and, in December 1975, petrol prices were raised considerably. Compensation in the form of treasury bonds was given to previous shareholders of the recently nationalised banks.

On 10 April 1976 the new Portuguese Constitution came into effect. The Constitution was essentially socialist, but nevertheless aimed at a mixed economy with the state being the major partner. It laid down certain post-coup political changes that were to be considered irreversible, for example, the principle of collectivisation and the dismantling of the old economic monoliths and the large agricultural estates that were often owned by the absentee landlords. By the beginning of the summer of 1976, the Agrarian Reform and collective bargaining had been regulated. With the Agrarian Reform, it was decided that land areas under 30 hectares could not be expropriated, the limits of the Agrarian Reform Zone were defined and regulations which allowed landowners to keep part of their expropriated land were passed. A foreign investment code was produced, along with a new export credit scheme. The regulations defining state intervention in the private sector were revised and methods were made available for the calculation of compensation for previous shareholders in the nationalised industries. By the end of the year, a national prices and incomes board had been set up, direct taxation had been increased and a surtax imposed on imported goods.

Governments and the economy, 1976–84

From the creation of a new Constitution in April 1976 until April 1984 Portugal saw the rise and fall of nine constitutional governments. The first two of these were transitional in the sense that they presided over the transition period to democratically elected civilian governments. The next three governments were governments of presidential initiative. They arose during a period when the parties refused to collaborate with one another and produce a stable government. It was as if the President wished the parties to have a breathing space so that they could regroup and reorganise in order to create effective, stable parliamentary parties. The problems were that two of the parties, the PSD and the CDS, were still struggling to establish their identity, while the PS did not wish to risk an alliance with the PCP, frightened that it could easily lose its own identity through the activities of the efficient, dedicated Communist Party members. The PCP was well-organised and stable, but did not have the electoral support it had hoped for.

The three governments that followed the presidential initiative governments were attempts by the right to reverse the revolutionary changes and create a free-market economy. These governments particularly wanted to see a change in the left-wing bias that had been built into the new Constitution. The ninth government resulted in the so-called 'centre-block coalition' of the PS and the PSD. This alliance had always been a possibility, since both are social democrat parties. President Eanes was always in favour of this alliance, but it only became politically possible after the 1983 elections. So, to summarise:

1.   The transition governments
      The first constitutional government (Soares)
      The second constitutional government (Soares)
2.   Presidential initiative governments
      The third constitutional government (Nobre da Costa)
      The fourth constitutional government (Mota Pinto)
      The fifth constitutional government (Maria Pintasilgo)
3.   The 'backlash' governments
      The sixth constitutional government (Sá Carneiro)
      The seventh constitutional government (Pinto Balsemão)
      The eighth constitutional government (Pinto Balsemão)
4.   The centre block (*bloco central*)
      The ninth constitutional government (Soares)

THE TRANSITION GOVERNMENTS

These governments had to hand over control to the civilians and had to deal with the military playing an overseeing role. They did not want to alienate the left, but at the same time, since they were supported by the electorate from the centre and the right, they could not only pass left-wing legislation. In the end, their ability to manoeuvre was constrained by the economic situation. The first government opened the negotiations with the EEC. These negotiations were to last almost ten years and the initial application to join the European Community was tantamount to a rejection of the radical socialist path that had been laid down in both MFA–Parties pacts.

Proudly alone, 23 July 1976–9 December 1977

On 23 July 1976 Portugal had its first constitutional government. It was a minority PS government under the premiership of Mário Soares, who insisted on a 'no-coalition', one party approach, in line with his pre-election campaign promises. Because he led a minority government, Soares had to seek support from the PCP or the PSD, which he did according to the nature of the legislation.

Although by July 1976 the GDP had not substantially decreased from its pre-revolutionary figure (despite nationalisations, three-quarters of the GDP was still produced by the private sector), there were serious economic problems. Inflation was about 25 per cent, unemployment was about 15 per cent, the balance of trade showed a deficit (following a pre-revolutionary trend) and the economy had had to absorb several hundreds of thousands of Portuguese returning from the colonies. The Soares government's response was to introduce a programme of economic austerity and to call for political restraint on the part of the workers. The programme cut back aid to ailing nationalised and private firms and increased prices of the service industries and direct taxation. Surtaxes were also put on imported goods, but, by the end of 1976, there was little improvement in the economy. In an attempt to improve the balance of payments situation, the escudo was devalued by 15 per cent and a crawling-peg devaluation of 1 per cent per month was introduced. The bank rate was also increased by 1 per cent to reduce credit and slow down growth, and prices of some essential goods were unfrozen. In order to relieve some of the hardships brought about by these measures, the government increased a minimum industrial wage to 4,500 escudos a month. They also created a special measure known as *cabaz de compras* (the 'shopping basket'). This was a list of some thirty essential goods which the government intended to subsidise, or regulate the supply of, in order to fix their prices at a reasonably low level for a set period.

The preceding economic measures were not sufficient to reduce the negative balance of payments. In order to prevent Portugal's gold reserves from being run down, Soares's government borrowed money from abroad. By the end of 1977, it had obtained short-term loans of more than one billion US dollars from European banks and the IMF. In the summer of 1977, the government was forced to approach the IMF in order to release a 750 million US dollar medium-term loan from an international consortium (see chronology). The conditions imposed by the IMF involved further unpopular measures aimed at reducing growth, inflation and the negative balance of payments. The minority government needed to show that it was in control of the country in order to negotiate the 50 million IMF stand-by credit (see chronology). However, on 8 December 1977, Soares's government lost the vote of confidence aimed at restoring its credibility, and it fell. The PCP, for the first time, voted with the opposition.

The odd couple, 23 January–28 July 1978

President Eanes asked Soares to form another government. After a series of negotiations, Mário Soares reached an agreement with the CDS whereby some CDS leaders would participate in government. In return, the CDS would give its support in passing a common legislative programme. This association of two rather unlikely political partners from the centre left and right of Portuguese politics seemed incongruous. Even in 1984, the exact reasons for their association were still unknown. One theory is that the CDS was the only party which would form an association, as it wished to obtain political power. Another possibility is that Mário Soares, recognising a powerful equal in Sá Carneiro, the leader of the PSD, did not favour any association with that party. In order to uphold Soares's election pledge of no-coalition, the new government was not officially known as a PS/CDS coalition.

On 13 April 1978 a new austerity budget was introduced which contained some of the measures advocated by the IMF. On 9 May 1978 an agreement was signed by the IMF and, through clever use of the overseas press and with the support of the West German government, the second constitutional government was able to obtain better IMF terms than those originally demanded. The IMF loan allowed the government access to a medium-term loan of some 750 million US dollars at reasonable rates, which would enable the government to pay back its short-term loan. Its intention also was to relieve the negative balance of payments and obtain another long-term loan from private foreign banks of some half a billion US dollars.

Although the agreement with the IMF helped stabilise the economic situation, political instability continued as politicians from the PS and CDS clashed over the Agrarian Reform. The CDS wanted a quick and full implementation of the legislation proposed by Antonio Barreto (see part 2, chronology), but the PS was afraid that rapid implementation would dramatically increase unemployment in the Alentejo region. On 24 July 1978 the CDS withdrew its members and support from the government, allegedly because of these problems over the Agrarian Reform. However, it has subsequently been argued that the reason it withdrew support was because it wanted to re-establish itself as the right-wing party. Out of government, Sá Carneiro and the PSD had been effective in their attacks on the PS/CDS arrangement and they were attracting many would-be CDS supporters. Out of office, the CDS hoped to recover its more right-wing following.

Without the CDS, Soares said he would continue as prime minister of a minority government. The economic policies of the second government had been successful in reducing the negative balance of payments to zero. This was achieved at the cost of a slow-down in the rate of growth, an increase in domestic prices and a reduction of capital investment.

GOVERNMENTS OF PRESIDENTIAL INITIATIVE

These governments were created by the President, since the parliamentary parties were unable to form a stable government. President Eanes was in favour of a PS/PSD coalition, as was the leadership of the PSD. However, the PS opposed it. The Constitution allowed the President to create governments, however, as soon as he exercised this prerogative, the parties refused to give him their support and, despite extensive consultations with the parties, President Eanes was unable to appoint a really viable government. The civilian parties felt that parliament was being threatened and losing power to the presidential office. The result was three governments in quick succession.

The technocrat government, 29 August–15 September 1978

It came as something of a surprise when President Eanes dismissed Soares and the second constitutional government. Then, in a televised speech, he proposed three possible solutions to the crisis. One, that there could be a setting-up of a coalition with a stable parliamentary majority; two, the setting-up of a non-party government with the support of the majority in parliament; or three, the dissolution of parliament and the holding of new parliamentary elections.

The parties could not agree on the composition of a coalition. Eanes decided it was too early to hold a general election and asked a technocrat, Nobre da Costa, to form a government. The government was formed and this 'technocrat government' was sworn in on 29 August 1978. The programme which was presented to parliament on 7 September was essentially similar to the austerity package of the second constitutional government. The parliament rejected the programme when the PS and CDS voted together against the programme. They clearly saw the formation of the Nobre da Costa government as an attempt by the President to reduce the power of the parties. As Mário Soares said at that time, 'It is impossible to govern against the parties.' Nobre da Costa's government, nevertheless, acting in a caretaker role, implemented the laws passed by the first two constitutional governments.

The consensus government, 22 November 1978– 11 June 1979

With the failure of the Nobre da Costa government to pass its programme, President Eanes went back to the parties and asked them to propose someone who would be acceptable to them all. After much consultation, it was agreed that a Coimbra university law professor, Mota Pinto, should be the new prime minister. His cabinet was not much different from Nobre da Costa's, but his policies were slightly more to the right. Pinto's programme was accepted in parliament; the PS abstained in the vote, while the PCP voted against the programme.

The more right-wing aspects of Mota Pinto's policies were

222   *The post-revolutionary period*

particularly felt in the Agrarian Reform Zone. Land was returned to previous landowners, rents were increased on existing collectives and co-operatives and bank credit to these co-operatives was reduced.

In the spring of 1979, the 50 million dollar stand-by credit from the IMF was up for renegotiation. By then, the negative balance of payments had steadily been reduced to almost zero and at the same time growth had been limited. This was a result of the monetarist policies implemented by all the constitutional governments in accordance with the original conditions proposed by the IMF. In the new negotiations, the IMF, content that the current balance of payments had been equilibrated, demanded that there should be a reduction in the budget deficit from 10 per cent to 7 per cent of the GDP. Pinto's government attempted to achieve this by withdrawing support from some 300 firms, increasing taxes on the price of fuel and by reducing the subsidy to the 'shopping basket' by 21 per cent. By then, the 'basket' accounted for some 11 per cent of the government's budget expenses. These unpopular measures were narrowly defeated in parliament in March, which resulted in the fall of the Mota Pinto government. The PSD became split at this time: one faction, led by Sá Carneiro, voted against these measures in an attempt to bring down the government and force new parliamentary elections, in the hope that they would gain a majority; the rest of the PSD sided with the CDS and voted for the government. After this defeat, Mota Pinto offered his resignation, but the President refused to accept it!

During May the CGTP/Inter. and UGT separately organised political strikes and demonstrations, aimed at bringing down Pinto's government. Although he managed to pass another budget, it was greatly altered, after having passed through the committee stages of parliament. Opposition to his government had continued to grow amongst the unions, socialists and communists. Finally, in June, Pinto resigned before the PS and the PCP could present a motion of censure.

The caretaker government, 31 July–27 December 1979

President Eanes now accepted Pinto's resignation and declared that general elections would be held later in the year. He set up a caretaker government with Maria de Lurdes Pintasilgo as the prime minister. Previously, she had been the Portuguese ambassador to UNESCO. She was a trained engineer, a staunch Catholic and had been an advisor when the last five-year economic plan of Marcello Caetano's regime had been produced. Her government was considered more left-wing than the previous one and it had the support of the PS and the PCP. It increased the minimum wage and, after violence in the Agrarian Reform Zone, called a halt to the implementation of Barreto's law. Her government also cancelled the wage ceiling. It was unsuccessful in reducing the bank rate and escudo devaluation, because of opposition from the Bank of Portugal. It increased the price of fuel and essential goods.

THE BACKLASH GOVERNMENTS

The AD emerged when politicians realised, after analysing the electoral system and voting patterns, that a majority could be obtained in parliament, if certain parties were to get together and form an alliance. However, AD was presented to the people as an alliance that would remove the left-wing bias from the Constitution, so that a true free-market economy could be created and the country would be allowed to move to the right. But the alliance's failure to replace President Eanes with their own candidate at the presidential elections prevented AD from changing the Constitution in the way they would have liked. The alliance had to meet the demands of the PS and the ASDI (Associação Socialista Democrática Independente, Association of Independent Social Democrats) in order to obtain the two-thirds majority required to change the Constitution. Thus, the changes they made were not as far reaching as they hoped. The AD alliance eventually collapsed over a leadership crisis.

The launching of AD, 3 January–4 December 1980

The Constitution then stated that parliamentary elections had to be held every four years and, if elections were held before the four years were up, any elected parliament could exist only to the end of that four-year period. Thus, the 1979 parliamentary elections would be for a parliament that, under the Constitution, would have to be dissolved in 1980. Hence, any government elected in 1979 knew that its term would finish in 1980, and it had been argued, perhaps somewhat cynically, that any government elected during this interim period might act in such a way as to gain electoral support so that they would have a good chance of being re-elected for a four-year period.

The December parliamentary elections resulted in the predicted victory of the AD (see chronology below) and similar results were obtained in the local government elections. Sá Carneiro became the prime minister and in January 1980 his government was sworn in. For the first time since the 1974 coup a prime minister had a majority in government, even though he headed an alliance. He took charge of a country which still had a low growth rate and an unbalanced domestic budget and rising unemployment. However, the balance of payments had at least reached equilibrium.

The programme of the AD was based upon an economic recovery through stimulation and expansion of the private sector. However, the government's attempts to privatise some of the public sector were blocked by the Council of the Revolution, which declared that this legislation was unconstitutional. The Council of the Revolution based its decisions on reports it obtained from the Constitutional Commission, a body which consisted mainly of civilians and had been created in accordance with the Constitution.

In an attempt to by-pass these constitutional constraints, Sá Carneiro and the AD attempted to use referenda as a means of changing the Constitution. The alliance proposed that parliament should pass laws allowing referenda to take place. However, these laws were never passed, since the Constitution explicitly stated that referenda for such purposes were illegal. In an attempt to pass their referenda laws, the AD put up a candidate to oppose General Eanes in the forthcoming presidential elections.

The alliance, under Sá Carneiro, reinflated the economy. They revalued the escudo and reduced crawling-peg devaluation which resulted in cheaper imports and less competitive exports. They decreased direct taxation, increased pensions and, although initially increasing the price of the 'shopping basket', they then froze it for the whole of 1980. Their overall aim was to increase the GDP and private consumption. The consequence of such policies was an improved standard of living for the middle and upper classes, but the net result was a massive increase in the balance of payments deficit. The AD government benefited from the austerity measures carried out by a previous, more left-wing government.

Parliamentary elections in October 1980 saw the AD returned with an increased majority. The PS had formed an electoral front to fight these elections, the FRS (Frente Republicana Socialista, Republican Socialist Front). It was composed of the PS and ASDI and also one of its splinter groups the UEDS (União de Esquerda Democrática Socialista, Union of the Social Democratic Left). On 4 December 1980, Prime Minister Sá Carneiro died in an aeroplane crash and three days later the AD candidate, Soares Carneiro, was beaten by Ramalho Eanes in the presidential elections. Because of the death of the prime minister, the AD government resigned.

The Constitution changers and the leadership crisis, 9 January–14 August 1981 and 4 September 1981– 23 December 1982

One of the founder members of the PSD and director of the influential weekly Lisbon newspaper *Expresso*, Francisco Pinto Balsemão, became the PSD's new leader. In January 1981 the seventh government was sworn in, with Balsemão as the new prime minister. Its economic policies were, at least at the outset, unchanged from Sá Carneiro's government. Thus, in the first part of 1981, growth continued, but, as a result of the simultaneous increase in inflation, and their policy of reduced devaluation, imports continued to increase sharply, while exports fell. The result was a continued downward trend in the balance of payments so that by the end of the year the imbalance had reached some 2.7 billion US dollars. The government was forced to take action and in December 1981 it increased the rate of devaluation of the escudo and also, in an attempt to limit growth, both the bank rate and taxation were increased, along with a reduction in government subsidy on some products. In June 1982, as a result of European currency parity adjustments, the escudo was effectively devalued by 9.4 per cent. By 1982 growth was at 2 per cent, having fallen from a 1980 value of 5.5 per cent and risen slightly from its 1981 value of 1.7 per cent.

In the 1981–2 period, economic conditions in Portugal were made worse by the most serious drought that Portugal had suffered since the beginning of the century. This drought increased the food and energy import bill, since an important fraction of Portugal's energy supply comes from hydroelectric power. The end of 1982 saw the balance of payments deficit increased to about 3 billion US dollars. Negotiations were reopened with the IMF for a new two-year stand-by credit of 300 million US dollars.

One of the major political debates during the 1981–2 period and the following year centred around changes to the 1976 Constitution. The Constitution defined a four-year transitional period during which it could not be revised, but, in 1980, changes could be made. The major change which was to be introduced (because of the second MFA–Parties Pact) was the abolition of the Council of the Revolution and its substitution by a number of bodies, which would carry out its function (see chronology below). Debate focused on issues such as the need to change doctrinaire articles, which defined the Portuguese state as socialist, and many wanted to curb the power of the President. They argued that over the previous four years the interplay between government and President had been a source of political instability. Furthermore, the precise role of the military in the Portuguese state needed to be defined, since there was to be a vacuum created by the dissolution of the Council of the Revolution.

To carry out any constitutional changes, the Constitution required that there be a two-thirds majority in parliament. The AD, lacking this majority, had to negotiate with the PS, UEDS and the ASDI. After much debate, the Constitution was finally revised on 12 August 1982. The Council of the Revolution's role was taken over by a variety of bodies whose composition reflected the political parties' representation in parliament. The power of parliament was thus greatly increased and the military subject to the civilian institutions, i.e. parliament and government. The President no longer had the same ability to dismiss governments and so both his power and function were reduced.

Pinto Balsemão's leadership of the PSD was never fully accepted by the whole party. This led him to resign his premiership on 10 August 1981, but, following the party's pledge to support him, he was reinstated with the result that the eighth constitutional government was sworn in on 4 September 1981. However, in December 1982, when the leader of the CDS, Freitas do Amaral, resigned from the government (he said he wanted to take up a university post), Pinto Balsemão resigned again. The PSD designated Vitor Crespo (no relation to Admiral Victor Crespo) as a substitute for Balsemão, but, by the end of 1982, it was clear that the AD was unable to produce a strong government. This led President Eanes to reject Crespo as a new prime minister, and he dissolved parliament once again and called for another general election on 25 April 1983.

Although Balsemão had resigned as prime minister on 10 December 1982, he and his government were forced by the Constitution to continue as a caretaker government until elections were held in April. During this period as a caretaker government, they were unable to introduce any new legislation. Some economic measures were passed with the approval of the majority in parliament, and throughout this period they continued negotiations with the IMF.

The AD collapsed, basically because its two original leaders, Sá Carneiro and Freitas do Amaral, were no longer in office. Sá Carneiro had died and Freitas do Amaral had withdrawn from the political scene. The economic measures brought in by the caretaker government in February 1983 included price increases in most consumer goods, the raising of import duties and, since inflation was about 22 per cent, the escudo was devalued by 2 per cent in March.

THE CENTRE BLOCK

As a result of the collapse of the AD leadership and its inability to control the economy, the PS recovered its lost ground in the next elections. But, once again, it did not gain an overall majority.

The obvious alliance, 9 June 1983 onwards

Parliamentary elections were held on 25 April 1983; the results were inconclusive, even though the socialists and communists increased their number of delegates. On 10 May the PS and the PSD opened negotiations to form a coalition government and, later in that month, President Eanes invited Mário Soares, as leader of the PS, to form a coalition government. The final alliance was with their natural allies, the social democrats (PSD and ASDI) and with other socialist groups (UEDS).

During May, the caretaker government obtained a loan of 400 million US dollars from the Bank of International Settlements, using Portugal's gold reserves as a collateral. Later, this government borrowed 300 million US dollars from a consortium of twelve international banks. In June, the PS and the PSD finally reached an agreement on a common programme and formally decided to create a coalition for a four-year period (see chronology below). After being sworn in, the new PS/PSD government almost immediately devalued the escudo by 12 per cent. On 24 June 1983 parliament approved its programme of economic austerity, which, in order to please the PSD rank and file, contained measures to gradually move Portugal towards a more free-market economy. In July, a law was passed allowing private firms to compete in the banking, insurance, cement and fertilizer industries, and, in October, another law went through parliament enabling firms to lay off workers for limited periods of time. In the summer of 1983, a new feature of Portuguese industry began to reach serious proportions, when the number of workers still at work, but without pay, reached a figure of 100,000. Also, many employers were then not paying their employees' state contributions for health and pensions.

The economic austerity measures of the government were apparent when its budget was presented to parliament in September 1983. This budget included a 28 per cent retrospective increase in income tax, and everyone leaving the country had to pay a 1,000 escudo exit tax. Economic austerity was further increased by new measures that were taken as part of the requirements of the letter of intent the government signed with the IMF on 7 October 1983. Portugal obtained a 750 million US dollar loan from the IMF, but, by doing so, committed itself to cuts in state spending, tighter credit and the lifting of some import restrictions. Two days after signing the letter of intent, Soares's government increased the bank rate by 2 per cent and increased the price of telephone and postal charges, and car and other insurance premiums were increased. To ease these measures a little, the PS/PSD coalition abolished part payment for state health services and reduced the price of some seventy medicines by state subsidy. By signing the letter of intent, Portugal was then able to obtain a further 350 million US dollars seven-year loan, in order to pay off short-term debts, incurred through its massive balance of payments deficit. By the end of 1983, the trade deficit had improved from a 1982 value of 4,550 million US dollars to about 2,800 million US dollars. However, by the end of 1983, inflation was running at 33 per cent, although for the year it averaged out at 26 per cent.

At the beginning of 1984, the IMF once again returned to Portugal to renegotiate a new loan. In an attempt to improve conditions for the lower-paid workers, the government raised the minimum salaries.

An issue which nearly split the PS/PSD coalition was the new abortion law. The law, which was probably one of the least liberal in Western Europe, was opposed by the CDS and PSD. The President, who was also against the law, signed it on 22 March 1984. The next month saw official demonstrations throughout the country, celebrating the 25 April 1974 coup d'état. It was the end of a decade.

Housing, health and education: the post-revolutionary period

HOUSING

The housing occupations that took place during the revolution symbolised the radicalism of the mass movement, but they were never really extensive, nor did they provide a solution to the housing problems that were described in part 1.

These occupations, if anything, had an adverse effect on the popularity of the radical movement, since they frightened and alienated many of the property-owning middle classes, who began to oppose what was called the 'excesses of the revolution': many became afraid that their own houses might be occupied. A second consequence was that the emigrants became apprehensive of these occupations, as many of them had invested money earned outside Portugal in housing: the Salazar/Caetano regime offered no other secure investment. This capital was an important feature for the continuation of a house-building programme: as less money was sent back, so the house-building slowed right down; house occupations deterred the emigrants from sending back their capital. The emigrants were also subject to propaganda from the political right and they were pressurised by governments, hostile to the revolution, who made it difficult for them to send money back to Portugal.

The housing situation in Portugal was also a direct result of Salazar's economic policy for, in 1984, Salazar's laws regarding rents were still operating and effectively causing a rent freeze. In 1984 it was remarkable that in a modern European city like Lisbon, which has a tremendous housing shortage, 69 per cent of the rents were less than £5 a month! Houses were not being built for the purpose of letting, only for owner-occupiers. The figures speak for themselves: in 1970, 41 per cent of all the houses built in Portugal were available for renting: twelve years later this figure had dropped to only 1.3 per cent. Although the law allows that new rents can be set, once set, they are fixed, and with inflation running at 25 per cent, to build housing for letting was not a good investment. In Portugal, the building society system, important in the United Kingdom for home-ownership, was never implemented. Thus, the number of private houses built in Portugal in 1970 was 27,193; in 1974 it was up to 42,580; but, by 1982, this number had fallen to 39,790.

By the end of the decade, the housing situation was, if anything, worse than before. Most of the houses occupied in Lisbon and elsewhere during the revolutionary period had been returned to their original owners. With the return of the people from the colonies, there was a chronic housing shortage, but the government's investment in housing and urbanisation had fallen between 1979 and 1983, when it was halved from 22 billion escudos to 11 billion escudos. What had improved by 1984 was energy distribution, and water and sanitary conditions, largely due to the efforts of the local authorities.

HEALTH

The major changes that took place after the revolution were the introduction and rationalisation of state medical care. Although still incomplete by 1984, the rationalisation had involved the fusion of separate state services to create an embryonic national health system in an attempt to make medical care available to all.

Prior to the 25 April coup, there had been some moves to improve the health system, when some rationalisation had taken place between 1970 and 1972, in the Caetano regime; the most important measures taken were the extension of the hospital network to a number of towns in the country and the formation of health centres, whose main function was to carry out preventive medicine. But, at the time of the 1974 coup, medicine was still concentrated in the three major cities (Lisbon, Oporto and Coimbra) and was basically a non-integrated structure made up of at least three separate systems: private practice; several different hospital networks (e.g. general hospitals, psychiatric hospitals, centres for the treatment of tuberculosis, and so on); and the caixas system (see part 1). The caixas system was under a different state ministry from the other two systems.

The improvement in health care did not occur immediately after the fall of the Salazar/Caetano regime. Several provisional governments carried out legislation in a piecemeal fashion and these legislative measures were not always implemented. Finally, in September 1979, a true National Health Scheme was created by law, but, by the end of the post-coup decade, it was not fully operational. Nevertheless, many measures had been taken which were important and have brought about genuine improvements in health care. For example, hospitals that were built but lacked equipment and staff were now functioning. By 1984, there had been a significant increase in the number of trained doctors. Post-graduate training now required doctors to work in rural areas, with the result that regional hospitals were more fully staffed and, as the doctors settled in the country, there was an increase in the number of general practitioners who worked in these regions. The caixas system, health and social welfare came under one minister. The health centres dedicated to preventive medicine were active in many areas and school medicine had grown substantially. Infant mortality by 1984 had fallen to half its pre-1974 coup value, mainly through the creation of the primary health care centres in the countryside.

Although nowhere nearly as well-developed as the United Kingdom's National Health Service, medical care is no longer held back in Portugal by the archaic structures and practices of the previous regime, and has a real potential for dramatic improvement; its main limitations are of a technical nature. Also, there had been a continuous struggle between governments (excluding the AD governments) wanting to implement the National Health Scheme and the Portuguese Medical Association. The Association wanted an insurance scheme with doctors acting as free agents, as, for example, exists in Switzerland.

EDUCATION

In Salazar's time, education was a highly selective system favouring the middle and upper classes. Marcello Caetano, in 1973, appointed Veiga Simão as minister of education and Simão tried to bring some changes into the educational system by introducing a comprehensive system. But, in 1974, Caetano was brought down and Simão became Portuguese ambassador to the United Nations. The coup d'état brought about radical changes and most of the transformations were the direct outcome of the formation of a democratic society.

During the revolutionary period, there was a spontaneous emergence of a number of different collective bodies. These took the form of neighbourhood committees, workers' committees, village committees, parents' committees, co-operatives, trade unions, and so on; all these bodies exerted pressure on the provisional governments, the MFA, the schools themselves and the local authorities, with the result that there was a general improvement in the primary and secondary educational system. In the immediate post-coup period, schools were opened in hastily improvised buildings, run-down schools were restored, safety and health in the existing schools were improved and there was an explosion in the number of extra-curricular activities, which included sports, music and drama. Nursery schools were created and adult education dramatically increased. Children and adults rediscovered the joy of learning and students, teachers and the local communities increasingly participated in the activities of the schools. The creation of debate and dialogue between the schools and local communities should result in a more articulate and more politically aware Portuguese citizen.

Without doubt, chaos existed in many schools and universities in the early months of the revolution, partly because of the explosion in the student population that had occurred during the last part of the previous regime. Sottomayor Cardia became minister of education in Soares's first constitutional government, in July 1976. Cardia removed a number of left-wingers from the ministry of education and the chaotic conditions in the educational system allowed Soares's government to pass legislation restructuring the whole system.

In the primary schools, the very rigid system of evolution which prevented flexibility in teaching and introduced career selection at a very early stage was abolished. In Salazar's time, although there was six years of obligatory schooling, this was never legally enforced, so that in the fourth year there was an examination (a diploma was awarded) with the result that many students left school at this stage. After the revolution, this examination was abolished, syllabi were radically changed and new courses, such as social studies, introduced into the curriculum. A reasonable degree of flexibility and independence in the implementation of syllabi was also permitted. In the later post-revolutionary period, there was a formal introduction of much extra-curricular activity. In many areas local authorities introduced free school transport, some free lunches and free morning milk.

At secondary school level, democratic management of the schools was introduced whereby, for example, the school would be run by an elected body of teachers. The state decreed that regular meetings between teachers and parents were obligatory. Teaching became more investigative and disciplines which emphasised social and political studies were introduced. The ministry of education published detailed syllabi, provided free text books to help with the teaching and schools were given independence in the way they implemented curricula. But perhaps the most important change was the creation of a single-stream system at secondary level. This law created one stream by combining a technical stream (equivalent to the British former secondary modern school and usually attended by lower-class children) and an academic stream (equivalent to the British former grammar school and usually attended by children from middle- and upper-class families).

At university level the number of courses available was increased and the number of places in university was limited, thus removing the situation whereby thousands of students could be reading a course at any one time. There were some new universities, a modest recruitment of university staff, and universities were democratised. Rectors (equivalent to the British vice-chancellors) were now elected, as were all the bodies that ran the universities. There was not a large reinstatement of former anti-regime university staff and some of the university procedures, with regard to appointments and higher degrees, were antiquated when compared to the rest of Europe.

After the 1974 coup, school teachers became unionised and these unions have played an important role in defending teachers' rights and in fighting with governments for better conditions in the schools. In 1984, teacher training, which in the past involved teachers attending specific 'training high schools' before they could progress in their careers, was then carried out at the teacher's own school. This meant that, through such in-service training, each school was responsible for the professional improvement of their own teachers.

In conclusion, ten years after the coup, education in Portugal had markedly improved when compared to the pre-revolutionary situation. It was fast approaching the level of that in other parts of Western Europe.

Ten years on

By 1984, Portugal was a democracy and all the institutions of formal democracy were functioning well. Since 1974, there had been a real redistribution of wealth in the urban areas, but this was less marked in the rural areas. There had been great improvements in communications, and slowly the local authorities had obtained more resources which they were gradually making available to an ever-increasing number of people. The Church still played an important social and political role, but the armed forces were out of the political scene and well under the control of the civilians.

Politically, ten years on from the coup, there was a clear left–right divide, with the left split and unable to form an alliance either in parliament or for the purposes of elections. Many Portuguese were eagerly awaiting entry into the EEC, hoping that this would be the panacea for their economic problems. The country still had serious problems: since 1974, unemployment had risen from 5 per cent to 10 per cent and, although wages had increased by 500 per cent over the decade, prices had outstripped this increase. Over the ten years, inflation was always around 20 per cent and the balance of payments nearly always negative, only reaching equilibrium in 1979 as a result of the stringent financial policy of the second constitutional government.

By 1984, the trade balance was negative by almost 2 billion US dollars and, since 1974, the public sector economy had shown a negative return, owing to the large size of the public sector and the state assisting numbers of ailing firms. The almost continuous negative balance of payments forced Portugal to make successive applications to the IMF and governments were required to comply with the economic constraints set by the IMF. One of the effects of this economic austerity was the concomitant increase in a 'parallel economy', that is the formation of an economy based upon illegitimate activities, such as smuggling, moonlighting and tax evasion. Unhappily, in 1984, corruption in both the public and private sector appeared to be a major problem.

But in 1984 Portugal still remained politically one of the freest countries in Europe. It was, however, a country of contrasts. The almost third-world conditions in the countryside were slowly changing, while already on the southern Algarve coast sophisticated hotels and resorts catered for the tourists. In a walk through the streets of Lisbon, at any time of the year, it was possible to enjoy the vitality of one of Europe's most beautiful cities. The almost total lack of censorship had not produced a London Soho or a Paris Pigalle. The avenues were wide, tree-lined and sunny, the people were open, noisy and friendly. Colourful political graffiti still gave their messages and perhaps one of the most simple, but most poignant, was: 25 de Abril sempre, 25 April always!

Chronology, 1977–84

1977

21 January   A Lisbon newspaper published a cost of living comparison in four of the major cities of Europe. Based on the price of 35 articles (which included such items as bread, pasta, flour, rice, sugar, etc.) available in supermarkets, the following results were obtained:

Amsterdam	6,380 escudos
Lisbon	5,560 escudos
London	4,890 escudos
Zurich	8,640 escudos

To buy these articles one needed in:

Amsterdam	34.5 hours of work
Lisbon	92 hours of work
London	44 hours of work
Zurich	36 hours of work

3 March   The first constitutional government announced an economic package, which included a 15 per cent devaluation of the escudo and the introduction of a monthly devaluation of 1 per cent (crawling-peg devaluation). Some support was given to ailing firms under state control.

28 March   First application to the EEC for full membership. From this date onwards every government in power pursued negotiations for entry.

31 March   Loureiro dos Santos was appointed vice-chief of the general staff of the armed forces. He had been a member of the 'operationals' (see part 2, chronology) under Ramalho Eanes.

14 July   The ministry of education stated that in future there would be limited access to universities. From then on, the number of places per faculty was to be fixed. Prior to this, there had been no limit on the number of students attending a course. For example, under Salazar, courses could be over-subscribed by a factor of ten.

22 July   The IMF published a report on the serious situation in the Portuguese balance of payments. In the summer of 1977 Soares's first constitutional government opened negotiations with the IMF for an IMF conditioned consortium loan. This meant that before a consortium (made up of banks from industrialised countries) would give us a loan, Portugal would first have to qualify for 50 million US dollars of stand-by credit from the IMF.

24 September   The chief of staff of the army replaced Brigadier Pires de Veloso, commander of the northern military region, with Brigadier Delgado.

November   During the first week of November, Soares interrupted negotiations with the IMF and his government developed a new economic plan. He refused to form a coalition government with either the right or the left.

25 November   Loureiro dos Santos was dismissed from the post of vice-chief of the general staff of the armed forces.

8 December   The Soares first constitutional government lost a vote of confidence and fell. The PCP voted with the PSD, CDS and the UDP. The government was defeated by 159 votes to 100.

9 December   Dissolution of first constitutional government.

28 December   President Eanes asked Prime Minister Soares to form another government.

30 December   The US ambassador to Portugal, Frank Carlucci, left the country to take up the number two position in the CIA.

1978

13 January   Prime Minister Soares was sworn in as head of the second constitutional government. Soares, not wanting to form a coalition with any other party, formed an 'agreement' with the CDS.

23 January   The second constitutional government was sworn in.

22 March   The minister of education under Caetano, Veiga Simão, stated that he intended to join the PS.

13 April	The second constitutional government budget was passed. It was an austere one, compatible with the IMF's demands for economic restraint. The price of water, transport and gas was increased by 30 per cent and there was a 20 per cent ceiling put on wages. The 'shopping basket' was increased by 20 per cent, but unemployment benefits were increased.
9 May	The IMF formally offered Portugal 50 million US dollars credit on reasonable terms. This released a 750 million US dollar consortium loan. The IMF stand-by credit brought with it demands, which were met by the government, for a 6 per cent devaluation, an increase in the bank rate to 18 per cent, crawling-peg devaluation up to 1.25 per cent per month and the removal of most import restrictions.
11 May	President Eanes declared that ex-President Américo Thomaz could return to Portugal from Brazil, if he so wished.
19 May	The patriarch of Lisbon denounced the corruption and the opportunism that existed in Portuguese society.
9 June	A group of American banks gave a 300 million US dollar loan to Portugal at low interest rates.
12 June	Soares declared that his second constitutional government was more left-wing than the first.
23 July	Ex-President Thomaz returned to Portugal.
24 July	The CDS withdrew its support for the PS government. It complained that the changes in the Agrarian Reform laws were again too slow.
28 July	Dissolution of the second constitutional government.

9 August   President Eanes asked an engineer, Nobre da Costa, who had been a very successful manager for the Portuguese oil company SACOR (and previously a manager in one of Salazar's economic monoliths owned by Champalimaud), to form a government.

29 August   The first government of presidential initiative (third constitutional government) was sworn in with Nobre da Costa as the new prime minister.

7 September   Nobre da Costa presented his programme to parliament. The debate on this programme lasted five days.

15 September   Nobre da Costa's government failed to pass its programme, and so the third constitutional government fell. The voting was as follows:
for the programme: 71 (PSD and 2 Independents)
against: 141 (PS, CDS, UDP and 6 Independents)
abstentions: 40

26 October   President Eanes, after discussions with all the political parties, asked Mota Pinto to form a government. He had been minister of tourism and commerce in Soares's first constitutional government.

4 November   The chief of staff of the army prevented Otelo from visiting the USA.

18 November   Deficit of 98 million escudos in 1978 in the public sector economy.

22 November   The second government of presidential initiative (fourth constitutional government) was sworn in under Prime Minister Mota Pinto.

4 December   Mota Pinto's programme was presented to parliament.

13 December   The programme was finally approved. The voting was as follows:
                 rejection of programme: 44 (PCP, UDP and some Independents)
                 acceptance of programme: 109 (PSD and CDS)
                 abstentions: 97 (PS and 1 Independent)
                 By the end of 1978, the balance of payments deficit had been cut from 1.5 billion US dollars in 1977 to 920 million US dollars.

1979

13 January   Sá Carneiro, leader of the PSD, announced in the national council of his party that he intended to put forward plans to reform the Constitution.

22 March   The Mota Pinto government just failed to pass its budget (46 against the budget, 43 for, with everyone else abstaining). Mota Pinto immediately offered his resignation, but this was not accepted by President Eanes.

13 June   Mota Pinto resigned as prime minister because the PS and PCP announced that they would present motions of censure.

July   In the early days of July, the AD was formed under Sá Carneiro. With the results of the previous elections in mind, politicians realised that, if the PSD, the CDS and the PPM formed an alliance, they would have a good chance of winning a large majority in parliament, even though they would receive fewer votes than a combination of the PS and the PCP. The formation of AD marks the emergence of Sá Carneiro as a leading politician.

13 July   Since Mota Pinto's government could not pass its budget, President Eanes announced the dissolution of parliament and that new parliamentary elections were to be held. President Eanes asked Maria de Lourdes Pintasilgo to form a third government of presidential initiative.

31 July   The third government of presidential initiative (fifth constitutional government) sworn in under Prime Minister Pintasilgo.

28 September   The Republican Guard killed two agricultural workers and wounded two others during riots which occurred when land was handed back to the original landowners in the Agrarian Reform Zone.

November   An amnesty law was passed for those incriminated for having participated in the events on 11 March 1975 and 25 November 1975.

1 December   Parliamentary elections for a new constitutional government took place, which resulted in a majority for the AD and a victory for Sá Carneiro. The voting was as follows: (percentage of the total number of votes lost):

               AD   42.52% (121 delegates)
               PS   27.33% (74 delegates)
               APU   18.8% (47 delegates)
               PSD   2.35% (7 delegates)
               UDP   2.18% (1 delegate)

               Turn out: 87.5%
               PSD party shown here was for the Azores and Madeira. The AD was composed of the PSD, CDS and PPM. APU (Aliança Povo Unido, United People's Alliance) was an alliance of PCP and the MDP/CDE.
               This government was to be only short-lived, because the Portuguese Constitution then stated

that elections were to be held every four years, and so parliamentary elections had to be held again in October 1980.

16 December   Elections were held for local government. Overall results were as follows:

AD	47.2%
PS	27.7%
APU	20.5%

Turn out: 73.8%

1980

3 January   The sixth constitutional government headed by Prime Minister Sá Carneiro was sworn in.

4 July   The ASDI was formed from dissident members of the PSD.

5 October   Parliamentary elections were held in accordance with the Constitution. Prime Minister Sá Carneiro was re-elected, with the AD obtaining an increased majority. Results were as follows:

AD	47.12%
FRS	28.03%
APU	16.90%
POUS	1.39%
UDP	1.38%

Turn out: 84.45%

(Total number of registered voters: 7 million. The FRS (Frente Republicana Socialista, Republican and Socialist Front) was an alliance of the PS and other socialist parties. The POUS was a left-wing workers' party.)

4 December   Prime Minister Sá Carneiro died in an aeroplane crash, along with Amaro da Costa, the second most powerful figure in the CDS.

7 December	Presidential elections were held in accordance with the Constitution. President Eanes was re-elected. Results were as follows:

R. Eanes	56.4%
Soares Carneiro	40.27%
O. S. de Carvalho	1.47%
G. Melo	0.83%
P. Veloso	0.78%
A. Rodrigues	0.21%
Turn out:	84%

1981

9 January	The seventh constitutional government was sworn in under Prime Minister Francisco Pinto Balsemão. Balsemão became the new leader of the PSD, following the death of Sá Carneiro, and negotiated with the rest of the parties in the AD to become the new prime minister.

29 January	President Eanes, with the support of the Council of the Revolution, appointed Garcia dos Santos as chief of staff of the army. He had been one of the 'operationals' on 25 November 1975.

February	A transport ministry enquiry declared that there was no evidence of sabotage in the plane crash that killed Sá Carneiro.

25 April	The AD presented a proposal to parliament for a revision of the Constitution. The proposal had fifty articles fewer than the existing Constitution. Amongst its proposals were: the removal of the irreversibility of nationalisations; the limitation of some of the powers of the President, but the retention of a semi-presidential system; and the replacement of the Council of the Revolution by a Council of State. The Council of State was to be composed of the President of the Republic,

the prime minister, a parliamentary president, the president of the supreme court of justice, the president of the supreme military court, the heads of the regional governments, five members of parliament and the attorney-general.

May

In this month Mário Soares was re-elected general secretary of the PS. He had stepped down following the party's backing of Ramalho Eanes's presidential campaign.

6 May

A bomb exploded at the Royal British Club in Lisbon. FP25, a terrorist organisation, claimed responsibility.

June

In this month workers' strikes resulted in a loss of 4.3 million working hours, and involved 450,000 workers in thirty different firms from five different sectors of the economy.

17 July

Government announced increases in petrol, electricity and gas. The finance minister reported that the public sector deficit had risen from 90 thousand million escudos in 1974 to 591 thousand million escudos in 1980. The balance of payments deficit had risen from 46 thousand million escudos in 1974 to 5 million, million escudos.
On the same day, the Council of the Revolution declared that the law passed by parliament defining the limits between the private and public sectors was unconstitutional. As a result of this declaration, the law was not passed.

10 August

Prime Minister Balsemão announced that he would resign as prime minister, as he considered that he did not have sufficient support within the coalition.

11 August   Prime Minister Balsemão resigned.

14 August   Dissolution   of   seventh   constitutional
                 government.

25 August   Balsemão agreed to form a new government.
                 The government announced that the cost of
                 living rose 20 per cent between July 1980 and
                 July 1981. Illiteracy in Portugal was 23 per cent,
                 three times that of any other Western European
                 country.

4 September   The eighth constitutional government was
                 sworn in with Francisco Pinto Balsemão as
                 prime minister of an AD coalition government.
                 The alliance had promised to give him better
                 support. Balsemão made the CDS leader, Freitas
                 do Amaral, a cabinet minister.

14 September   Balsemão presented his new government's pro-
                 gramme to parliament.
                 In September South Africa invaded southern
                 Angola, ostensibly to fight SWAPO guerillas,
                 and fires in Portugal destroyed half a million
                 acres of pine forest.

29 October   Balsemão's   programme   was   approved   by
                 parliament.
                 In October, the FRS electoral front was dis-
                 banded.

19 November   The government decided to introduce a 14.2 per
                 cent ceiling on wage increases.

16 December   The first financing convention of EEC pre-
                 accession aid to Portugal was held. The conven-
                 tion promised to provide 700 million escudos to
                 support small- and medium-sized enterprises.
                 In December Eanes visited Mozambique. An
                 austerity budget that was presented to parlia-

ment by the AD was approved by 132 votes to 100.

1982

January   In the first week of January there was a transport strike in the Lisbon area.

12 February   A general strike against the policies of the AD took place. Many considered it a success.

12 August   A revised (second) Constitution was passed in parliament with 180 votes for and 40 against, after an agreement between the AD and the PS. The old Constitution required that a two-thirds majority in parliament was necessary before any article could be changed. The AD, PS, UEDS, and ASDI voted for changing the Constitution, while the PCP, UDP and MDP/CDE were against. The new Constitution resulted in the abolition of the Council of the Revolution, whose function was taken over by a number of newly-created bodies. The government was no longer responsible to the President of the Republic, which meant that the President was unable to dismiss governments in the same way as he had done previously.

30 September   The new Constitution came into effect.

29 October   The Council of the Revolution held its last meeting. It was attended by all its members and presided over by President Eanes.

30 October   Sixteen members of the Council of State were sworn in by the President. The Council was composed of the president of parliament, the prime minister, the presidents of the Azores and Madeira governments, president of the Constitutional Tribunal and the ombudsman. Five of

the other ten members were to be appointed by the President and the other five by parliament.

12 December
Elections for local government were held. AD obtained a majority of the votes. Voting was as follows:

AD	43.0%
PS	31.4%
APU	20.6%

19 December
Prime Minister Balsemão resigned from the government, arguing that he did not have the full support of the AD.

23 December
Dissolution of eighth constitutional government.

29 December
The PSD proposed to President Eanes that its new leader, Victor Crespo, be made prime minister.
The end of the year saw a 12 billion US dollar foreign debt, a 3 billion balance of payments deficit, annual inflation at about 23 per cent and unemployment at 13 per cent and increasing.

1983

3 January
Petrol prices were increased by 19 per cent.

4 February
President Eanes rejected the proposal for a new AD government under Victor Crespo. Eanes dissolved parliament and called for new elections on 25 April 1983. Francisco Balsemão was forced by the Constitution to continue as prime minister, until the new government was sworn in. This event marked the beginning of the dissolution of the AD.
In February there were increases in the prices of most goods and import duties were also increased. Inflation was about 22 per cent.

23 March   The escudo was devalued by 2 per cent and
                  crawling-peg devaluation increased to 1 per cent
                  a month. An agreement was reached with the
                  World Bank for a 19,000 million escudo loan.
                  In March Francisco Balsemão was replaced by
                  Mota Pinto as leader of the PSD.

25 April   Parliamentary elections. Results were as
                  follows:

		1980
PS	36.12% (99)	(74)
PSD	27.24% (72)	(82)
APU	18.20% (44)	(39)
CDS	12.40% (29)	(46)
PPM	−0	
UDP	−0	

                  Turn out: 58%
                  (Number of seats obtained in parliament shown
                  in brackets. For comparison the results of the
                  1980 election are included.)

10 May   The PS and the PSD began negotiations to form
                  a coalition government.

27 May   President Eanes invited Soares to form a
                  government.
                  In May 1983 the outgoing AD government put
                  up 30 tons of the state's gold reserves as col-
                  lateral for a 400 million US dollar loan from the
                  Bank of International Settlements. Portugal
                  later received a 300 million dollar loan from a
                  consortium of 12 international banks. This
                  money was needed to pay off 1.3 billion US
                  dollars owing from interest due on previously
                  obtained short-term loans and to help meet a
                  state spending deficit of 1.5 billion US dollars.

2 June   The PSD approved the terms of a coalition with
                  the PS.

4 June   An agreement between the PS and the PSD was signed to form a coalition (bloco central). The agreement was to be valid for four years and encompassed the following: economic austerity; anti-corruption; independence and impartiality of the media; an opening-up of the nationalised sector to competition from the private sector in banking, insurance, and the cement and fertilizer industries; new land reform policies; improvements in the social and health services; a review of the rent laws and a social contract between employers and employees to be sought.

9 June   The ninth constitutional government was sworn in under Prime Minister Mário Soares (leader of the PS) and deputy Prime Minister Mota Pinto (leader of the PSD). The government was a PS/PSD coalition.

13 June   Devaluation of the escudo by 12 per cent.

24 June   The PS/PSD programme was approved in parliament. In June, there were price rises for basic food-stuffs, government spending cuts and tax increases. The government calculated that taxes had risen by 807 per cent since 1975, prices by 373 per cent and wages by 325 per cent.
In the first six months of 1983, there had been a 33 per cent improvement in the trade deficit.

5 July   Parliament voted to allow private firms to compete with the nationalised industries in the banking, insurance, cement and fertilizer sectors.

9 August   A new agreement was signed with the IMF.

September   The government passed an economic austerity package that included a retrospective 28 per cent increase in income tax and a 1,000 escudo exit tax on people leaving the country.

6 October   The government passed a law allowing firms to lay off labour for a limited period.

7 October   Negotiations were completed for a 750 million US dollar loan from the IMF. The PS/PSD government signed a letter of intent to reduce state spending, to implement tighter credit schemes and tougher import restrictions. The IMF loan encouraged foreign banks to issue further loans to help Portugal service its large foreign debt.
The President of Mozambique visited Lisbon, which marked an improvement in relationships with Portugal's former colony.

9 October   The bank rate was increased by 2 per cent; car insurance premiums, telephone and postal charges were also increased. Part payments for state health services were abolished.

3 November   A law was passed authorising the creation of private banks and insurance companies parallel to the state sector.
In November, floods killed 9 people and 4,500 were made homeless.

2 December   Portugal signed an agreement with a consortium of sixteen US, European and Japanese banks for a seven-year loan of 350 million US dollars.

3 December   Portugal obtained a loan of 45 billion escudos under the sponsorship of the IMF.

10 December   Garcia dos Santos, the last officer of the MFA to hold an important post in the armed forces, was removed as chief of staff of the army.

13 December   Portugal and the USA signed an agreement giving the US use of the Lajes air base in the Azores.

14 December   FP25 exploded bombs near the police and Republican Guard headquarters in Lisbon.

1984

1 January   The minimum salary was increased to 15,000 escudos a month, except for agricultural workers and domestic servants, where it was set at 13,000 and 10,000 escudos a month respectively.

27 January   An IMF delegation arrived in Portugal to renegotiate the previous August's agreement. Their main concern was the current account deficit on the budget.

1 February   Petrol prices were increased (97 escudos per litre for 4-star).

23 February   The first use (by the German firm Bosch) of the lay-off law. The law allowed firms to lay off people for a period, provided that government approval had been given.

16 March   The Constitutional Tribunal approved the new abortion laws, which allowed abortion on medical grounds. This legislation had been very controversial and almost split the PS/PSD alliance.

23 March   President Eanes signed the law on abortion.

25 April   Official demonstrations and speeches to celebrate 25 April 1974 coup d'état.

Programme of the Movement of the Armed Forces

Considering that after thirteen years of fighting overseas, the present political system has not been able to define concretely and objectively an overseas policy which would lead to peace among Portuguese of all races and creeds;

Considering that such a policy can only be defined after the purging (saneamento) of the present internal policies of government and all its institutions in order to make them, by democratic means, indisputable representatives of the Portuguese people;

Considering also that the replacement of the present political system will have to take place without internal social upheaval which would affect the peace, progress and well-being of the nation;

The Movement of the Armed Forces, with a profound conviction that it interprets the aspirations and interests of the overwhelming majority of the Portuguese people and that its action is wholly justified in the name of saving the country, and using the power conferred upon it by the nation through its soldiers, proclaims and promises to guarantee the adoption of the following measures, which are considered necessary for the resolution of the great national crisis prevailing in Portugal.

A. Immediate measures

1. Political power will be exercised by the Junta of National Salvation [Junta de Salvação Nacional, JSN] until the formation in the near future of a civilian provisional government.

The choice of the President and Vice-President will be made by the Junta.

2. The Junta of National Salvation will decree:

a) The immediate dismissal of the President of the Republic and of the present government, the dissolution of the National Assembly and of the Council of State, measures which will be accompanied by the public announcement of the convocation within twelve months, of the National Constitutional Assembly elected by direct and secret universal suffrage, according to an electoral law which will be produced by the future provisional government.

b) The dismissal of all district governors on the continent, of the governors of the autonomous districts in the Portuguese islands, and of the Governors-General in the overseas provinces, as well as the immediate dissolution of the National Popular Action [Acção Nacional Popular, the only political party before the 25 April coup, editors' note].

i) the general governments of the overseas provinces will be taken over by the respective secretaries-general, who will be invested with the functions of local government until the appointment of new Governors-General by the provisional government;

ii) All matters pertaining to the civil governments will be dealt with by the respective legal substitutes during the period when no new governors have been appointed by the provisional government;

c) The immediate dissolution of the DGS, the Portuguese Legion [Legião Portuguesa] and the political youth organisations. In the overseas provinces the DGS will be restructured and purged and will be organised into a police of military information, while the military operations so demand it;

d) Individuals guilty of crimes against the political order will be handed over to the armed forces, for the duration of the supervisory period of the Junta of National Salvation, so that decisions can be made as to whether individuals will be brought to trial;

e) Measures which permit the vigilance and rigorous control of all economic and financial operations with foreign countries;

f) An immediate amnesty of all political prisoners with the exception of common criminals, who will be handed over to the respective authorities, and the voluntary reinstatement of civil servants dismissed for political reasons;

g) The abolition of censorship and prior examination;

i) The need to safeguard military secrets is recognised, and in order to avoid any disquiet in public opinion caused by the ideological aggressiveness of reactionary sectors, an ad hoc, temporary committee will be created which will control the press, radio, television, theatre and cinema; it will be directly responsible to the Junta of National Salvation, and will be in operation until the publication of new laws by the future provisional government on the press, radio, television, theatre and cinema;

h) Measures for the reorganisation and purging of the armed forces and paramilitary forces (the Republican Guard (GNR) the police (PSP) and Fiscal Guard (GF) and so on);

i) Frontier control will be in the hands of the armed forces and paramilitary forces until a special force for this is set up;

j) Measures which will lead to an efficient fight against corruption and speculation.

B. Short-term measures

1. Within a maximum period of three weeks after taking power, the Junta of National Salvation will choose [from] among its members someone to be President of the Republic, whose powers will be similar to those outlined in the present Constitution.

a) The remaining members of the Junta of National Salvation will assume the functions of General Chief of Staff of the Armed Forces, Vice-Chief of Staff of the Armed Forces, Chief of Staff of the Navy, Chief of Staff of the Army, Chief of Staff of the Air Force. They will be members of the Council of State.

2. After taking office, the President of the Republic will appoint a civilian provisional government which will be made up of members representing groups and different political ideologies and independents who identify with this present programme.

3. During the 'period of exception' of the provisional government, a period imposed by the historical necessity for political transformation, the Junta of National Salvation will remain in power in order to safeguard the objectives proclaimed here.

a) The period of exception will finish, in agreement with the new Political Constitution, as soon as the President of the Republic and the Legislative Assembly are elected.

4. The provisional government will govern by decrees, which of necessity will adhere to the spirit of the present proclamation.

5. The provisional government, bearing in mind that major reforms can only be adopted within the framework of the future National Constitutional Assembly, will immediately promote:

a) Application of measures that will guarantee the exercise of formal government and the study and application of preparatory measures of a material, economic, social and cultural nature, which will guarantee the effective future exercise of political freedom by all citizens;

b) Freedom of meeting and of association. In the application of this principle the formation of 'political associations', possibly the embryos of future political parties, will be allowed and the freedom of trade unions will be guaranteed in accordance with a special law regulating its exercise;

c) Freedom of expression and thought in any form;

d) The promulgation of a new law covering the press, radio, television, theatre and cinema;

e) Measures and arrangements which will ensure in a very short time the independence and the restitution of dignity to the Judiciary;

i) The abolition of 'special tribunals' and the restitution of dignity to the penal process, in all its phases;

ii) Crimes committed against the state in the new regime will be dealt with by judges and tried in ordinary tribunals. All guarantees will be given to the defendants. Criminal investigations will be carried out by the Judicial Police.

6. The provisional government will launch the basis of:

a) A new economic policy, which will serve the Portuguese people and, in particular, all the sectors of the population which until now have been less favoured, with the immediate preoccupation of fighting inflation and excessive rises in the cost of living and this will of necessity imply an anti-monopolistic strategy;

b) A new social policy which in every sector will have as its essential objective the defence of the working classes and the progressive, but accelerated, improvement in the quality of life for all Portuguese.

7. The provisional government will be guided in matters of foreign affairs by the principles of independence and equality between states, of non-interference in the internal affairs of other countries, and of the defence of peace. It will enlarge and diversify international relations on the basis of friendship and co-operation.

a) The provisional government will respect all international commitments resulting from existing treaties.

8. The overseas policy of the government will take into consideration that its definition rests with the nation. It will be guided by the following principles:

a) The recognition that the solution to the wars overseas is political and not military;

b) The creation of the conditions for a frank and open debate, at a national level, of the overseas problem;

c) The development of foundations of an overseas policy that will lead to peace.

C. Final considerations

1. As soon as the Legislative Assembly and the new President of the Republic are elected, the Junta of National Salvation will be dissolved and the action of the Armed Forces will be limited to the specific task of defending national sovereignty.

2. The Movement of the Armed Forces, with the conviction that the principles and objectives proclaimed here translate a commitment to the country and to the better interests of the nation, addresses itself to all Portuguese people in a vehement demand for their sincere, enlightened and resolute participation in public life, exhorting them to guarantee by their work, and by their peaceful co-existence, whatever their social position, the necessary conditions for the definition within a short time of a policy, which will lead to the solution of the grave national problems and to harmony, progress and social justice, all indispensable to the cleansing of our public life and to obtaining for Portugal its deserved place among the nations.

The first MFA–Parties Pact (or the constitutional platform between the parties and the MFA, 11 April 1975)

A. Introduction

1. The revolutionary movement initiated by the Armed Forces on 25 April 1974 acquired a growing dynamism either in response to the just aspirations of the Portuguese people, or to successive acts of reactionary aggression which were increasingly more violent.

2. The serious counter-revolutionary events of 11 March imposed the necessity for the institutionalisation of the Movement of the Armed Forces. So the constitutional law no. 5/75 created the Council of the Revolution which took over the functions previously carried out by the Junta of National Salvation, by the Council of State and by the Council of the Chiefs of the General Staffs of the Armed Forces.

3. Law no. 5/75 does not aim at substituting or reducing the importance of the political parties which are truly democratic and sincerely committed to the completion of the Programme of the MFA; the law aims at the dynamisation and overseeing of the revolutionary process which will be carried out in close alliance with the Portuguese people and with those political parties which defend their most legitimate interests.

4. The MFA, represented by the Council of the Revolution, establishes a public political platform with the parties which are committed to the principles of the Programme of the MFA and to the consolidation and expansion of the democratic victories already achieved.

5. In the development of this platform, the results of dialogues which occurred with the different parties and the situation resulting from the smashing of the counter-revolutionary coup of 11 March were taken into consideration.

B. The objectives of the platform

1. It is intended to establish a common political platform which will make possible the continuation of the political, economic and social revolution, which was initiated on 25 April 1974, within a framework of political pluralism and a socialising trend which would allow us to carry out, in freedom, a common plan of national reconstruction, without antagonism between the parties which is sterile and divisive.

2. The terms of the present platform must be integrated in the future Political Constitution to be developed and approved by the Constitutional Assembly.

3. The present platform will be valid for a period which will be known as the transition period, with the duration of between three and five years to be fixed in the new Constitution, which will end with the revision of the Constitution.

C. Elections for the Constitutional Assembly, the working of the Constitutional Assembly and the preparation and promulgation of the Political Constitution

1. The Council of the Revolution reaffirms its determination to enforce what has already been established for truly free and responsible elections for the formation of a Constitutional Assembly.
2. During the preparation of the future Political Constitution there will be a committee of the MFA, which, in collaboration with the parties signing this agreement, will follow the proceedings of the Constitutional Assembly, in order to facilitate co-operation between the parties and to speed up the preparation of the future Political Constitution within the spirit of the Programme of the MFA and of this agreement.
3. Once the new Constitution has been prepared and approved by the Constitutional Assembly, the Constitution should be promulgated by the President of the Republic after consultation with the Council of the Revolution.
4. Until the new organs of sovereignty, defined by the new Political Constitution, start functioning, the Council of the Revolution, the Assembly of the MFA and the provisional government will maintain their present functions.
5. Since the sole aim of the next elections is the formation of the Constitutional Assembly, whose only task will be to draw up and approve a Constitution, any alterations to the Constitution of the provisional government, up until the election of the Legislative Assembly and the consequent formation of a new government, will be made only on the initiative of the President of the Republic, after consultation with the Prime Minister and the Council of the Revolution.
6. The parties which sign this agreement commit themselves not to question the institutionalisation of the MFA, in the terms explained below, and to include it in the new Constitution, together with the remaining points agreed in this document.

D. Future power structures and their functions

1. Organs of Sovereignty

The organs of sovereignty of the Portuguese Republic during the transition period will be the following: a) the President of the Republic; b) the Council of the Revolution; c) the Assembly of the MFA; d) the Legislative Assembly; e) the Government; and f) the Tribunals.

2. The President of the Republic

2.1 The President of the Republic will automatically be the President of the Council of the Revolution and the Supreme Commander of the Armed Forces.

2.2 The President of the Republic will have powers and functions given to him by the Constitution, amongst which will be: a) to preside over the Council of the Revolution; b) to carry out the functions of Supreme Commander of the Armed Forces; c) to choose the Prime Minister after consultation with the Council of the Revolution; d) to appoint and dismiss members of government in line with proposals from the Prime Minister; e) to dissolve the Legislative Assembly, according to decisions of the Council of the Revolution, fixing the date for the new elections within a maximum period of 90 days; f) to promulgate and publish laws of the Council of the Revolution and the Legislative Assembly, as well as decree-laws of the government.

2.3 The President of the Republic will be elected by an electoral college created for that purpose by the Assembly of the MFA and the Legislative Assembly.

2.3.1 Enrolment as a candidate requires the signatures of a minimum of 80 elected members of the college.

2.3.2 Election will be by absolute majority in the first term or by simple majority in the second term, and only those candidates who had more than 20 per cent of the votes in the first term will be admitted to the second term.

2.4 In the case of death or permanent disability of the President of the Republic, his functions will be taken over by a person appointed by the Council of the Revolution, and new elections should be held within sixty days.

3. Council of the Revolution

3.1 The Constitution of the Council of the Revolution will be as defined in the constitutional law no. 5/75, of 14 March.

3.1.1 Any alteration to the composition of the Council of the Revolution can only be made by legislation of the Council itself, in agreement with the decisions of the Assembly of the MFA.

3.2 The functions of the Council of the Revolution will be:

a) To define, within the spirit of the Constitution the required programmatic orientations of internal and foreign policies and to see that they are carried out.

b) To decide, with general obligatory force, on the constitutionality of laws and other legislative diplomas, without prejudicing the competence of the tribunals to appraise formal inconstitutionality.

c) To appraise and approve legislative diplomas produced by the Assembly or the government when they deal with the following matters: 1) the general lines of economic, social and financial policies; 2) foreign relations, in particular with new Portuguese-speaking countries and with the overseas territories still under Portuguese administration; 3) the exercise of freedom and fundamental rights; 4) the organisation of national defence and the definition of the duties deriving from it; 5) the regulation of political activity, in particular that which pertains to elections.

d) To carry out legislative power in matters of national interest which require urgent resolution, when the Legislative Assembly or the government cannot do it.

e) To ensure that ordinary laws are obeyed and to appraise the acts of the government or of the administration.

f) To propose to the Legislative Assembly alterations to the present Constitution.

g) To exert legislative power in military matters, and when such diplomas are produced which involve any increase in expenses which cannot be covered by the approved state budget, they will have to be referred to the Prime Minister.

h) To authorise the President of the Republic to make war, in case of actual or imminent aggression, and to make peace.

i) To give an opinion to the President of the Republic on the choice of Prime Minister and of ministers who must have the confidence of the MFA.

j) To deliberate on the dissolution of the Legislative Assembly whenever it considers it necessary for the resolution of situations of political impasse.

k) To authorise the President of the Republic to declare a state of siege and to give an opinion on all emergencies which seriously affect the life of the nation.

l) To give an opinion about the temporary or permanent physical disability of the President of the Republic.

m) To choose a provisional President of the Republic in the case of death, or impediment to the functioning of the President of the Republic.

3.3 The Council of the Revolution will function on a permanent basis, according to regulations drawn up by itself.

4. The government

4.1 The Prime Minister will be chosen by the President of the Republic after consultation with the Council of the Revolution, and such political forces and parties which he thinks should be consulted.

4.2 The government will be chosen by the Prime Minister, taking into consideration the representation of the parties in the Legislative Assembly and possible coalitions, and will be sworn in by the President of the Republic.

4.3 In the cases of an initial formation or of a ministerial reshuffle which includes at least one third of the ministers, the new government will have to submit to a vote of confidence of the Legislative Assembly at its first session.

4.4 The Prime Minister is politically responsible to the President of the Republic and to the Legislative Assembly.

4.5 The Legislative Assembly can vote motions of no-confidence in the government. Approval of two motions of no-confidence which take effect with the interval of less than thirty days require a ministerial reshuffle.

4.6 The government will have the power to legislate by decree-laws on matters which are not restricted to the Council of the Revolution or to the Legislative Assembly.

It can also, through its own initiative, present proposed laws to the Legislative Assembly.

4.7 The Ministers of Defence, Internal Administration and Economic Planning must have the confidence of the MFA, so that their appointments cannot be made without prior consultation with the Council of the Revolution.

5. The Legislative Assembly

5.1 The Legislative Assembly will be elected by universal, direct and secret suffrage and will have a maximum of 250 deputies.

5.2 The legislative powers of the Assembly will be limited only by the necessary sanction of the Council of the Revolution in the matters outlined in 3.2 c); it will not be allowed to legislate on exclusively military matters.

5.3 In the case of a declaration of a state of siege, this cannot be prolonged for a period of more than thirty days, without being ratified by the Legislative Assembly.

5.4 The Legislative Assembly, together with all its members, forms part of the electoral college for the election of the President of the Republic.

5.5 The Legislative Assembly can be invested by the Council of the Revolution with constitutional powers, when, through the initiative of the Council of the Revolution, proposals for alterations to the Constitution are presented.

5.6 The legislative diplomas produced by the Assembly, which have not obtained the approval of the Council of the Revolution, can be promulgated in their initial form, if in a second vote, they are approved by a majority of two-thirds of the total number of deputies.

6. The Assembly of the MFA

6.1 The Assembly of the MFA will be made up of 240 representatives of the armed forces, 120 from the army, 60 from the navy and 60 from the air force, and its [the Assembly's] composition will be determined by a law produced by the Council of the Revolution.

6.2 The Assembly of the MFA, of which the Council of the Revolution is an integral part, will be presided over by the Council of the Revolution, through its president or the president's substitute.

6.3 The Assembly of the MFA, along with all of its members, forms part of the electoral college for the election of the President of the Republic.
6.4 The Assembly of the MFA will function on a permanent basis, according to its own regulations, which are part of the legislative powers of the Council of the Revolution.

E. Other provisions

1. The Constitution, its revisions and terms

1.1 The future Constitution to be prepared by the Constitutional Assembly will remain in force for a period equal to the transition period, and that will be between three and five years.
1.2 At the end of the transition period, the Legislative Assembly will be dissolved and a new assembly elected, which will begin its mandate with constitutional powers, and will proceed to the revision of the Constitution.
Only when this Constitution is revised, approved and enacted will the transition period be considered to be at an end.

2. 'Programmatic points to be included in the Constitution'

Besides the regulations which constitute the basis of this agreement, the Constitution will have to embody the principles of the Movement of the Armed Forces, the victories legitimately obtained throughout the process, as well as developments to the Programme imposed by the dynamism of the revolution, which is openly and irreversibly moving the country along the original path to Portuguese socialism.

3. The Armed Forces

3.1 Throughout the whole transition period, military power will be independent of civilian power.
3.2 The Commander-in-Chief of the Armed Forces will be the General Chief of Staff of all the Armed Forces, who is directly dependent on the President of the Republic.
3.3 The General Chief of Staff of all the Armed Forces will be assisted by a Vice-General Chief of Staff of all the Armed Forces, who will be his substitute in case of disabilities.
3.4 Each branch of the Armed Forces will be headed by a Chief of Staff.
3.5 The General Chief of Staff of all the Armed Forces, the Vice-General Chief of Staff of all the Armed Forces and the Chiefs of Staff of the three branches of the Armed Forces will have ministerial status.
3.6 The Armed Forces will be the guarantors and initiators of the revolutionary process, which will lead to a true political, economic and social democracy.

3.7 Besides their specific role of defending national integrity and independence, the Armed Forces will participate in the economic, social, cultural and political development of the country within the scope of their Movement.

The second MFA–Parties Pact

1. The ruling bodies

The ruling bodies during the transition period will be the following:
(a) The President of the Republic;
(b) The Council of the Revolution;
(c) The Legislative Assembly;
(d) The Government;
(e) The Tribunals.

2. President of the Republic

2.1 The President of the Republic will be elected by a universal, direct and secret suffrage.

Candidates standing for President of the Republic need to have the support of no less than 7,500 and no more than 15,000 citizens of the electorate.

2.2 The President of the Republic will also be the President of the Council of the Revolution and the Supreme Commander of the armed forces.

2.3 The President of the Republic will have powers and functions given to him by the Constitution, which will include the following:
a) To preside over the Council of the Revolution;
b) To be Commander of the Armed Forces;
c) To declare war or make peace within the terms of the Constitution, and only with the authorisation of the Council of the Revolution;
d) To declare a state of siege or state of emergency, only with the authorisation of the Council of the Revolution, in the whole of or any part of the national territory. In accordance with the Constitution;
e) To appoint or dismiss the Prime Minister after consultation with the Council of the Revolution and the political parties, taking into account their electoral representatives in the Legislative Assembly;
f) To appoint or dismiss members of the government, in accordance with the wishes of the Prime Minister;
g) To promulgate and order the publication of laws of the Legislative Assembly, law-decrees and regulating decrees, as well as legislative diplomas and diplomas of the Council of the Revolution; to sign any remaining decrees;
h) To dissolve the Legislative Assembly and to select dates for new elections, which have to be held within a maximum of ninety days from the dissolution;

i) To dissolve bodies of the autonomous regions after consultation with the Council of the Revolution.

2.4 A state of siege or state of emergency cannot be prolonged for more than thirty days without first being ratified by the Legislative Assembly.

2.5.1 The President may exercise the right of veto after consultation and proper debate with the Council of the Revolution and demand a new discussion of the diploma, if, within fifteen days, counting from the day of reception of a decree of the Legislative Assembly to be promulgated as a law, or after the period defined in no. 3.8.3, the Council of the Revolution will not declare the decree unconstitutional.

2.5.2 The President must sign a law if the Legislative Assembly passes a decree by an absolute majority vote. A two-thirds majority of those members of parliament present will be required to pass decrees dealing with the following matters:

1) The limits between sectors of state property, collective property and private property;
2) Foreign relations;
3) The organisation of national defence and the definition of rights and duties related to it;
4) The regulation of electoral acts, described in the Constitution.

2.6 The exercise of power to dissolve the Legislative Assembly by the President of the Republic requires the agreement of the Council of the Revolution, except in cases where the dissolution is obligatory as set out in no. 4.4.

2.7 In the case when the post of President of the Republic becomes vacant, the functions of President of the Republic will be taken over by the President of the Legislative Assembly. The new election must take place within a maximum period of sixty days.

2.8 If the President of the Republic resigns from his post within a period of thirty days after legislative elections, which have taken place as a consequence of the dissolution of the Assembly, he will be unable to present himself for re-election in the immediate presidential elections.

3. Council of the Revolution

3.1 The Council of the Revolution will be composed of:
a) The President of the Republic, who will preside over it;
b) The General Chief of Staff of the Armed Forces, the Vice-General Chief of Staff of the Armed Forces (if he exists), the Chief of Staff of the Army, the Chief of Staff of the Air Force, the Chief of Staff of the Navy, and the Prime Minister, if he belongs to the Armed Forces.
c) 14 officials, 8 being from the Army, 3 from the Air Force and 3 from the Navy; they will be designated by the respective branches of the Armed Forces.

3.2 In the case of death, resignation or permanent impediment, to be verified by the Council, of some of the members referred to in c) of the previous number, their place will be filled by representatives designated from the respective branch of the Armed Forces.

3.3 The Council regulates its own organisation and function.

3.4 The Council of the Revolution will function in permanent session according to regulations decided by itself.

3.5 The Council of the Revolution has the functions of counsel to the President of the Republic, of guarantor of the normal functioning of democratic institutions, guarantor of the implementation of the Constitution, and guarantor of loyalty to the spirit of the Portuguese revolution of 25 April 1974. It also acts as a political and legislative body in military matters.

3.6 In its role as counsel to the President of the Republic and guarantor of the normal functioning of democratic institutions, the Council of the Revolution advises the President of the Republic in the exercise of his duties and also:

a) It authorises the President of the Republic to declare war or make peace;

b) It authorises the President of the Republic to declare a state of siege or emergency in the whole of or in any part of the national territory;

c) It authorises the President of the Republic to travel outside national territory;

d) It declares whether the President of the Republic is physically incapable of fulfilling his role. Furthermore, it verifies any temporary impediment to his functioning.

3.7 In its role as guarantor of the implementation of the Constitution, the Council of the Revolution:

a) Will, on its own initiative, or, at the request of the President of the Republic, give its opinion on the constitutionality of laws before they are signed;

b) It will oversee the drawing up of measures necessary for the fulfillment of constitutional norms, and it can make recommendations for that purpose;

c) It will pronounce opinions, which will be obligatorily enforced, about the constitutionality of any laws already published, at the request of the President of the Republic, of the President of the Legislative Assembly, of the Prime Minister, of the Attorney-General, of the purveyor of justice, and also in the cases which are cited in no. 3.10.

3.8.1 In order for a) of the previous number to be fulfilled, every decree which is submitted to the President of the Republic so that it can be signed as a law or as a law-decree, or, when treaties or international agreements have to be signed, they will have to be sent simultaneously to the Council of the Revolution, and cannot be signed before a period of five days from receipt by the Council has lapsed, except in cases of emergency, which will be defined by the President of the Republic, who will then inform the Council of the Revolution that he intends to sign immediately.

3.8.2 Should the Council have any doubts about the constitutionality of a decree, after proper debate, and should it decide to analyse the decree, it will inform the President of the Republic within the following five days so that he does not sign the decree.

3.8.3 When an opinion about the constitutionality of a diploma is either deliberated by the Council or requested by the President of the Republic, the Council of the Revolution will have to give its opinion within the following twenty days. This period may be shortened, if the President of the Republic so wishes.

3.8.4 If the Council of the Revolution decides that a given diploma is unconstitutional, before it is signed, the President of the Republic must exert his right of veto, according to 2.5.1; in the case of a decree of the Legislative Assembly, a qualified majority of two-thirds of the MPs present will be required, before the decree can be signed. If it is a decree concerning government, it cannot be signed.

3.9 If the Council of the Revolution finds that the Constitution is not being obeyed, because the necessary legislative measures are not being taken to implement the constitutional norms, it may recommend that the competent legislative bodies adopt them within a reasonable time.

3.10.1 In matters judged in court, tribunals cannot apply norms which are against the Constitution or against principles stated in the Constitution; they have the ability to assess or to decide whether there is unconstitutionality. However, inherent or formal unconstitutionality of treaties or international agreements will not inhibit its application to Portugal's internal affairs, provided that these unconstitutionalities are enforceable in the internal order of the other party or parties.

3.10.2 Whenever the tribunals refuse to apply a norm, which is part of a law or law-decree, or regulating decree, or equivalent diploma, on the basis of its unconstitutionality, and, once the ordinary resources available are exhausted, there will be an obligatory, free appeal to the Public Prosecutor, which will be confined to the question of unconstitutionality for the purpose of passing judgment on the case by the Constitutional Commission.

3.10.3 There will also be free appeal to the Constitutional Commission, which is binding on the Public Prosecutor, over decisions applicable to a norm, previously judged unconstitutional by that Commission.

3.10.4 If the Constitutional Commission decides that, in three clear cases, the same norm is unconstitutional, the Council of the Revolution may declare the unconstitutionality of that norm, and this has to be obeyed without prejudicing cases that have been tried.

3.10.5 When unconstitutionality is inherent or deliberate, it will be enough to have a decision of unconstitutionality by the Constitutional Commission so that the Council of the Revolution may declare that it is unconstitutional, and this decision is binding.

3.11.1 The Constitutional Commission will be presided over by a member of the Council of the Revolution who will have the deciding vote and, besides the President, will be composed of:

a) Four judges, one of them being designated by the Supreme Court, the others being designated by the Supreme Council of Magistrates, one being from the High Court of Justice, and two being from the County Court;

b) One meritorious person designated by the President of the Republic;

c) One meritorious person designated by the Legislative Assembly;
d) Two meritorious persons designated by the Council of the Revolution: one of whom must be a competent lawyer.
3.11.2 The members of the Constitutional Commission will be appointed for the whole of the transition period; they will be independent, permanent, and the rules which guarantee impartiality and independence when applied to judges will be applicable to them when they exercise their powers of jurisdiction.
3.11.3 The organisation and function of the Constitutional Commission will be approved by the Council of the Revolution. The rules of the procedure will be approved by the Council of the Revolution without prejudice of the possibility that the Legislative Assembly may change them.
3.12 The functions of the Constitutional Commission will be:
a) To give an obligatory opinion about the constitutionality of the laws that have been assessed by the Council of the Revolution, in agreement with nos. 3.7a) and 3.7c);
b) To give an obligatory opinion about the existence of violations of constitutional norms by omission, in agreement with, and for the purpose considered in no. 3.7b);
c) To assess the nature of unconstitutionality, submitted in agreement with nos. 3.10.2 and 3.10.3.
3.13 In its role as guarantor of loyalty to the spirit of the Portuguese revolution, the Council of the Revolution will:
a) Give an opinion to the President of the Republic about the Prime Minister;
b) Give an opinion or advise the President about the exercise of the right of suspensive veto, in agreement with no. 2.5.
3.14 In its role as a political and legislative body in military matters, the Council of the Revolution has the following functions:
a) Exclusive rights to legislate about organisations, functioning and discipline in the armed forces;
b) The right to improve treaties or international agreements which deal with military matters.
3.15.1 The acts of the Council of the Revolution which represent the exercise of rights indicated in 3.3, 3.11.3 and 3.14 will have the form, according to each case, of a legislative diploma from the Council of the Revolution or a diploma from the Council of the Revolution and will be signed by the President of the Republic, only requiring a ministerial referendum for those which would involve an increase in expenditure or a decrease in income.
3.15.2 The legislative diplomas of the Council of the Revolution are on a par with laws and decree-laws, and the diplomas of the Council of the Revolution are on a par with the regulating decrees or the acts of the Legislative Assembly or the government, which has approved treaties or international agreements: the remaining acts of the Council of the Revolution will have the form of resolutions and will be published without the signature of the President of the Republic.

4. Relationships between the President of the Republic, the Legislative Assembly and the Government

4.1 The government is politically responsible to the President of the Republic and to the Legislative Assembly.

4.2 The political responsibility of the government to the Legislative Assembly takes effect through appreciation of the programme of the government, through a refusal by parliament to approve a vote of confidence proposed by the government, or through the approval of motions of censure in terms defined by the Constitutional Assembly.

4.3 When the government resigns, the members of the government which resigned will continue to carry out their duties until a new government takes power.

4.4 The President of the Republic is obliged to dissolve the Legislative Assembly when, for whatever reasons, a vote of no-confidence or a vote of censure is passed three times for the same legislature.

5. Final temporary arrangements

5.1 The first legislative period will last four years.

5.2 The first mandate of the President of the Republic will cease either three months after the end of the period of transition or five years after his election, depending on which comes first.

5.3 If the Legislative Assembly is dissolved, or the post of President of the Republic becomes vacant, the period of the new legislature or of the new mandate will not commence until the remainder of the period of the previous legislature and mandate has been completed, in accordance with the terms laid out in the above paragraphs.

5.4 In the second legislative period, the Legislative Assembly will have mandatory powers to revise the Constitution, and the President of the Republic cannot refuse to promulgate this revision. The period of transition will end, when this new law is promulgated.

5.5 The present pact will be enforceable during the transition period, which will have a minimum duration of four years, and cannot be revised during this period without the agreement of the Council of the Revolution.

5.6 The present pact substitutes or revokes the previous one, and the parties which sign it are bound to include it in the text of the Constitution.

APPENDIX 4

The Document of the Nine (Melo Antunes document, 6 August 1975)

1. Recent developments in the political situation in Portugal, including what has been happening inside the armed forces, have forced a group of officers to look critically at certain events which have taken place during several episodes which have set the pace of the perturbed political life of the Portuguese over the last weeks.

It seems to these officers that a crucial point has arrived in the revolutionary process, initiated on 25 April 1974, a point full of options that are to be seized with calm and unyielding energy, in relation to the future of the country.

It also seems to them that now is the moment to clarify ideological and political positions and to end the ambiguities, which were seeded and fed progressively by all those who, within and outside the Armed Forces, were interested in discrediting some sectors, so that they would be better able to assert and impose their own ideas.

These officers refuse from the start the term 'divisionists', with which they have been denigrated. The scandalous suggestion has even been put forward that they should be expelled from the Armed Forces. They do not renounce their right to criticise, a right that at such a serious moment in national life becomes a patriotic duty.

2. The Movement of the Armed Forces was born from the spirit and heart of a group of democratic, patriotic and anti-fascist officers who decided to put an end to the long fascist night and to begin, with all the Portuguese people, a new march of peace, progress and democracy, on the basis of a universally accepted and respected Political Programme. We know how the large popular mass movements opened up new perspectives on the democratic revolution initiated on 25 April 1974 and how, starting above all from the general elections for the National Constitutional Assembly, the way to socialism assumed an irreversible quality.

The Programme of the Movement of the Armed Forces was the theoretical element of the democratic revolution, but it already contained the essential political proposals which aimed at a basic socialist model. In view of this, the left-wing ideology underlying the Programme was in no way harmed by the so-called 'advances of the revolutionary process', when and where these 'advances' corresponded effectively to the destruction of political, economic and social structures of the previous regime, and where these 'advances' resulted in their substitution by new effective structures which are the basis of a new socio-political organisation, of socialist origin.

269

Unfortunately, however, hardly ever did transformations of this type take place.

Instead, we watched the dismantling of half a dozen large financial and monopolistic groups; but, in parallel, and as nationalisations took place (the rate of nationalisations was impossible to absorb, however dynamic the process was and however high the degree of support from the people, without the risk of breaking the pre-existing social and cultural fabrics of society – and that is what is happening at present), we have watched the very rapid disintegration of the structures of social and economic organisation, which have served as support for wide sections of the petite and middle bourgeoisie, without any new structures being created that are able to guarantee the management of productive units and economic circuits and to maintain an essential minimum of normality in the social relations between all the Portuguese.

Meanwhile, and in parallel, there is a progressive disintegration of the structures of state. Power was exercised in an unbridled and anarchic way nearly everywhere (even within the Armed Forces), and the organisations of party groups with the most experience and eager to control the centres of power profited from this disorder. The MFA, which initially claimed to be above the parties, found itself more and more trapped in the political manipulations of the parties and mass organisations, and found itself being compromised and committed to a particular political project which did not correspond either to its initial vocation or to the role which the population of the country was expecting from it: that is, as guide and leader of a process of profound transformation of Portuguese society, with a clear political project for the transition to socialism, which would be independent of the parties, although it would not dispense with their co-operation nor with the widest possible social basis of support.

3. The country is profoundly shaken and cheated of the great hope with which it watched the emergence of the MFA. The most acute moment in a very serious economic crisis has arrived; its consequences cannot fail to be felt as a rupture, which is already imminent between the MFA and the majority of the Portuguese people. Each day there is a widening of the gap between very small minority social groups (part of the Lisbon proletariat and part of the Alentejo proletariat), carrying out a certain revolutionary project, and practically the rest of the country, which violently opposes the changes that a certain 'revolutionary vanguard' endeavours to impose, without taking into account the complexity of the historical, social and cultural reality of the Portuguese people.

Finally, the most acute phase of decolonisation (Angola) is drawing near, without the fact being taken into account that it is not possible 'to decolonise', and guarantee an effective, peaceful transition to true independence, without a solid internal cohesion of political power and without, above all, a consideration that 'decolonisation' should continue to be, until it is complete, the principal national objective. We are faced now with a problem in Angola with which we will probably not be able to deal: a conflict of national proportions is being generated, which will, in the short term, have catastrophic and tragic consequences for both Portugal and Angola. In any case, the future of a real revolution in Portugal is endangered, as a result of the course of events in Angola, to which we are tied by undeniable, historical responsibilities, beyond those immediate human and social responsibilities towards the Portuguese who work and live there.

4. All these very serious aspects of national life have been systematically concealed, more than that, profoundly adulterated by a large fraction of the media through a rigid party control over them – in particular, over the nationalised media – and we witness today the degrading and shameful spectacle of a good part of the population racing to listen to the news given by foreign broadcasting corporations, instead of by those in our own country.

As if this were not already enough, we are at the height of preparation of a diploma, which, in establishing a 'commission of analysis' (and why not a 'commission of censure?') will serve as a javelin aimed at the last resistent bulwarks of the free press in this country.

5. This document does not claim to be an exhaustive criticism of the actions of the regime, installed after 25 April or, in particular, of the institutions created after 28 September 1974. Recently, a lot of criticism has come from the public, which essentially clarifies the fundamental weaknesses of the present regime.

It is important for this group of officers, who thought that the moment had come to take a stance, to define themselves as clearly as possible in front of the Portuguese people and in relation to the various levels of political power and, in particular, in front of the MFA, and so they have decided to make the following statements:

– They reject the Eastern European model of a socialist society, to which we will be fatally led by a political elite that stubbornly believes that a 'vanguard', which has a very narrow social base, will carry out the revolution in the name of the people, and which has, in practice, allowed every infiltration of this 'vanguard' into the centres of political power and military structures.

The bureaucratic dirigisme typical of totalitarian regimes is steadfastly opposed by those who in the past fought against fascism, and now coherently ready themselves again at the prospect of a fight against the new forms of totalitarianism.

– They reject the model of a social democratic society, in force in many countries in Western Europe, because they believe that the major problems of Portuguese society cannot be solved by the reproduction in our country of classical systems of advanced capitalism.

It will be a tragic mistake at present, when everything leads us to believe that a general and global crisis of capitalism is approaching, to attempt, even at the cost of losing immediate real benefits, although manifestly illusory, a repetition of the social democrats' experience.

– They fight for a left-wing political project, where the construction of a socialist society – that is, a classless society, where the exploitation of man by man has been eradicated – will be achieved at rhythms appropriate to the precise Portuguese social reality so that the transition will be made gradually, without convulsions, and peacefully.

This purpose will only be attained if, in opposition to the Leninist theory of 'revolutionary vanguard', which imposes its political dogmas in a sectarian and violent manner, an alternative strategy is set up, which involves the formation of a very wide and solid social bloc of support for a national project of transition to socialism.

This model of socialism is inseparable from political democracy. It should be built, then, within a political pluralism, with the parties capable of adhering to this national project. This model of socialism is inseparable also from liberties, rights and fundamental guarantees. We do not deny that it can suffer changes to its content, as the historic process continues. However, a revolutionary concept of socialism, introduced in the geo-political and strategic context of a European country like Portugal, which has a historic and cultural past of its own, cannot separate the fundamental problem of human freedom from the construction of socialism.

– They demand and fight for an authentic national independence (political as well as economic) which means the coherent application of a foreign policy, which is appropriate to our historic, cultural and geo-political realities, and which implies:

– the opening of relations with every country in the world, on the basis of equality, mutual respect and non-interference in the internal affairs of each country, bearing in mind the need for independence with regard to the great powers;

– the maintenance of our connections with Europe, the reinforcing and deepening of our relationships with certain economic groups (the EEC and EFTA);

– the frank opening-up of relations with the Third World (in particular with our previous colonies) and the Arab countries;

– the deepening of our relations with the socialist countries of Eastern Europe;

– the development of a strategy in the Mediterranean area, in conjunction with all interested countries, European and Arab alike.

– They fight to recapture the original image of the MFA, in the sense that the MFA was only universally acceptable while it was an autonomous body for the production of policies and ideologies.

In this way the consensus that took place around its programme is explained. It is considered indispensable for the correct resolution of the very serious crisis affecting the country that the Movement of the armed forces not only declares itself to be above the parties, but also develops a political practice, which is free from any and every influence of the parties. Only then will it have the conditions to regain its credibility and also to fulfill its historic vocation to be a respected arbiter, and driving force of the revolutionary process.

It is only then, as well, that we can expect the support of a wide social bloc, encompassing the rural and urban proletariat, the petite bourgeoisie and very large fractions of the middle bourgeoisie (including technocrats and progressive intellectuals), to be in a position to create a basis of support, indispensable to the practical realisation of the large transformations Portuguese society must undergo.

– They reject the institution of a politics based upon demagogical measures and practices, whatever their character, which are nothing more than a proof of their real inability to define the great problems of Portuguese society and to find just and adequate solutions, in terms of balanced and truthful politics, the only legitimate way to obtain ample mobilisation of the social bases of support.

– They think that the so-called 'authority crisis' reflects the more general question of 'political power'. Where is the political power? Who holds the political power? How does he use it?

We think that the question of power is not so much the problem of power at government level, but at the level of the MFA. That is, the question of power is the question of power inside the MFA.

The clarification of this problem is a priority task. Without it, it is not possible to attack the fundamental problem of state organisation, without completely ruining it. The divisions which arose in the heart of the MFA reflect distinct ideological positions. The positions are incompatible, since it is not possible to reconcile a totalitarian conception of the organisation of society with a democratic and progressive conception, or even with vague populist conceptions of an anarchic nature.

It is necessary to vigorously denounce the fascist spirit underlying the position that, calling itself socialist, will end, in practice, in a bureaucratic dictatorship, directed against a uniform and inert mass of citizens of this country.

It is necessary to energetically repel anarchism and populism, which will lead inevitably to the catastrophic dissolution of the state, in a period of development of society in which, without state, no political project is viable.

The resolution of the power crisis inside the MFA – and thus the question of power at state level – will not, however, be resolved, while only treated at the level of different ideologies. It is essential, in practice, to find an adequate solution to the problem of dispersion of the 'centres of power'. Without a minimum of 'unity of command', political direction will reveal itself to be each time more fluid, floating, lost in an agitated sea of arbitrary decisions of the Fifth Division of the General Chief of Staff of the Armed Forces, of the Assembly of the MFA, of ad hoc military assemblies, unexpectedly and mysteriously formed, of the Cabinets of Dynamisation, of the Council of the Revolution, of the COPCON, of the unions, etc. What political space for manoeuvre exists for a government under these conditions, and what is its real authority? No plans can be coherently conceived and applied without a government, which, on one hand, does not leave any margin for doubt as to its ability to execute the overall political project defined by the MFA, and, on the other, is invested with the necessary authority to govern.

6. Every day and every hour that passes there are evident signs of a social

agitation which tends to spread dangerously and multiply itself, submerging the country in a wave of uncontrollable violence.

Factors are accumulating which promote a very wide social basis of support for a return to fascism. It is ridiculous to say, as do certain political groups and certain channels of the media, that they are the 'manoeuvres of reaction'. The discontent, bad feeling and anguish are real and too evident, and they have a profound cause in errors of political direction, accumulated over the last few months, and in grave disorientations within the MFA itself.

What has to be done?

We find ourselves increasingly at a crossroads in history, and it is once more the MFA which has to assume the major weight of responsibilities in relation to the Portuguese people.

It is imperious to consciously choose a path to socialism, without violating the wishes of the vast majority of the Portuguese, winning over those who are hesitant or discontented through persuasion and example. It is incumbent upon the MFA, completely independently of the political parties, but taking into account the role that they can and should have, to define the political project of transition to socialism.

It is necessary to regain the confidence of the Portuguese, putting an end to calls to hatred and incitements to violence and resentment. It is a question of constructing a society of tolerance and peace and not a society which is subject to new mechanisms of oppression and exploitation, and that cannot be realised with the present leadership, even though it has been partially renewed, given its lack of credibility and its manifest inability to govern.

Finally, it is necessary to lead the country with justice and equity, and according to firm and steadfast rules, in the direction of socialism, democracy and peace.

The COPCON Document (working proposal for a political programme, 12 August 1975)

I. The present situation

1. The situation prevailing in the country as a consequence of the inability, at every level, to solve the real problems which had faced the power structures, has unleashed a general, economic decline, widening the gap between the urban zones and the rural zones, and the Lisbon industrial zone and other less developed industrial zones. The emphasis on dirigisme and attempts at controlling the state apparatus by the parties, particularly highlighted by the PCP, led some officers with responsibilities in the revolutionary process to present a document which aimed at clarifying the present situation. In practice, a greater confusion resulted, as a result of the ambiguities contained in the said document.

2. In view of this it becomes essential to clarify, de facto, the present situation and so show the country our position in this matter, for we considered that the MFA should recognise the mistakes it has made up until now, denouncing without hesitation, their causes.

3. The decline of the economic situation and the respective social and political implications for large sections of the popular masses is due mainly to the lack of definition of a clear political line, and to the lack of a consequential governmental programme; there has not been a set of economic measures able to fill the vacuum created by the disintegration of the pre-existing capitalist structure, and on the other hand, dependence on imperialism, with all its consequences, still manifests itself, with, for example, the closing of factories, the flight of capital, unemployment and brazen political pressures on our sovereignty.

4. The workers of the towns and country, as well as large sectors of public employees, supported by their class organisations, and in a noble tradition of struggle, have achieved a more efficient defence of their economic situation against an increase in the cost of living, even though it is they who are most affected by the spread of unemployment.

5. Although well advertised, the creation of structures and policies of support for small and medium-sized businesses and industries is clearly totally inefficient, and, on the contrary, it has been found that the situation has considerably worsened as a result of an increase in taxes and other expenses.

6. Owners of small and medium-sized farms in the north and middle of the country have seen their situation constantly worsen since 25 April, as a result of the increase in the cost of living, of materials and products essential to farming, as well as difficulties in the distribution and selling

of their products. Internal commerce has not been organised in order to eliminate speculation from the middle-men, nor to create a distribution network that would simplify distribution from the producer to the consumer with mutual benefits. It is, without doubt, the owners of small and medium-sized farms, who, at the moment, suffer the effects of economic decline.

7. In the field of health care, the material and human resources capable of responding minimally to the most pressing needs of the population were not delivered to the provinces.

8. At the same time, there was a development among rural populations of campaigns of enlightenment and dynamisation, which, because of inadequate prior planning, often did not respect the socio-cultural characteristics of the environment in which development was taking place and in some cases a real violation of people's customs took place. These campaigns, supported by words that were devoid of significance when they were addressed to many of the rural population, were, in the majority of cases, prejudicial, because they were not accompanied by any real measures capable of demonstrating to the people that the objective was a real improvement in their living conditions.

9. There is a climate of disenchantment and disbelief on the part of the populus, making them lose their faith in the revolution, in which they should be principally and directly interested. The causes of this fact are fundamentally the following:

a) The replacement of local authority fascist administrations was effected, in the majority of cases, through elements of the petite and middle bourgeoisie, local supporters of the PCP–MDP/CDE, who showed themselves to be incapable of solving the main present problems;

b) The concession of benefits through the Leagues of Owners of Small and Medium-sized Farms, whose creation met the former wishes of these classes, was carried out favouring those who were followers of the political line of those people who dominated the above-mentioned leagues;

c) The commissions which were meant to liquidate the former 'farming *grémios*' were totally incipient and they have not liquidated anything to date, rather they have followed, in respect of the concession of benefits, identical criteria referred to in the (above) case of the Leagues of Owners of Small and Medium-sized Farms.

As a result of this and the consequent growing discontentment, the reactionary forces have exploited, manoeuvred and instrumentalised this more than just disenchantment, and have been able to provoke an escalation of contentious violence, leading the people to an open opposition of the MFA, because they identify them with a political line responsible for this situation.

10. The conditions under which elections took place helped to confuse people concerning the instruments that could be used for the control of the apparatus of state and of power, given that:

– the bourgeois structure in which Portuguese society was, and is, organised does not permit the revolutionary consciousness to be carried to the widest popular masses;

– in a bourgeois structure of universal suffrage, only one thing can be achieved ... bourgeoisie;
– in a bourgeois structure only the bourgeois and reformist parties have the financial means to carry their own voice to the whole country;
– in a bourgeois structure there is no attempt to debate and resolve real problems, but only a political demagogy made up of word-games, destined to intoxicate and confuse the people, who, after forty-eight years of fascism, were not in any condition to distinguish any of these word-games.

It has to be recognised that the MFA is largely responsible, since they made the holding of elections a point of honour, an aspect which was well exploited by the forces interested in this type of election.

11. The inability of FOUR PROVISIONAL GOVERNMENTS to function is not only the result of the dirigisme forced by the PCP, which infiltrated the state apparatus and the media, since the PS, the PPD and the MDP/CDE who were also there share these responsibilities, from which, today, they seek to disassociate themselves. We cannot expect more from the parties on the right of the PS, and that includes the party leadership, than an attempt to stop and reverse the march of the revolutionary process, so that they can guarantee the privileges of the high bourgeoisie and the unbridled exploitation of the workers.

12. The insistence of the MFA in seeking to solve contradictions through compromised solutions negotiated with bourgeois parties and the cover it has been giving to partisan manoeuvres have discredited the military amongst the workers.

II. An analysis of the Document of the Nine

1. But the solution to the present situation, for which the MFA is mostly responsible, will not be found in right-wing measures, as proposed by the document, and which led to our taking-up this position. It is certainly not government coalitions which will permit an advance in the construction of socialism. It is not by simultaneously rejecting SOCIAL DEMOCRACY, STATE CAPITALISM, POPULAR DEMOCRACY, and the conquests of the working classes, will they (the working classes) be allowed to take control of the (revolutionary) process, or even consolidate positions already achieved. The proposal presented will lead to a RECOVERY BY THE RIGHT, opening up the field of manoeuvre for the destruction of the revolution, despite the patriotic and democratic intentions, in the minds of the signatories to the document.

2. The economic perspective presented, which strengthens the links with the EEC and EFTA, will reinforce the subjection of the country to a shameful ECONOMIC–FINANCIAL and POLITICAL dependence, and whatever illusions there are about its aims are lost completely with the presentation of final demands for the realisation of 'FINANCIAL HELP TO PORTUGAL'. To revitalise private enterprise through massive investment of foreign financial capital will simply result in the loss of NATIONAL INDEPENDENCE. It is not enough to mask such a disaster by saying that we also have to deal with the Third World and the countries of the East.

Nor is it by opening the doors to imperialism that we can manage to carry out a fitting decolonisation of the territories, which are still under Portuguese administration and still the victims of imperialist exploitation.

3. It is not by taking up a position above the parties, without disassociating themselves from the parties of the right, that they (the Group of Nine) can recover credibility, and affirm that they claim to construct socialism and not to achieve a bourgeois, but still capitalist, democracy, and that is what will happen. How can a project call itself a left-wing project, when it conceals the role of the masses and refuses the action of the vanguards?

How is it possible to 'criticise' the rate of nationalisations?

Can it be that the people will be served by leaving in the hands of the bourgeoisie the ownership of the means of production?

How can we ignore the *caciquismo* [term used to denote having control or power over people, editors' note] and the role of the class struggle in its destruction?

How can we appeal for concord without distinguishing between the exploiters and the exploited?

4. Crystallizing this phase of the critical analysis of the document, we refer to the fundamental point which was not forgotten by its signatories. The central point is the present political situation and its relation to the growing activity of fascism. Real facts demonstrate that fascism has now abandoned its defensive caution, in order to deliberately and clearly launch an offensive, through violent acts which are openly committed. Historically, it has been demonstrated that moderates who claim to abhor violent acts of fascism by taking up conciliatory positions are the first victims of fascism, or in other cases, transform themselves into oppressors of the masses, whom they pretend to liberate.

III. Proposals

1. A revolutionary programme for a solution to the situation has to include, above all else, the realisation of the MFA–People's alliance project, which will guarantee that the workers will be in control of the resolution of their problems. Without this participation socialism is impossible. We have to build an organisational structure of the popular masses, through the creation and recognition of councils of villages, factories and districts, which will be the organs through which workers can take decisions, in order to solve their own problems. These organs of workers' power have to be an instrument for economic solutions, for social planning (schools, hospitals, housing and transport), and they have to be, finally, true organs of political power, the only barrier capable of victoriously opposing fascist and imperialist aggression.

2. The economic solutions for this country have to be based on structural changes, and the economy redirected to give total and effective support for agriculture, so that we are quickly able to produce an increased quantity of food, the buying of which from abroad is at the moment one of the main causes of a deficit in our balance of payments. With that aim

in mind, it is necessary to plan agriculture, and to carry out an agrarian revolution, in agreement with the expressed view of the Village Assemblies and other organs of expression of the owners of small and medium-sized farms, and (the farmers) in the south. All of them should have financial and technical support, which will guarantee profitability and conditions for farm workers, similar to those of workers in the towns.

3. Ways should be created which will enable effective and immediate support for small and medium-sized businesses and industries, developing at the same time conditions which will favour associationism and co-operativism.

4. On the other hand, Portugal is to end its dependence on imperialism, a dependence which is the cause of the present economic crisis. Thus, it has to end its financial and technological dependence on imperialist countries, even if we have to suspend or reconvert industries, which were implanted in our country in order to exploit the cheap labour of Portuguese workers.

In this sense we have to cease our subjection to the EEC and to EFTA, who have practised a policy of blackmail in relation to Portugal. We have to move towards an economic policy of true national independence, so that our country can:

a) Align itself with countries of the Third World, favouring co-operation with former Portuguese colonies, in new terms of equality and fraternity.

b) Maintain and establish commercial relations and co-operation with every country in the world on the basis of reciprocity and mutual advantage.

Under these conditions our country will be in a position to be able to win the blockade of imperialism, by using imperialism's internal contradictions, one of which is the public opinion of the respective countries (in which imperialism exists), and, principally, the solidarity of the respective working classes and of the people of the Third World, for whom our revolutionary process constitutes a great hope and stimulus for uniting the people and aiding them in their struggle.

5. The problem of hundreds of thousands of unemployed should be solved by economic planning aimed at full employment. With that purpose in mind there is a need to create jobs in agriculture and in civil construction. We are aware that the reconversion of the economy in these terms, the initiation of socialist planning, independence from imperialism and a policy of full employment, imply great difficulties and sacrifices which will have to be shared by all. We cannot demand that only the workers support it. Because of this we have to severely cut the maximum national wage, and remove privileges from certain minority sectors of society.

6. In relation to housing we have to create a just policy, which will frontally attack the grand landlords who made speculation their way of life, and defend the small landlords who, with reasonable incomes, were able to guarantee their livelihood and that of their families. In relation to this, we have to put a ceiling on rents, taking into account the location,

type of construction, number of rooms, etc. The residents' associations will play a decisive role in establishing an adoptable criterion.

7. In relation to the health problem, we have to socialise medicine, guaranteeing the delivery of medical care to every province (non-urban areas), and this includes using all the human and technical resources of the Armed Forces. As a complementary measure we have to proceed likewise to nationalise the pharmaceutical industries, regulating the manufacture of medicines so as to reduce the number of medicines which only differ by the brand name, and in this way reducing the present large public expenditure, which puts an extraordinary burden on the cost of medicines.

8. In relation to EDUCATION conditions have to be guaranteed so that basic education is provided for everybody, with secondary and higher education being immediately subordinated to the interests of the working classes.

9. Besides this generic programme, applicable in the medium term, and which has to be discussed, corrected and planned in detail, with the collaboration of all the organs of popular and military expression, we think that, amongst others, the following URGENT MEASURES have to be taken:

– Lowering the prices of fertilizers and buying agricultural products at prices which guarantee a just remuneration for the work of small and medium-sized farms;

– Using, whenever necessary, the means of transport of the Armed Forces for the distribution of agrarian products;

– Lowering the prices of animal fodder, and the guarantee of just prices to small and medium-sized producers of cattle, sheep, pork, as well as chickens;

– Putting conditions on the importation of food, whenever it can be substituted by similar food produced in the country;

– Guarantee of concession of credit at a very low or no interest rate, according to each case, in amounts able to guarantee its effective and reproductive application;

– Repressive action on the Liquidating Commissions of the former farming *grémios*, and Leagues of Owners of Small and Medium-sized Farms, whenever political discrimination in the delivery of subsidies is found;

– Creation of conditions of veterinary and technical support to the owners of small and medium-sized farms and to producers;

– Emergency measures in relation to displaced people from Angola, including them in a general policy of employment and full housing, such as: requisition of hotels, construction of prefabricated houses and other measures which may be found appropriate as a solution, although only a temporary one;

– Adoption of measures for children, very old people and the handicapped who live in circumstances incompatible with a minimum of social security;

– Drawing up of plans which allow rapid conversion, in useful ways, of

closed industrial firms resulting from sabotage by capitalists and reactionaries or by the action of imperialism;
– Creation of conditions which can guarantee the physical and moral safety of people in the sense of preserving the right to own property, whenever this does not constitute an effective means of exploitation.
10. The media should serve this programme, stimulating a frank, free and total debate, without reservations, destroying, once and for all, any form of manipulation and following the fundamental principle that it is only in this way that the interests of the working classes are served, and that the contradictions that exist among the people can be resolved.
11. To guarantee the execution of this programme, it is necessary to define the executive power which will be responsible for it; which will be the power during the transition. This transition power will be constituted by the MFA, and by all the political organisations which are truly revolutionary and that claim and defend the power of the workers. As such, there will be the guarantee of the creation, de facto, of the MFA–People's alliance as a first measure to be taken and as the prop for the creation of the new power structure. This power will be the directive political power during the transition period until the creation of a National Popular Assembly.

IV. Internal organisation of the armed forces

1. The development of a proposal like this which calls itself revolutionary, essentially supported by the MFA–People's alliance and which only touches upon the popular sector, not dealing, even superficially, with the internal aspect of the Armed Forces would be a very serious mistake, whose evident contradictions would assume counter-revolutionary appearances.
2. Thus, and in a very succinct way, we think it is essential that the internal structure of the Armed Forces be rethought, at very short notice, with the aim of achieving the following:

a) Form of class organisation

– The military should organise themselves in agreement with the different existing classes, debating freely their problems of class, electing democratically their representatives to the ADU (Assembly of Unit Delegates) which would be the spokesperson for the conclusions arrived at;
– The solutions proposed by the ADUs and which have implications for the collective life of a military unit should be debated in the AGU (General Assembly of a Unit), in such a way as to make possible a general consensus, which is the indispensable basis for cohesion and discipline.

b) Social rights

– All measures should be taken so that a considerable elevation in the standard of living of privates should be achieved, mainly through the modernisation of barracks, a substantial increase in their wages, general rights, and family allowances, etc.

c) Reinforcement of discipline

– Intensification of the internal dynamisation of the units, debating and analysing together the problems, without restrictions, consolidating the cohesion by means of a consentive discipline which is achieved through enlightenment, and only then will it enable to the total delivery of the military to their patriotic mission of intransigent defence of the interests of the Portuguese people.

Conclusion

The present project constitutes the only viable and realistic proposal which is offered to the Portuguese people for the socialist society which we want to achieve and constitutes a firm refusal of FASCISM, SOCIAL DEMOCRACY, and STATE CAPITALISM, which are forms of exploitation which deny the real emancipation of the working classes.

LONG LIVE THE ALLIANCE BETWEEN THE WORKERS AND THE PEASANTS!
LONG LIVE THE INDESTRUCTIBLE ALLIANCE BETWEEN THE WORKERS AND THE REVOLUTIONARY ARMED FORCES!
LONG LIVE THE MFA–PEOPLE'S ALLIANCE!
LONG LIVE THE SOCIALIST REVOLUTION!
LONG LIVE PORTUGAL!

APPENDIX 6
The Agrarian Reform Law (Decree-law no. 406–A/75, 29 July 1975)

The large farm owners, and in the last decades, the big agricultural capitalists have constituted a dominating social stratum in the country-side during fascism. This domination, of which the fascist state apparatus was both a vehicle and a guarantor, was based on the ruthless exploitation of the mass of farm workers and on the plunder and submission of the owners of small farms.

The liquidation of fascism and of its bases implies in the countryside the destruction of the social economic power of those strata, which, although now deprived of the power of state and of the control of large areas of the state apparatus by the political process initiated on 25 April 1974, continue under various forms to exert their control over the people in the rural areas.

In effect, the ownership of large tracts of land and of the fundamental means of farm production by these strata of society, even in a trans-formed political context, not only represents a prolonging of the exploitation and plunder, but also causes a reproduction of the same conditions of their social and ideological control.

If the Agrarian Reform, which is meant to be launched, responds to an imperative for the liberation of the productive forces, in relation to the bottlenecks produced by the forms of land ownership and of the means of production that are against the development of those forces, we should not forget for a moment that today, in Portugal, an Agrarian Reform concretely becomes a fundamental political process of liquidation of the (control of) the owners of the big farms, of the liquidation of those strata of society which have dominated the countryside until now.

The liquidation of the control of the owners of big farms is an integral part of, and essential for, the process of the destruction of fascism and its social bases, and emerges as a fundamental condition for the liberation and emancipation of the farm workers, the owners of small farms and for the construction of a democratic society.

This process does not constitute however, in its essence, a deed or an initiative of the power of the state: and all in all it cannot be considered as a set of administrative and legal measures in the tracks of which an Agrarian Reform, commanded from the central administration, would be carried out. The Agrarian Reform must result – as it largely does already – from the power of the initiative, the imagination, the organi-sation, the struggle and the work of the farm workers and the owners of small farms. In the introduction of a law like this the important

283

contribution that these strata of society have given to the advance and acceleration of the reform process, after 25 April 1974, should be recognised. It is in the tradition of the historical struggles that were fought by the casual rural workers of the Alentejo region against the owners of large farms and against fascism which reached a peak in the beginning of the 1960s.

The legal mechanisms contained in this law only constitute a general framework for an attack on extensive ownership and on large-scale capitalist exploitation of the land. It is a political result of the tradition of struggle, of the initiatives and conquests of the agricultural workers and the owners of small farms and one is now aiming to produce an instrument that will be a stimulus for these social classes.

It is a moment in the life of the state in which the principal protagonists of the social process are the dominated classes of the countryside, and whose dynamic is eminently local. It is important that there should be seen to be, on the one hand, in this law, a partial synthesis of the experiences and conquests and, on the other hand, an appeal and a framework so that the popular initiative can develop and implant itself on a base of multiple local assemblies whose function would be to launch their own reform – without prejudice, moreover, of the contribution of the irreplaceable class associations and other specific organs.

At this point in the life of the state, the deliberately partial nature of this law should also be underlined, seeing that it effectively limits itself to foresee and regulate the process of expropriation of land from the large landowners and from the grand capitalist exploiters, who were, until now, dominant and their agents most powerful.

The way forward is projected in the institutionalisation of embryonic forms of initiative and local social organisations, which have a role to play in the dynamics of the liquidation of the big farms and the construction of new forms of production and of livelihood. However, it will be left to later, when laws will be passed which will define new forms of organisation of production, the definition of a new legal statute of the land, of water, of the forest, as well as land usage, ownership and circulation.

That regime and that statute cannot, and should not, come unilaterally from the state: they have to be born, in a large measure, from the local initiatives and struggles, from the will of the assemblies, throughout the countryside, from village to village, and this will signal the control of the productive process by the working classes.

In these terms:

Using the faculty which is conferred by article no. 3, no. 1, item (3) of the constitutional law no. 6/75, 26 March, the government decrees and I promulgate, so that the following will become law:

Article 1

Under the terms of the present law, the country dwellings [that is buildings, land etc.] which are in the following situations will be subject to expropriation:

a) If they belong to individuals, societies or collective groups of private ownership, although they may be for public use, who are proprietors, in the national territory, of country dwellings that, in their entirety, calculated through the appended tables [not included here] of this diploma, correspond to more than 50,000 points or, independent of this requisite, correspond to an area of more than 700 hectares;
b) If they belong to individuals, societies or collective groups of private ownership, although they may be for public use, which correspond to those situations mentioned in the decree-law no. 660/74, 25 November and complementary legislation;
c) That are not cultivated or do not reach the minimum levels of farming, established or to be established by a regulation of the Ministry of Agriculture and Fisheries.

Article 2

1. The owners whose land was expropriated and who are not under the conditions of items b) and c) of the previous article are entitled to the right of reserve [portion of land which cannot be expropriated, editors' note] of an area of land, to be staked out as a function of the overall planning of the explorations that have yet to be established, up to a limit equivalent to 50,000 points, in agreement with the table appended [not included here] to this diploma, providing that they cumulatively fulfill the following conditions:
a) they directly work the land they own;
b) they and their family live exclusively or predominantly from farming their land;
c) they have not already exerted the right of reserve which has been defined in any other law.
2. If one of the above conditions a) and b) ceases to exist the reserved area will be subject to expropriation.
3. Collective groups either as commercial societies, or civilians in commercial firms, or foundations or other associations do not have the right of reserve.
4. Ownership resulting from the exercise of the right of reserve can only be transmitted, by succession, to legitimate heirs, or through negotiations between the living, to the state.

Article 3

1. The right of reserve defined in the previous article ceases to exist, if it is not exerted through a written declaration sent to the Institute of the Agrarian Reorganisation, within fifteen days to be counted from the day on which the owner or whoever represents him was notified.
2. Independently of the notification referred to in the above number, the right of reserve ceases within twenty days counting from the putting up of public notices in the local councils or in the town councils in the area in which the dwellings [buildings and land, editors' note] are going to be expropriated.

3. The declaration of the exercise of the right of reserve should be accompanied, otherwise it will become invalid, by another (declaration) in which is stated the relationship between the rural and urban dwellings owned by the proprietors, bearing in mind articles 15 and 16 of this law.
4. The notification in no. 1 above of this article, and the declaration of the exercise of the right of reserve will be made by a registered letter which must be signed for on receipt.

Article 4

Without prejudice for the following articles, following expropriation, all rights and expenses of the expropriated dwellings cease.

Article 5

The rules to be used in the fixation of indemnities to be given to the owners, or other holders of rights or of responsibilities, which were encompassed by expropriation measures or by requisition, will be defined in a law to be published within 180 days from the date of promulgation of this law.

Article 6

1. The rights of those who, for any reason except ownership, exploit an area of an expropriated dwelling, which, when added to the areas of any other dwellings which they are exploiting, does not, at the time of expropriation, exceed the number of points referred to in article 1, will be respected.
2. To those who, for any reason except ownership, work an area of an expropriated dwelling which, when added to all the others who also work an area at the time of expropriation, exceeds the number of points referred to in article no. 1, a right to a reserve is guaranteed in relation to their contractual rights, which is on a level with the one which is given to the owners and they are to have the same working conditions.

Article 7

1. In the whole of national territory, nobody, whether individually or collectively, as a society or a group can own or can work, directly or indirectly, for any reason, an area of land which exceeds that defined in item a) of article no. 1.
2. The judicial proceedings taken against that which is defined in the previous number, will be in proportion to the violation, regardless of whether either a total or partial violation has taken place.
3. The prohibition established in no. 1 applies to an individual in any one group, even if it is, de facto, a collective group.
4. The prohibition established in no. 1 does not apply to the state, the recognised public collectives and co-operatives which will be regulated by special laws.

Article 8

The expropriation or the measures to readjust the working of the land, in terms of the previous articles, will be legislated by regulations passed by the Ministry of Agriculture and Fisheries, under a proposal from the Institute of Agrarian Reorganisation, from the Regional Councils of Agrarian Reform or from local assemblies whose composition and operations will be regulated by a law still to be published.

Article 9

The publication of the act of expropriation has, as an immediate effect, the nationalisation of the area to which it applies and the ownership by the Institute of Agrarian Reorganisation of the same, independent of any previous contract or payment or indemnities.

Article 10

The actions or omissions, intentional or by negligence, of owners, leaseholders, other farm businessmen and their delegates which affect the use of the land, the infra-structure and equipment, or lead to the diminution, destruction or loss of production, will result in the loss of the right of reserve as well as any other rights which are acquired through it. Any other legal sanctions that can be applied in this case will appertain, and, according to the seriousness, a reduction or elimination of the indemnity which should have taken place as defined in article 5 above will also apply.

Article 11

The Institute of Agrarian Reorganisation may requisition from the owners or the leaseholders or others, who are affected by expropriation measures, the mechanical industrial equipment, cattle and other components of the exploitation of their farms, in excess of their needs in the area they will cultivate. The Institute will in every case have first choice whenever the above (owners, ... etc.) carry out any transfer of goods or property.

Article 12

In the farm year subsequent to this expropriation the Institute of Agrarian Reorganisation may compulsorily rent the reserved area without the consequences foreseen in no. 2 of article 2.

Article 13

It is the function of the Institute of Agrarian Reorganisation through the Regional Centres of Agrarian Reform, whenever they exist:

a) To promote and support the installation of units of production in the expropriated areas;
b) To co-ordinate, control and support technically and financially the farming of the expropriated areas;
c) To proceed to the demarcation of the reserved areas, under the terms of articles 2, 3, and 6;
d) to make an inventory for the benefactors, of equipment, cattle and other goods existing in the farmed areas situated in the expropriated areas and to proceed to requisition them, as it finds appropriate.

Article 14

If from acts resulting from the application of the present law there are unlawful offences carried out contrary to the rights of the owners, leaseholders and other interested parties, they can appeal only for simple devolution to the Regional Councils of Agrarian Reform. They can also appeal against their decisions, and when they have not yet been constituted, to the Ministry of Agriculture and Fisheries.

Article 15

1. So that the measures established in this law can be applied, any acts since 25 April 1974, which have benefited relatives or the like, that in any way resulted in a reduction of the area of the country dwellings of each owner will be declared void. Similarly, by the expropriation law or regulation any such acts practised since that date also be declared void.
2. Rent contracts or any other contracts, which involve concessions in the use of land, and which were entered into after 15 April 1975, by owners or other people to whom the measures of expropriation defined in this diploma are applicable are also void.

Article 16

For the effects of the present diploma, married couples who are co-owners of their property, or co-owners of other property, or the recipients of an undivided inheritance and other similar recipients of autonomous inheritances or other similar groups will be treated as a sole owner, leaseholder or farm businessman.

Article 17

1. Doubts which may emerge in an interpretation and execution of the present diploma, with regards to the use of the appended table [not included here], will be resolved by regulations passed by the Ministry of Agriculture and Fisheries.
2. The table to be applied in the counties, not included in the appended table, will be approved and published in a regulation by the Ministry of Agriculture and Fisheries. [Portugal is divided into districts and each district is sub-divided into counties or *concelhos*.]

Article 18

This diploma will be valid immediately. It is signed by Vasco Gonçalves, Alvaro Cunhal, Francisco Pereira de Moura, Joaquim Magalhães Mota, Mario Murteira, José Joaquim Fragoso, Fernando Oliveira Baptista. It was published on 29 July 1975 and was promulgated by President Costa Gomes.

APPENDIX 7

The structure of the armed forces

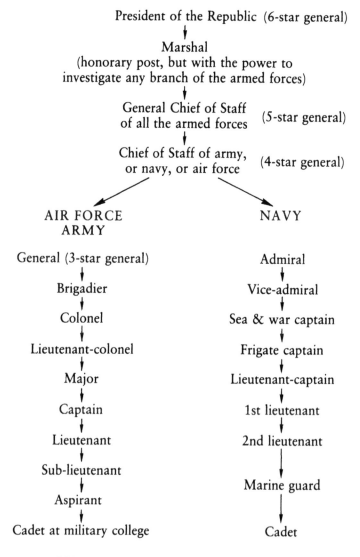

President of the Republic (6-star general)
↓
Marshal
(honorary post, but with the power to
investigate any branch of the armed forces)
↓
General Chief of Staff
of all the armed forces   (5-star general)
↓
Chief of Staff of army,
or navy, or air force   (4-star general)

AIR FORCE
ARMY

NAVY

General (3-star general)
↓
Brigadier
↓
Colonel
↓
Lieutenant-colonel
↓
Major
↓
Captain
↓
Lieutenant
↓
Sub-lieutenant
↓
Aspirant
↓
Cadet at military college

Admiral
↓
Vice-admiral
↓
Sea & war captain
↓
Frigate captain
↓
Lieutenant-captain
↓
1st lieutenant
↓
2nd lieutenant
↓
Marine guard
↓
Cadet

APPENDIX 8
The number of workers employed in the Agrarian Reform Zone

	Thousands
Before Agrarian Reform 1974	21.7
1975–6	71.9
1976–7	64.2
1977–8	59.0
1978–9	43.0
1979–80	26.0
1980–1	25.0
1982–3	22.5

The rise and fall of the military in government

Provisional governments	Duration of government	Prime Minister	Composition of cabinet
First	16.5.74–11.7.74	Adelino da Palma Carlos	1 member of the armed forces 5 Independents 3 PS 2 PCP 2 PPD 1 MDP 1 SEDES
Second	18.7.74–30.9.74	Vasco Gonçalves	8 Members of the armed forces 4 PS 3 Independents 1 PCP 1 PPD
Third	30.9.74–26.3.75	Vasco Gonçalves	9 members of the armed forces 4 PS 2 Independents 1 PCP 1 PPD
Fourth	26.3.75–8.8.75	Vasco Conçalves	8 members of the armed forces 4 Independents 2 PS 2 PCP 2 MDP 2 PPD 1 ex-MES
Fifth	8.8.75–12.9.75	Vasco Gonçalves	7 members of the armed forces 6 Independents 4 MDP 1 PCP

| Sixth | 19.9.75–22.7.76 | Pinheiro de Azevedo | 6 members of the armed forces
4 PS
3 Independents
2 PPD
1 PCP |

Constitutional governments

| First | 23.7.76–9.12.77 | Mário Soares | 3 members of the armed forces
13 PS
2 Independents |
| Second | 23.1.78–28.7.78 | Mário Soares | 1 member of the armed forces
11 PS
3 CDS
1 Independent |

Epilogue

The Portuguese political scene in the eighteen months that followed the celebrations to mark the decade of the 1974 coup-d'état has continued to change.

The PS–PSD alliance pursued their policy of economic restraint in their attempts to equilibrate the balance of payments problem and reduce inflation: they had some success. Inflation fell from 32.1 per cent (from July 1983 to July 1984) to 21.5 per cent for the same period from 1984 to 1985. The forecast rate for 1985–6 was 20 per cent. Compared to 1983, the negative balance of payments was 3.5 per cent less in 1984. Exports have risen more than imports since 1983 as a result of the devaluation of the escudo. But Portugal had to import over 900 million US dollars worth of basic food-stuffs during 1984, and unemployment increased in 1984 to reach about 11 per cent in 1985. There was also the continuing problem of employed people not being paid their salaries.

It was surprising that the PS–PSD alliance was so short lived. The alliance collapsed probably because of continuous conflicts within the PSD and, also, because of the unpopularity of the government's economic policies. The conflicts resulted in Mota Pinto's being replaced as PSD's leader, his enemies claiming that he was too much under the influence of the PS. The replacement, caretaker leader, Rui Mauchete, was unable to unite the PSD, whose upper hierarchy were divided and unable to produce a candidate for the forthcoming presidential elections. A young economist, Anibal Cavaco Silva, gained instant popularity with his bold proposals for the solution of the problem of the PSD's presidential candidate. For the party leadership it was a surprise when the rank and file elected him as the new leader: to the rank and file he appeared to have features of the party's old hero, Sá Carneiro.

Prime Minister Soares and the PS considered that the new,

almost unknown PSD leader, Cavaco Silva, would have little popular support and refused to agree to a number of conditions that Silva required from the PS, if the PSD was to continue in the alliance. Soares gambled that President Eanes would not dissolve parliament and, in the unlikely event of his doing so, that they would have a majority in the next parliament. Cavaco Silva withdrew the PSD from the coalition in June 1985. Eanes dissolved parliament when he realised that the PS would not have the support of the other parties and so be able to govern as a minority government.

The prospect of parliamentary elections speeded up the creation of a new party. This party, the PRD (Partido Renovador Democrático – Party of Democratic Renewal) is a centre-left party, with the claim that Eanes will become its leader when his presidential term comes to an end. Although Eanes has never formally given his support to the party, his wife actively campaigned on their behalf in the run-up to the elections.

On 5 October 1985, Portugal went to the polls yet again. The main result was the emergence of the PRD as the third most powerful political force in the country. It was a defeat for the PS, but, as in all elections since the 1974 coup d'état, the left and centre-left had the majority of the votes. The results were as follows:

PSD	29.8%	(27.2%)
PS	20.8%	(36.1%)
PRD	18.0%	(–)
APU	15.6%	(18.2%)
CDS	9.7%	(12.4%)

The results in parentheses are from the 1983 elections; percentages are the total number of votes cast.

After the elections Mário Soares stepped down as prime minister and President Eanes asked Anibal Cavaco Silva to form a minority government. The electoral results were a serious setback for Mário Soares's attempt to become Portugal's new President.

President Eanes has soon to step down as President, under the dictates of the Constitution, but it is probable that he will continue to play a key role in Portuguese politics as leader of the newly formed PRD. The next President is likely to be either Mário Soares (supported by the PS), Freitas do Amaral (supported by CDS and PSD), or Maria de Lurdes Pintasilgo (independent). Pintasilgo has been ahead consistently in the opinion polls.

On 12 June 1985, after eight years of negotiating, Portugal (together with Spain) signed the Treaty of Accession to enter the EEC on 1 January 1986.

In November 1985 Otelo Saraiva de Cavalho finally went on trial for his alleged leadership of the urban guerilla group FP25. Charismatic as ever, he dissociated himself from FP25, but declared he had had the intention of setting up a clandestine movement, with an armed branch, to prevent the return of fascism and with an ultimate aim of carrying the workers to power. For many people on the left, during his imprisonment and during the trial, the hero of the 1974 coup d'état still carried Portugal's revolutionary torch.

Bibliography

Abreu, P. de 1983. *25 de Abril ao 25 de Novembro*. Editorial Intervenção, Lisbon

Almeida, D. de 1977. *Origens e Evolução do Movimento de Capitães*. Edições Socidis, Lisbon

Almeida, D. de 1979. *Ascensão, Apogeu e Queda do MFA* 2 volumes. Author's edition, Lisbon

Antunes, J. F. 1983. *O segredo do 25 de Novembro*. 3rd edition. Publicaçoës Europa-América, Lisbon

Archives of *Anglo-Portuguese News*, a Cascais-based newspaper

Archives of *Diário de Noticias*, a Lisbon-based newspaper

Archives of *Expresso*, a Lisbon-based newspaper

Archives of *O Jornal*, a Lisbon-based newspaper

Bandeira, A. R. 1975. *Military Interventions in Portuguese Politics – Antecedents of the Armed Forces Movement*. Brazilian Studies, Canada

Bissio, R. R. 1984. *Third World Guide*. Rio de Janeiro, Brazil

Carvalho, O. S. 1977. *Alvorada de Abril*. Livraria Bertrand, Lisbon

Clement, D. 1976. *Elementos para a compreensão do 25 de Novembro*. Edições Sociais, Lisbon

Domingos, H., Gago, J. S. and Matos, L. S. 1975. *A revolucão num regimento. A polícia militar en 1975*. O Armazem das Letras Lda, Lisbon

Ferreira, F. A. G. 1985. *15 Anos da História Recente de Portugal*. António Coelho Lda, Lisbon

Ferreira, J. M. 1983. *Ensaio Histórico sobre a Revolução do 25 d'Abril*. Imprensa Nacional, Lisbon

Figueiredo, A. de 1976. *Portugal: Fifty Years of Dictatorship*. Holmes and Meir, London

Fonseca, R. 1983. *A Questão do Estado na Revolução Portuguesa*. Livros Horizonte, Lisbon

Freitas, A. J., Cruz, F. and Guerra, A. (undated) *Setembro, 28 A negra madrugada*. Ediguia Publicaçoës, SARL, Lisbon

Frio, J., Leitão, F. and Pina, C. 1975. *11 de Março: Autópsia de um Golpe*. Agéncia Portuguesa de Revistas, Lisbon

Gomes, C. and Manuel, A. 1979. *Sobre Portugal. A Regra do Jogo*, Lisbon

Harsgor, M. 1976. *Portugal in Revolution. The Washington Papers, 32*. Sage Publications, Beverly Hills and London

297

Harvey, R. 1978. *Portugal, Birth of a Democracy.* Macmillan, London
Kohler, B. 1982. *Political Forces in Spain, Greece and Portugal.* Butterworth European Studies, London
Livermore, H. V. 1976. *New History of Portugal.* Cambridge University Press
Macedo, J. B. and Serfaty, S. 1981. *Portugal Since the Revolution: Economic and Political Perspectives.* F. A. Praeger, New York
Mailer, P. 1977. *Portugal: The Impossible Revolution.* Solidarity, London
Marques, A. L. de 1980. *História de Portugal.* volume 3. Palas Editores, Lisbon
Martins, M. B. 1975. *Sociedade e Grupos em Portugal.* Editorial Estampa, Lisbon
Melo, F. R. de 1976, 1977. *Dossier á Republica.* 2 volumes. Ediçoës Afrodite, Lisbon
MFA 1975. *Relatório Preliminar do 11 de Março de 1975.* MFA Publications, London
Minter, W. 1972. *Portuguese Africa and the West.* Penguin Books, Harmondsworth
Morrison, R. J. 1981. *Portugal in Transition: Revolutionary Changes in an Open Economy.* Auburn House, London
Mota, J. G. 1976. *A Resistência.* Ediçoës Jornal Expresso, Lisbon
Neves, O. 1977. *Diário de uma Revolução.* Mil Dias Editoria, Lisbon
Newitt, M. 1981. *Portugal in Africa.* Longman, London
Pereira, M. 1979. *Política e Economia em Portugal nos Séculos XIX e XX.* Livros Horizonte, Lisbon
Robinson, R. 1979. *Contemporary Portugal.* Allen and Unwin, London
Rodrigues, A., Borga, C. and Cardoso, M. 1974. *O Movimento dos Capitães e o 25 Abril.* Morais Editores, Lisbon
Rodrigues, A., Borga, C. and Cardoso, M. 1976. *Portugal depois de Abril.* Intervoz Publicidade Lda, Lisbon
Rodrigues, A., Borga, C. and Cardoso, M. 1979. *Abril nos quarteis de Novembro.* Livraria Bertrand, Lisbon
Serrão, J. 1982. *A Emigração Portuguesa.* 4th edition. Livros Horizonte, Lisbon
Soares, M. 1976. *Portugal Struggles.* Allen and Unwin, London
Woolf, S. J. 1970. *European Fascism.* Weidenfeld and Nicolson, London

Index

For EU product safety concerns, contact us at Calle de José Abascal, 56–1°, 28003 Madrid, Spain or eugpsr@cambridge.org.

www.ingramcontent.com/pod-product-compliance
Ingram Content Group UK Ltd.
Pitfield, Milton Keynes, MK11 3LW, UK
UKHW042151130625
459647UK00011B/1288